TOWARD EFFICIENT DEMOCRACY
The Question of Governmental Organization

THE BROOKINGS INSTITUTION

The Brookings Institution—Devoted to Public Service through Research and Training in the Social Sciences—was incorporated on December 8, 1927. Broadly stated, the Institution has two primary purposes: the first is to aid constructively in the development of sound national policies; and the second is to offer training of a supergraduate character to students of the social sciences.

The responsibility for the final determination of the Institution's policies and its program of work for the administration of its endowment is vested in a self-perpetuating board of trustees. It is the function of the trustees to make possible the conduct of scientific research under the most favorable conditions, and to safeguard the independence of the research staff in the pursuit of their studies and in the publication of the results of such studies. It is not a part of their function to determine, control, or influence the conduct of particular investigations or the conclusions reached, but only to approve the principal fields of investigation to which the available funds are to be allocated, and to satisfy themselves with reference to the intellectual competence and scientific integrity of the staff. Major responsibility for "formulating general policies and co-ordinating the activities of the Institution" is vested in the president. The by-laws provide also that "there shall be an advisory council selected by the president from among the scientific staff of the Institution."

Authors of studies published by the Institution have had the advice, criticism, and assistance both of an administrative officer and of a co-operating committee selected from the staff. In manuscript accepted for publication, the author has freedom to present his final interpretations and conclusions, although they may not necessarily be concurred in by some or all of those who co-operate with him or by other members of the staff. The Institution in publishing the work assumes the responsibility that it meets reasonable tests of scholarship and presents data and conclusions worthy of public consideration.

TOWARD EFFICIENT DEMOCRACY

The Question of Governmental Organization

By

ARTHUR C. MILLSPAUGH

Washington, D.C.
THE BROOKINGS INSTITUTION
1949

Printed in the United States of America
George Banta Publishing Company
Menasha, Wisconsin

PREFACE

This book deals with an extremely comprehensive and complex problem of national organization. The nature of the study is such as to raise highly debatable issues and to involve an unusual degree of individual interpretation and judgment. Dr. Millspaugh's conclusions are therefore in no sense to be regarded as an institutional pronouncement. It is recognized that many will disagree with the author at specific points and even on major conclusions. On various subjects which are here discussed there is naturally disagreement within the Brookings Institution. The purpose of the book is to stimulate, clarify, and focus discussion with reference to fundamental problems of government organization.

The author's point of view may be briefly summarized as follows: Our system of government came into being 160 years ago. Soon after its adoption, it began to change; and the process of change, often unobserved, has continued to this date. Yet, the great central institutions of government remain substantially unaltered, so far as fundamentals and essentials are concerned. This is true of Congress, the plan of representation, the presidency, the relations between president and Congress, and the relations of both with the administration. As we look back at the development of the over-all organization, we see a growth in size, an increasing complexity, and a marked expansion of power, of responsibility, and of activity; but we do not see much change in the general pattern.

From time to time, the author points out, criticisms have been directed at one feature or another, and many proposals have been made for changes. Generally speaking, these proposals have concerned themselves with a part of the legislative-executive setup rather than with the whole of it. For example, we may cite the legislation of 1946 that dealt with certain features of the internal organization and procedures of Congress, or the current discussion of a modification of the Electoral College system. Such reforms and movements for reform may be sound and desirable. It is not intended to condemn the method of gradual or step-by-step improvement. But something more is needed.

In this age, according to the author, some of the political objectives that we have in view are very different from those that guided the deliberations of the founding fathers at Philadelphia in 1787. In view of conditions in the United States and in the world and in view of the responsibilities that our national government has assumed, a serious question arises whether our general pattern of government is fundamentally adapted to the age in which we live, whether it is so founded and constructed as to give reasonable assurance of effective democratic action. We can answer such questions only by understanding the whole of government, the foundation as well as the superstructure, the basic and causative as well as the secondary and derivate factors. We should not be content with standing on the doorsteps of the structure: we should go to the inner seats as well as to the ultimate sources of governmental power and see how power is exercised and how or in what measure it is democratically controlled. The author's analysis leads him to the conclusion that only a fundamental reorganization of our government would be adequate to meet the requirements of the modern age. The somewhat novel type of governmental organization suggested is not proposed for immediate adoption but as a focus for discussion in order to reach beyond minor questions and consider basic problems of governmental structure and organization.

The reader will find in Chapter I an explanation of the scope and method of this study. It is in a sense a sequel to Dr. Millspaugh's *Democracy, Efficiency, Stability*, published by the Brookings Institution in 1942. That study was a diagnosis. This one is diagnostic, too, but it is also and principally intended to help in the making of a prescription.

H. G. Moulton,
President

February 1949

CONTENTS

vii

PART II. A SUPPORTING ANALYSIS

CHAPTER I

INTRODUCTION

This is a book about American government; and it may help us to get started if we bring up at once a familiar comparison. You own an automobile. You are worried about the service that you have been getting from your car, and you wonder whether it can meet the demands that you are obliged to put upon it. Before you decide what to do, you will, if you are wise, give first thought to the machine itself. Is it up to date? Is it adapted to your particular transportation needs? Is it saving of time, fuel, oil, and energy? Is it safe? If your answers to these and similar questions should be "No," you will consider whether adjustments, repairs, or replacements can make the machine work better. You will also do some thinking about yourself and others who care for your automobile and drive it; but you will not expect even the best of operators to get good results from an out-of-date and defective machine.

If you are a house-wife, your thinking about your refrigerator or washing machine will be equally uninhibited. You are not likely to cling to it solely because you have had it a long time, because you are sentimentally devoted to it, or because you are against change. Your prejudices, such as they are, will be in favor of the new rather than the old. And you will share the general respect of Americans for the scientists, engineers, and technicians who apply themselves to the remaking of the vehicles, appliances, and tools that make our work more efficient and our living happier.

Our governmental machine is hardly to be compared with an automobile: it is more like an altered and enormously enlarged stage-coach. This governmental machine belongs to us, and its sole purpose is to do certain tasks for us and the nation. We are not wholly satisfied with the operations of the contrivance; but we do little except tinker with it, make small repairs, attach gadgets, and change drivers.

1

A comparison of this sort should not be carried too far. A government is not a material mechanical thing. It is an organization of men. Among its institutions and agencies, powers, duties, and tasks are distributed, relationships and procedures established. For many reasons, we cannot repair, overhaul, or discard this creation as we would an automobile, a refrigerator, or a washing machine. "Prudence, indeed, will dictate," says the Declaration of Independence, "that governments long established should not be changed for light and transient causes."

But nothing can be gained and much may be lost by closing our eyes and minds to the problem. As the young Woodrow Wilson wrote in his *Congressional Government* more than sixty years ago:

The Constitution is not honored by blind worship.... When we shall have examined all its parts without sentiment, and gauged all its functions by the standards of practical common sense, we shall have established anew our right to the claim of political sagacity; and it will remain only to act intelligently upon what our opened eyes have seen in order to prove again the justice of our claim to political genius.

Entirely apart from the promise and menace of atomic energy, there has perhaps never been a time, certainly not since the eighteenth century, when problems of government presented such crucial and sweeping challenges to the theorist and the statesman. We are living in an age of world-wide revolution. Beyond our borders, political instability, institutional strain, and governmental change are almost universal phenomena. In various spheres and phases of postwar action, the question of how to organize government is insistent. Americans act as constitutional architects and political tutors in the Philippines, Germany, Japan, and Korea. Our foreign policy is vitally involved in the political systems of Eastern Europe, Greece, Turkey, Palestine, Iran, Latin America, and China. We are more than detached observers of the trend toward political union in Western Europe and of great governmental experiments in India, Burma, and Indonesia. We are intimately affected by constitutional developments in France and Italy, by governmental realities and prospects in Spain and Argentina, by the possibilities of evolution or revolution in the Soviet Union, and by Soviet methods of political penetration and conquest in other states. Throughout all the critical areas, men occupy themselves in some fashion with problems of fundamental statecraft.

In the course of the current revolutionary contest, the United States has become the champion of certain historic political principles; but our championship is unlikely to prevail unless democratic government can be made to justify itself. It must prove its worth and strength here in the United States, as well as abroad.

Our eighteenth-century government, which in some respects has changed so much and in other respects so little, has taken on itself tremendous responsibilities. It has undertaken to guarantee, legislatively and administratively, the economic progress and social welfare of the American people, if not of all the world's peoples outside the Soviet sphere. To carry out its responsibilities, government has acquired a variety of controls and stimulants. These call for special functional qualities: foresight, certainty, speed, flexibility, co-ordination, continuity, intelligence, and leadership.

In the international sphere, in this fateful time of tension and alarm, the responsibilities that rest upon government are quite as difficult and present operational demands no less exacting. Our international obligations go much further than membership in the United Nations, economic rebuilding, military preparedness, or a balance-of-power diplomacy. Unless we are entirely bereft of hope and bankrupt of ideas, our government must lead not only this nation but also the world toward a secure regime of law and order. Such a goal poses a problem beyond all other political problems with which the human mind has grappled. It is a problem that we cannot postpone, except at our peril.

During the last fifty years Americans have been commenting more and more on the defects and shortcomings of their government, questioning whether we as a people possess the political capacity or the political means to meet successfully the difficult demands of the modern age. Most of the criticisms of government have dealt with details or with a single feature—Congress, the presidency, the administrative departments and agencies, or methods of election. From these limited appraisals have come many warnings of the danger that may confront us unless we put reforms into effect. A number of students, taking a larger view of the governmental system, have objected to some of its basic features and have proposed more or less drastic changes. Many of these proposals will be discussed in a later chapter.

Among the critics there is general agreement that the Constitution was a work of consummate statesmanship, for which Americans should be everlastingly grateful. It is agreed that the constitutional structure was well fitted to the conditions that existed at the end of the eighteenth century and admirably designed for the accomplishment of the purposes that seemed then of first importance. But, it is argued, both conditions and objectives have changed since that time; and, although alterations have occurred in the form and workings of government, these alterations have fallen short of adequate adjustments. Some look upon presidential leadership or the "strong executive" as something that will correct the basic and inherent faults of the system. Others see disadvantages and dangers in that development.

The purpose of this book is to survey systematically the problem of adjusting our national government to modern requirements. We shall be concerned with the basic or over-all organization, with the authorities and processes that practically decide the ends and means of national action, that determine policies, make laws, and supervise their execution. The problem is conceived to lie in the presidency, the Senate, the House of Representatives, the scheme of representation and election, the administration, and the party system. None of these alone creates the problem or can solve it. All must be understood in their relationships and interactions. For the purposes of this study, it is assumed that the following will remain for the present as they now are: the states and their governments, the division of powers between the federal government and the states, the enumerated powers of Congress, the constitutional prohibitions on Congress and the states, the constitutional guarantees of civil rights, and the judicial branch. While no doubt these features of government need careful and critical examination, they do not appear to be directly and necessarily involved in the problem that we have set for ourselves.

Though our survey is thus limited, it is still an extremely broad one. It rests on a multitude of facts and relationships, which in many instances can be variously interpreted. This is a brief and therefore a very much generalized discussion. In such a discussion it is seldom possible to prove anything beyond the shadow of a doubt. Some features of our national government, such as the workings of the two-chamber system of legislation, have not yet had sufficient detailed study. The whole problem calls urgently for systematic co-operative research. In this book the author's conclusions are his own. Many of them are debatable and should be debated.

It is here assumed that the American people are dedicated to the principle of free government. In common talk a free system is variously called democracy, government by the people, government by consent of the governed, and representative, republican, responsible, or popular government. Whatever name it may bear, it carries two sets of essential implications: one relating to the individual citizen and the other to the institutions and procedures of government. These two sets of implications are: (1) guaranteed and enforced civil rights and individual liberties, freedom of religion, of opinion, of speech, of the press, and of assembly; and (2) control of the government by a popular majority through free elections, or, to put it in another way, responsibility of the government to a popular majority. Free government, of course, does not mean the direct democracy of the Swiss cantons or of the New England town meeting; and neither popular control nor governmental responsibility can operate constantly or absolutely.

Because of the assumption that we have made, democracy

must become a matter of prime concern as we examine the forms and operations of our government; and the realization, implementation, and preservation of democracy must be kept in view as among our ultimate and essential objectives. We shall have, then, no reservations about free government; we want to keep what we have; we want as much more of it as we can get; and we want it all the time.

It is just as imperative that our democracy should work successfully. So another assumption, which likewise becomes an objective, is that we mus* have the greatest possible efficiency in our government. According to the dictionary definition, *efficiency* is "effective operation as measured by a comparison of production with cost in energy, time, money, etc."; and *efficient* means "highly capable or productive; effective in operation." Of course we cannot judge the efficiency of a government as easily as we can that of a machine, a shop, or a worker making tangible things. The products of government are policies and supervisory actions, and, with regard to these, there are usually great differences of opinion. Even after a long passage of time and with the full benefit of hindsight, it is not always possible to say whether government acted rightly or wrongly, or whether under the circumstances it could have taken any other course.

All human institutions function imperfectly; and when a defect stands out clearly, like the proverbial sore thumb, it is difficult to say whether it is something worse than we have a right to expect. The best that can be done is to decide in a common-sense way (1) how a government ought to act in order to meet its responsibilities, and (2) whether it is designed to act in that manner. That it is possible to reach a deliberate judgment on such a matter or at least to establish a strong presumption, was shown by two early American experiences. Both the Declaration of Independence and the Constitution originated in conclusions regarding the inappropriateness of a governmental set-up.

Democracy and efficiency, therefore, not only stand as assumptions and objectives, but they also offer criteria with which to judge the existing organization and establish principles for the future.

Americans tend to undervalue the importance of over-all governmental organization. In this tendency, we find four principal lines of thinking.

In the first place, it is often implied and sometimes asserted that our form of government *is* democracy. If this were so, no one devoted to democracy could advocate a different form. As a matter of fact, free governments may be, and in practice are, organized in a variety of ways. The parliamentary, cabinet, or ministerial type, exemplified by Great Britain, has been widely imitated; but few parliamentary governments have been set up in precisely the same manner. Our own form of government, which may be termed the presidential or presidential-congressional, is likewise subject to numerous variations. Differences are possible in the number, size, and composition of legislatures, in the scheme of representation, in the set-up of the executive, in the distribution of powers, and in the location of responsibility.

Secondly, it is very commonly declared that the kind of government we have depends on the people themselves. So far as this view goes, it is correct. That the operation, as well as the preservation, of free government depends on the minds, morals, and emotions of the citizenry has from the beginning been a commonplace in American political thinking. If we have as a people lost capacity to control our political life, no organization of government can save us.

On the other hand, people and government act on each other. Political institutions continuously and strongly influence popular attitudes. A government may be so organized as to stimulate leadership, crystallize and clarify issues, and fix responsibility, thus facilitating electoral control; or the organization may be such as to discourage or pervert leadership, lower the plane of discussion, confuse the public mind, and conceal responsibility. The channels of political action may be open or clogged. Organization can register the majority will, or frustrate it. A form of government in its day-by-day operation may be interesting or uninteresting. If interesting, it encourages citizens to participate; if uninteresting, it produces indifference and apathy. The mass of voters can give only a small share of their time and attention to their civic duties. One type of governmental organization may make their task as easy as possible, while another may place an excessive burden upon them. When we are tempted to blame the people, it might be well first to inquire whether they do not really act as their political organization presumes and compels them to act.

In the third place, it is said that democracies are inefficient anyway, that inefficiency is the price that we must pay for free government. Before accepting such a view, we should first make sure that we really have democracy, without qualifications or reservations. Our own government, for example, is in part undemocratic. Is it the democratic or the undemocratic features that stand in the way of efficiency? When this question is answered, we may find that it is not democracy but the frustration of democracy that produces inefficiency.

Appraisal and organization of democratic government certainly present special difficulties. Some would say that the efficiency of such a government lies in the accuracy with which it reflects public opinion. When public opinion is mistaken, as it sometimes is, the mistakes of government may be excusable. On the other hand, we should consider that public opinion is formed in large part by public leadership. When popular demands tend to become unreasonable and to exceed the capacity of government, or when public opinion is blind to a foreign threat, a truly effective democratic government will try through its leadership to enlighten the people, moderate their demands, or arouse them from dangerous apathy. As already suggested, such leadership, needed for both democracy and efficiency, may be encouraged or discouraged by the organization of government.

The fourth line of depreciative thinking appeared long ago in Pope's often-quoted couplet:

"O'er forms of government let fools contest;
That which is best administered is best."

Franklin expressed a similar sentiment when the deliberations of the Constitutional Convention of 1787 came to an end. He thought that there was "no form of Government but what may be a blessing to the people if well administered."

Not even a perfect form of government, if one could be conceived, would be able to run itself. To a large extent, the measure of an institution is the realized applied capacity of the men who direct it. To a large extent also, any institution operates in accordance with understandings that come from personal inclinations and accommodations and that are not and cannot be embodied in an organization plan. The living content of government is usually more important than its form. Any organization works best when it is composed of or controlled by men of character and ability.

But governments are themselves recruiting agencies. Men do not enter politics regardless of the atmosphere and the risks of politics. They do not go into government regardless of the opportunities, the prestige, and the rewards that government offers. A government can be so organized as to attract able men to its service or to discourage their participation. Once in the government, such men work best in a good organization. A qualified workman can do his job better with a good machine than with a poor one. Organization prescribes its characteristic rules and procedures. No man, either the best or the worst, can wholly ignore the constitutional pattern or long act in defiance of it. In many cases members of an organization, no matter what their personal inclinations or potentialities may be, act in ways that seem illogical and wasteful, not because they want to, but because they have to. The institution recreates its members in its own image.

It may help us to see that organization makes some difference if we take a hypothetical example. Suppose the Constitution were to vest legislative powers in a Congress consisting of five houses: A Senate composed of two members from each state, a House of Representatives elected by districts, a Regional Assembly made up of delegates from river basins, a Corporative Convention chosen by various organized groups, and an Economic Parliament representing industry, labor, and the consumers. For good measure, let us suppose that we have established in one of these bodies the principle of the *liberum veto* or unanimous consent, the principle that once helped to bring about the destruction of Poland and which is now partially applied to the Security Council of the United Nations. Let us suppose in addition that we have two executives, one chosen by an electoral college and the other by the five legislatures in joint session. Let us give each executive a veto on bills. Would such a form of government be democratic or efficient?

Between 1783 and 1789 thinking Americans believed that the form of government then existing presented a problem of extreme importance. This has often been called the "critical period" of American history. Was governmental organization at that time a matter of no importance?

PART I

A CASE FOR REORGANIZATION

CHAPTER II

EIGHTEENTH-CENTURY GOVERNMENT

It will help us to understand our government if we take a quick backward glance at the place and time in which it took form. What previous experience guided the builders? What were the feelings and ideas of Americans in 1787? Of still greater interest, what were the founding fathers specifically trying to do? What were their practical primary objectives? After recalling the answers to these questions, we shall note in this chapter the main features of the legislative-executive organization and the way it was expected to operate.

ENVIRONMENT

The attitudes and thinking that produced the Constitution were not in all respects universal and timeless. They were to an extent special, local, and transitory. They grew out of the environment as it then was; and the America of the founding fathers, compared with the America of today, seems like another country in another world.

An infant empire. The land liberated by the Revolution was even then so vast in extent as to stir the imagination; but most of it consisted of trackless wilderness. The inhabited territory did not exceed 100,000 square miles; and the census of 1790 showed for the original thirteen states a population of less than 4,000,000. In the presence of space and distance and of population movement and increase, transportation and communication were about as they had been in the time of the Roman Empire. A considerable foreign commerce had developed, and an increasing trade went on among the states and with the Indian tribes; but domestic commerce, other than that over water routes, was for the most part local. It was realized that the development of commerce and the unity of the country depended on the construction and improvement of roads and the build-

13

ing of canals. Since the fathers knew no other means of cheapening or quickening travel, they could hardly conceive the kind of economic unity that their country was to achieve.

An agricultural economy. The "landed interest" greatly outnumbered all other economic groups. Farmers made up 90 per cent of the total population. Only 3 per cent of the people lived in towns of over 8,000. Philadelphia, the largest, had some 40,000 inhabitants. In eighteenth-century America fishing, whaling, trapping, and lumbering had become profitable industries; but they offered few clues to the tremendous natural wealth that the nation possessed or was to possess. British policy had discouraged colonial manufacturers; and, in any event, America in the eighteenth century lacked mechanical power, as well as a sufficient supply of labor. Manufacturing was in general a household activity.

The economic interest. At the time of the framing of the Constitution, economic undertakings were usually carried on by individuals or partnerships. Workers fell into three classes: free laborers, indentured servants, and negro slaves. The free laborers had no organization or unions in the modern sense, no means of collective bargaining, and no rights or special legal protection as wage earners. The employer and his "help" generally worked together in a close personal association; and the employer dictated the terms and conditions of employment. To the bankers and businessmen of the time, commerce represented the most important interest and the most urgent concern. While capital was accumulating and demanding outlets, the war, the fiscal practices adopted for its prosecution, and the termination of British regulations produced economic dislocations and a depression. To make matters worse, the postwar commercial and financial policies of the states tended to promote instability, uncertainty, and lack of confidence.

Individualism. To the man who lived under colonial and frontier conditions, independence was an ordinary way of life and liberty an instinctive feeling and natural possession. Marked differences in regard to property, wealth, and social position had grown up in the older portions of the country, but the circumstances of colonization in the past and the presence of free land in the West created a general impression of economic opportunities open to all. A livelihood, with enough saved for "a rainy day" and for old age, was the chief personal ambition of the common man. This form of security, in whatever words it may have been expressed, resulted from liberty, as liberty was then conceived—liberty to acquire land and to pioneer, to take and to leave jobs, to exercise thrift and to save, and to engage in competition with others.

Aristocracy. In spite of the feelings and influences that emphasized and nurtured liberty and equality, America in 1787 was still pre-eminently an aristocratic society. At the top were the landed proprietors, the bankers and the merchants, the clergy, and, in general, the men of "substance" and education. At the bottom were the small farmers, the laborers, the propertyless, the uneducated, and the illiterate.

The family and the community. The typical family of the time was to a large extent a closely knit, self-contained social and economic unit. Similarly, the local community possessed a large measure of self-sufficiency, though the American of that time had developed a sense of loyalty to his state and, in some respects, a feeling of dependence on its government. Taken as a whole, the America of 1787 was an extremely decentralized society. This was so, not merely because the thirteen states were politically sovereign, but also and mainly because of physical and economic conditions and because communities within the states formed real functioning entities.

International danger. The situation in 1787 was one of grave international insecurity. The Indian tribes alone presented a difficult problem; but, in addition, we had on our borders two of the great European powers, Britain and Spain, either of which could be an enemy. Geographical isolation meant considerable protection; but we were only partially isolated. Some of Europe was over here.

POLITICAL EXPERIENCE

Americans in 1787 were acquainted by experience with four types of government: the British, the colonial, the state, and the Congress of the Confederation.

The British government. The British constitutional struggles of the seventeenth century had their counterparts and repercussions in colonial America. Educated Americans in the eighteenth century were acquainted with English political and legal writings and followed in the press the proceedings of Parliament and other happenings of political interest. During the preliminaries of the Revolution, American political thinkers had examined the philosophical foundations of the British Constitution; and, during the period of active resistance to British policies, the governmental institutions that produced the policies received their share of critical attention. Except for a dislike of monarchy and of hereditary nobility, Americans seem to have felt little hostility toward British institutions. The founding fathers admired the British form of government, as they saw and understood it, and were disposed to follow its pattern, so far as might be practicable.[1]

The British government had, or appeared to have, three branches: the legislative (the two houses of Parliament), the executive (King and ministers), and the judicial. The cabinet, which was responsible to Parliament, had already taken over much of the executive power; but, the founding fathers held that this form of government, as it was then, or as it had been "in its original purity,"[2] exemplified the theories of separation of powers and checks and balances.

Colonial governments. To govern the colonies, the British first improvised a variety of forms, but later adopted a fairly uniform type of organization. This type of organization embodied of necessity two different and largely antagonistic elements: imperial control and local representation. The royal governor appointed by the King exercised the executive power. A lower house or assembly, elected by the people, represented local interests and possessed certain legislative authority. In addition, a Council, generally appointed by the royal governor, served both as an upper house of the legislature and as an executive advisory body.

Now, if we include the courts, which were independent at least in theory, we again have the three distinct branches;

and these appeared to be checking and balancing each other. Both the governor and the British Government had the right to veto colonial legislation; while the popular assembly asserted its authority over the executive through the "power of the purse." Moreover, the assembly generally appointed a number of administrative officers. The antagonisms that developed between the royal governors and the popular assemblies indicated an unhealthy political situation, but, notwithstanding, seemed to support the idea that separation of powers and checks and balances were essential to the safeguarding of liberty.[3]

In colonial experience, therefore, the powers of government were partially separated mainly because it had been necessary to have two primary authorities represented—the British Government and the colonial people. In operation, fusion of powers rather than separation, and unified action rather than checks and balances, became the practical objective and the apparent trend.

State governments. The new state constitutions followed to an extent the colonial models. Twelve, adopted between 1776 and 1787, included provisions that affirmed the principle of separation of powers. Nevertheless, while paying lip-service to the principle, the states in large part disregarded it in practice. The new constitutions in most cases made the legislatures dominant and practically unified the legislative and executive powers. In eight states the legislature elected the executive; in ten states his term of office was only a year; and in eleven states he had no veto. Several states established a council of state to advise the governor; and as a rule the legislature appointed the council along with the chief administrative officers of the state.

Pennsylvania and Georgia in 1787 had single-chambered legislatures. All the others had established the two-house system.

Although the new constitutions proclaimed that governments rested on the consent of the governed, state laws restricted the franchise to taxpayers and property owners and prescribed property qualifications for holding office.

The policies of the states between the Revolution and the

Constitutional Convention were those of separate sovereignties, jealous of one another and each primarily concerned with the protection and promotion of particular interests. Each framed and imposed its own tariffs and raised commercial barriers against its neighbors, while several yielded to inflationary pressures. Prevailing conditions threatened traditional rights of property and sanctity of contracts. The men of "substance" charged these disturbing conditions, so far as the state governments could be held responsible for them, to the dominance of the legislature, which came closest to representing the multitude and which tended to reflect popular impulses.

The Confederation. A second primary cause of "the public misfortunes," lay in the absence of a real union and of a strong central government. During the war the thirteen states had agreed to the Articles of Confederation, which established not a nation or a government but "a firm league of friendship" declared to be "perpetual." The Congress of the Confederation rested on the states, not on the people. With respect to most matters within its jurisdiction, the Congress could take no action except with the assent of nine states. It had no power of its own to execute its decisions, enforce its law, or even to collect the revenue necessary for its own support. It could neither keep order at home nor win respect abroad.

In 1787 fate held the scales fairly evenly between unity and disunity. There had been significant co-operation among the states, and there were strong unifying influences; but such facts could not obscure the reality and persistence of basic tendencies toward separation. The sovereignty of the states and their relations with one another created on this side of the Atlantic an essentially international situation. Should much more time pass, localistic feelings appeared certain to crystallize into antagonistic nationalisms, making the New World another Europe.

Localistic representation. The America of 1787 was accustomed to the representation of states as states and to the idea that members of legislative assemblies should represent geographical districts or local units. The character of American communities in 1787 made representation on a geographical basis appropriate, if not unavoidable; and it had come to be customary on this side of the Atlantic for the legislator to be a resident of the district that he represented.[4] Experience with that kind of representation had not been a wholly happy one,[5] and the founding fathers saw the possibility of national, as contrasted with local, representation. The executive, in their view, might be considered to represent the whole people.[6]

IDEAS AND FEELINGS

The Constitution resulted from numerous currents and cross-currents of thinking and no single or simple explanation of it is adequate. The major contributions, however, came from environment and political experience, as interpreted by the men who composed the Constitutional Convention. These men belonged, generally speaking, to the aristocratic minority and represented pre-eminently the conservative thinking of the propertied class. They were nationalists, but also loyal citizens of their respective states.

Certain widely held theories served both to confirm the practical trend of the deliberations at Philadelphia and to provide arguments in the subsequent campaign for ratification; but, as practical men and patriots, the framers of the Constitution had to consider not only how to reach agreement among themselves, but also how to obtain acceptance of their handiwork by the state conventions. Thus, the Constitution made substantial concessions to the demands of strategy and tactics. When experience or theory did not suggest an appropriate model, the founders did the best they could by means of invention.

Partial eclipse of the democratic ideal. To the extent that democracy depends on constitutional guarantees of individual rights, the America of 1787 had embraced democracy. Despite this fact and despite the prevailing individualism and love of liberty, the tendencies and ideas that we now associate with popular government had not obtained either clear definition or wide acceptance. The term "democracy" was neither familiar nor in good repute. In the minds of the aristocracy the word stood for a leveling tendency, a wild radicalism, mobocracy, rule by the rabble.

In an age that had no perception of the function of public opinion and political parties in popular government,[7] "party" and "faction" seem to have meant pretty much the same thing[8] and to have been equally objectionable. Both represented something antisocial and disruptive, opposed to co-operation and unity, and bearing various sorts of evil fruit—instability, confusion, intolerance, "mutual animosity," and "violent conflicts." Factionalism seemed inevitably to accompany democracy.

Distrust of political power and of human nature. The founding fathers, as well as Americans generally, feared the possibilities of despotism. History, their own experience, and their immediate situation,[9] warned them of the dangers of military dictatorship while creating a general and deep-seated dislike and distrust of standing armies. In the presence of international insecurity, the fathers took into view not only the effect of war but also the likelihood that a feebly or improperly governed country would fall a victim to diplomatic intrigues or to infiltration and corruption from abroad.

The fate of free governments in the past pointed to the tremendously strong tendencies toward aggrandizement, usurpation, and seizure of supreme power; and Hamilton wrote: "History will teach us that . . . of those men who have overturned the liberties of republics, the greatest number have begun their career by paying an obsequious court to the people; commencing demagogues, and ending tyrants."[10]

With their distrust of political power and fear of despotism, the founding fathers brought to their task a remarkable though distorted view of human nature and of the social and political struggle for power. According to Hamilton, men are "ambitious, vindictive, and rapacious."[11] The trouble was not so much the corruptibility of men as their weakness, passions, and will to power. No governmental authority would by itself stay within its allotted sphere; it would naturally and inevitably tend to encroach on other authorities. A major argument for the Constitution was that it established a governmental mechanism which would automatically stop encroachment and resist tendencies dangerous to the public liberties. This mechanism was supported by the two great theories: separation of powers and checks and balances.

Separation of powers. The theory of separation of powers had long enjoyed influential and authoritative advocacy. Montesquieu thought, mistakenly, that the British Government exemplified the principle of separation; and the doctrine found a kind of confirmation in the form that the colonial governments took. In revolutionary America the theory was widely regarded as a political axiom; and it was written into most of the state constitutions, though, as we have seen, the governments thereby established did not fully conform to the theory.[12]

The powers ordinarily referred to were the assumed three powers of government: the legislative, the executive, and the judicial. The case for an independent judiciary could easily rest on its own historical premises, notably on the need for protection of the individual against the government. With respect to the legislative and executive spheres, separation of powers had little to do with division of work, specialization of function, or any other means of promoting efficiency. The theory, as it was advanced in the eighteenth century, rested largely on a belief that separation of powers was essential to free government.[13]

Checks and balances. The theory of checks and balances rested in part on other theories already mentioned. These had to do with the evils of concentrated power, the frailties of human nature, and the passions of the populace. The case for checks and balances has probably never been more clearly stated than in *The Federalist:*

But the great security against a gradual concentration of the several powers in the same department, consists in giving to those who administer each department the necessary constitutional means and personal motives to resist encroachments of the others. The provision for defence must in this, as in all other cases, be made commensurate to the danger of attack. Ambition must be made to counter-act ambition. The interest of the man must be connected with the constitutional rights of the place. It may be a reflection on human nature, that such devices should be necessary to control the abuses of government. But what is government itself, but the greatest of all reflections on human nature? If men were angels, no government would be necessary. If angels were to govern men, neither external nor internal controls on government would be necessary. In framing a government which is to be administered by men over men, the great difficulty lies in this: You must first enable the government to control the governed; and in the next place oblige it to control itself. A dependence on the people is, no doubt, the primary control on the government; but experience has taught mankind the necessity of auxiliary precautions.[14]

To this conception of governmental organization other feelings and ideas contributed; for example, the fear of legislative tyranny,[15] the purpose to compromise and balance opposing economic interests, the desire to curb popular impulse, party spirit and factionalism, the disposition to maintain the *status quo,* and the aim to ensure continued rule by the aristocracy and protection of its economic interests.[16]

An absolute separation of powers is inconsistent with checks and balances; and, when the Constitution came to be framed, it was found necessary to depart substantially from one theory in order to apply the other.

The two-house legislature. The choice of a dual legislative system found also theoretical defenses. It was contended that two houses would mean more deliberation, that one of them would make up for the shortcomings and correct the errors of the other, and that the two together would double "the security to the people, by requiring the concurrence of two distinct bodies in schemes of usurpation or perfidy. . . ."[17] Since it was tactically necessary to have a fairly numerous lower house representing the people, the framers of the Constitution believed that a second or upper chamber, if it had a special composition and permanence, would help to ensure continuity of policy, act as a salutary check on the impulsiveness and factionalism of the people's representatives, and thus "secure the rights of property and promote stability."[18]

Size of a legislative body. From the popular assembly, repretation was the prime expectation. According to *The Federalist*, the requirements of representation called for a fairly numerous membership (one that might eventually reach 400); but the founding fathers believed that the quality of an assembly was likely to vary inversely with its size. It was pointed out that assemblies of men act differently and usually on a lower plane than the individuals who compose them.[19]

Responsibility. "Responsibility is the great point," said Dickinson;[20] and Hamilton pointed out that "one of the weightiest objections to a plurality in the Executive, . . . is, that it tends to conceal faults and destroy responsibility."[21] With regard to bodies of men in general, he said: "Regard to reputation has a less active influence, when the infamy of a bad action is to be divided among a number, than when it is to fall singly upon one."[22] Unfortunately, other ideas that have been mentioned, as well as the practical attainment of major objectives, pushed the principle of responsibility into the background.

OBJECTIVES

The prime purpose of the Constitutional Convention was to "form a more perfect union." Other aims were: efficiency in foreign affairs, stronger government through a stronger executive, general limitations on governmental power, the curbing of popular control, prevention of despotism, protection and promotion of commerce, and general political stability.

A more perfect union. Although the word *nation* or *national* is nowhere used in the Constitution, the prime purpose of its framers was to build a nation. Because of strong local feelings and attachments, the "more perfect union" meant some form of federation, to replace the discredited confederation. The statesmen at Philadelphia had to overcome the fears of the small states while meeting the legitimate demands of the large ones, and to safeguard so far as might be possible those economic interests to which the sections were most devoted.

Efficiency in foreign affairs. It was hoped that the new nation might be made strong enough to hold the balance of power in the New World and thus to protect its boundaries at home, along with its maritime and commercial interests abroad.[23] The safe and proper conduct of foreign affairs in the perilous years ahead demanded a union of the states, a single foreign policy firmly conducted, sufficient military strength for defensive purposes, and a vigorous executive in charge of the country's diplomacy.

Stronger government through a stronger executive. The intention was to avoid the kind of weakness shown by the states and by the Confederation. The framers of the Constitution wanted a government capable of governing. For the requisite strength, energy, promptitude, secrecy, and dispatch—all particularly needed in the critical field of foreign affairs—they put their hopes chiefly in executive power. The presidency, introducing certain highly-prized qualities into the government, was to serve also as a unifying national institution, thus fitting into the complex pattern devised to make federalism feasible.

Curbing of democracy. Of the implications of democracy mentioned in Chapter I, the founding fathers accepted one set and largely rejected the other. Though they were more concerned with the broad interests of their class than with the political liberties of the people, they aimed to safeguard the individual against tyranny and agreed to the addition of a bill of rights to the Constitution. They did not intend, however, that the national government should be controlled by or be responsible to the people. The framers of the Constitution feared the tyranny of the majority as much as any other tyranny. "Complaints are everywhere heard," wrote Madison, "that measures are too often decided, not according to the rules of justice and the rights of the minor party, but by the superior force of an interested and overbearing majority."[24] The aim was to set up a government that the "prudent" and "virtuous" minority could control.

Madison argued that republican government in a large country offered the means of controlling the effects of party and faction. An extensive federation and the delegation of governmental power to representatives would make it possible "to refine and enlarge the public views, by passing them through the medium of a chosen body of citizens. . . ."[25] In this way, parties and factions were to be curbed and harmonized and the general interest protected, with heightened prospects for efficiency and stability. The Convention agreed that the governmental mechanisms must be contrived so as not to give free rein or quick response to popular impulsiveness.

Prevention of despotism. While intent on curbing democracy, the framers of the Constitution proposed to avoid one-man government, either in the form of monarchy, or in any other form, military or civil.

General political stability. The Constitutional Convention wished to set up a political regime which would ensure public order and make revolution in the future unnecessary and improbable. They anticipated constitutional change, but not by encroachment, usurpation, or violence; and, in the interest of conservatism, they desired to impose on the process of change controls similar to those that were to act as brakes on the government itself.

THE FRAMEWORK AND MECHANISM

Environment, experience, ideas, and feelings, marshaled and debated to attain practical objectives, resulted in the constitutional framework and mechanism of government. The need of reconciling divergent viewpoints and clashing interests produced political conclusions that did not give perfect satisfaction to anybody, but did provide ground on which many could stand. The grand attempt to form a more perfect union, with the compromises that it entailed, was enough alone to create a complicated organization; but, on the whole, it was one peculiarly adapted to the urgent needs and the dominant feelings of the time.

Federalism. The process of constructing a federation involved and affected in one way or another almost every aspect of government.

Unlike the Articles of Confederation, the Constitution established a genuine central government, with power to raise its own revenue and to make and enforce laws binding directly on the people. The Constitution, the laws made in pursuance thereof, and the treaties entered into by the United States were declared to be "the supreme law of the land." The House of Representatives directly and proportionally represented the people, and the president bore a relationship not precisely defined to the whole nation. On the other hand, the Constitution gave the states equal representation in the Senate; and the devices of proportional and equal representation were joined in the electoral college scheme and in the amending process.

A much qualified free government. The Constitution was not unreservedly democratic in origin, in intent, or in substance. Plans of representation and election were so devised as to make minority control of a part or all of the government possible and even probable. A minority could always prevent the making of treaties, and under certain circumstances it could block other legislative action. The constitutional framework, however, included a popularly elected House, and, with respect to the Senate and the president, established schemes of indirect choice that assumed and permitted popular elections in their first stages.

Supremacy of civil over military. The Constitution provided for the subordination of the military to the civil authorities. The power to declare war belonged to Congress; no appropriation of money for the army could be for a longer term than two years; and Congress was to make the rules and regulations for the land and naval forces and, in a measure, for the militia.[26] The Constitution expressed the ideal of a decentralized military force drawn largely from the citizenry. The militia, ordinarily distributed among the states and largely under state control, was expected to be the main reliance for the common defense. The president, a civil officer, was to be commander-in-chief of the army and navy, and of the militia also when in the actual service of the United States.[27]

Mixture of powers and separation of departments. The Constitution purported to vest "all legislative powers herein granted" in a Congress, the "executive power" in a president, and the "judicial power" in the federal courts. This is the nearest the Constitution came to a general declaration in favor of separation of powers. As a matter of fact, the principle was not incorporated in the Constitution. What the instrument provided for was a distribution of mixed powers among departments which were partially separate and partially under one another's control.[28]

The check-and-balance system. It was provided that each governmental authority should share in the power of the others and that each should exercise some control over the selection, the tenure, the compensation, or the operations of the others. The resulting intricate arrangements constituted the checks and balances of the Constitution, intended to keep the departments in equilibrium and provide "some practical security for each against the invasion of the others."[29] It is not to be inferred, however, that this system won acceptance solely because of a belief in its intrinsic merits. Much of the check-and-balance mechanism resulted from the compromises involved in the construction of a federal union.

Two assemblies. Two legislative bodies were required for the working out of the federal idea. The Senate and House of Representatives were intended to function independently of each other and to have practically no joint existence or joint responsibility.[30]

To keep each body as distinct as possible from the executive, the Constitution prohibited any member from serving as a presidential elector[31] and from being appointed during his term to a federal office created or given increased compensation during that time; and no one could be at once a federal officer and a member of either house.[32]

In the process of law-making, except for the conclusion of treaties, each house possessed an absolute veto on the proposals of the other. By failing or refusing to act, either might check, thwart, or embarrass the other or the president. They could also check the executive by affirmative action, if and when they agreed. They had considerable potential control over the president himself, since they fixed his salary and the amount of his official expenditures.

Under certain circumstances, the House of Representatives was to choose the president, and the Senate, the vice-president. Moreover, the two houses were to fix the date of the presidential election and determine what officer should act as president in the event of the death, resignation, or disability of both president and vice-president. Neither house, nor the two acting in agreement, could remove the president by simple vote; but the House of Representatives could impeach (that is, prosecute) him for treason, bribery, or other high crimes and misdemeanors, with the Senate acting as judge. If two thirds of the senators present voted for conviction, the president might be removed and disqualified from holding any federal office.[33]

Implicit in the ideas of separated departments and checks and balances was the belief that each governmental authority should be different from the others—different with respect to points of view, ways of thinking, amount of experience, and quality of judgment. The House of Representatives was to be the popular assembly, close to the people and directly representing them. Accordingly, the prescribed qualifications were liberal. A representative at the time of his election had to be twenty-five years old and to have been seven years an American citizen. To ensure accountability to his constituents, his term was made short—two years.

Representatives were to be apportioned among the states according to population; and, in its first session, the House consisted of sixty-five members. The Constitution said nothing about congressional districts; but these were generally assumed; and it soon became customary for members of the lower house to be elected from and by districts. The Constitution prescribed that the representative must be an inhabitant of the *state* in which he is elected. Custom soon decreed that under ordinary circumstances he must reside in a *district* in order to be chosen its representative.

Aside from its role in impeachment trials, the House had

one special power, that of originating all bills for raising revenue.

Of all the institutions set up by the founding fathers, the Senate satisfied the greatest assortment of purposes and figured in the largest number of compromises. Out of the differences that threatened for a time to wreck the Convention, equal representation of the states in the Senate emerged as an essential expedient for ensuring "the sovereignty and political safety of the smaller states."[34] In order further to satisfy the small states, the Constitution provided that no state should be deprived of its equal suffrage in the Senate without its own consent.[35]

To lend further assurance to the small states, the Constitution gave the Senate an important participation in the executive power. The comparatively small size of the upper house and its anticipated qualities seemed to equip it to exercise the functions of an executive council.[36] So the Constitution provided that the president should have power, "by and with the advice and consent of the Senate, to make treaties, provided two-thirds of the senators present concur; and he shall nominate, and, by and with the advice and consent of the Senate, shall appoint ambassadors, other public ministers and consuls, judges of the Supreme Court, and all other officers of the United States, whose appointments are not herein otherwise provided for, and which shall be established by law. But the Congress may by law vest the appointment of such inferior officers, as they think proper, in the president alone, in the courts of law, or in the heads of departments."[37]

To fit the Senate to its purposes and functions, the Constitution provided that this body should be composed of two senators from each state, chosen by the state legislatures for six-year terms. In the beginning, therefore, the Senate had only twenty-six members. That this institution might have permanence and stability, it was provided that one third of the senators should be chosen every two years. The Constitution fixed the minimum age at thirty and the period of citizenship at nine years, and required each senator to be a resident of the state for which he is chosen.[38]

Because of its small size, its indirect election, its expected stability, and its special powers, the Senate was intended to serve, more than any other institution, as a legislative balance-wheel and brake, protecting not only the small states but also the conservative men of "substance" against the presumed tendencies of the lower house.[39]

The presidency. The framers of the Constitution wanted the president strong enough to ensure executive and administrative efficiency, but not strong enough to become a dictator. They equipped the two legislative bodies, particularly the Senate, with power to check him; but, in accordance with the theory, it was necessary that he should have means of self-defense against legislative encroachment. The weapon they gave him was the qualified veto.[40]

The veto, besides serving as a means of defense, was expected to act as a further safeguard against the enactment of unnecessary or improper laws and as a device to preserve the *status quo*.[41] It enabled the president, when supported by a minority in House or Senate, to block action desired by majorities in both legislative bodies. Here, as in the two-chamber system, lay the possibility of delays and deadlocks, and the Constitution laid down no procedure for ending governmental paralysis should it occur.[42]

The president acquired through the veto a substantial share of legislative power. In addition, the Constitution provided: "He shall from time to time give to the Congress information of the state of the Union, and recommend to their consideration such measures as he shall judge necessary and expedient."[43] While this provision may not have implied any strong or extensive presidential leadership in legislation, his powers to recommend and to veto made the president a legislative, as well as an executive, authority.

To the president was assigned the conduct of foreign relations. Although treaties were declared to be a part of the law of the land, the Constitution provided a method for making treaties different from that for enacting statutes. As already explained, the president was to make treaties by and with the advice and consent of two thirds of the senators.

While the members of the House represented local constituencies and the senators the states, the president was conceived somewhat indefinitely to be the agent or champion of the nation, of the people as a whole, or of the general interest.[44] This conception fitted the presidency into the larger implications of the check-and-balance theory.[45]

The method of electing the president, however, excluded the idea of direct responsibility to the people. The Electoral College, presumably to be chosen by the several state legislatures and weighted in favor of the small states, was shrewdly contrived, as the statesmen of 1787 thought, to eliminate parties and factions, the intrigues of officeholders and legislators, and democratic influences in general. These specially chosen presidential electors were, it was believed, self-insulated against "tumult and disorder," "heats and ferments," "extraordinary or violent movements," "cabal, intrigue, and corruption," and "sinister bias."[46] In this manner, the framers of the Constitution thought they were guaranteeing the choice of eminently qualified men.

In case no person should receive a majority of the votes of the Electoral College, or in case two or more persons should tie, each having a majority,[47] the election, according to the Constitution, was to go to the House of Representatives, the voting there to be by states, each state representation having one vote.[48]

The person who received in the Electoral College the second highest number of votes for president was to become vice-president with the duty of presiding over the Senate. In case the president should die, resign, become disabled, or be removed, the vice-president was to succeed him. For the further succession to the presidency, Congress was authorized to provide by law.[49]

The founding fathers expected the electors to choose for president and vice-president the best two men in the country and, accordingly, fixed for the two offices some comparatively exacting qualifications. President and vice-president must be natural-born citizens of the United States or citizens at the time of the adoption of the Constitution and each must be thirty-five years of age or older and have resided in the United States at least fourteen years.

The executive departments. Various provisions of the Constitution made executive departments necessary, or implied that as a matter of course they would be established. No mention was made of a "cabinet," either as a group to be consulted by the president or as a responsible executive body in the English sense. Control of the administration was distributed among the president and the two houses of Congress. Legislative control could be exercised in many ways but chiefly through (1) the creation or abolition of agencies; (2) determining and changing their organizations; (3) specifying their powers, duties, and procedures; and (4) granting or withholding appropriations. The appropriating power or "power of the purse" was the most powerful of all the controls. The right of the Senate to confirm presidential appointments offered to the upper house an opportunity to check executive action and provided an additional legislative instrument for the control of the administration.

THE EXPECTED MANNER OF OPERATION

It is clear from what has already been said that the founding fathers were not concerned with forms alone. Then, as now, the important question was, "How will government actually operate?" The framers of the Constitution had a justified expectation that the mechanism would function in the manner that they desired. They did not want it to act democratically, in the sense of responding obediently or quickly to the will of the majority. They anticipated that delays enforced by one of the departments or in certain cases by the minority would preclude or mitigate actions springing from impulse, corrupt designs, and factionalism. In this way, as well as by other means, the government would work in conformity with the fathers' conception of efficiency.

Good government was to be furthered in the first place by

selecting able and virtuous men for the presidency and the Senate. This done, the executive, with authority concentrated in one man, was expected to perform his duties with a national view and the requisite vigor. In foreign affairs, he was to act with decision, secrecy, and dispatch. In the making of executive appointments, his shortcomings and errors would be measurably corrected by the Senate.

Efficient legislative operations were seen in a somewhat different light. "In the legislature," wrote Hamilton, "promptitude of decision is oftener an evil than a benefit."[50] It was hoped that checks and the resulting delays would compel deliberation. Certainly, the founding fathers did not think of legislation as a series of measures to meet urgent and rapidly changing situations. Nor did they anticipate any great need of co-ordinating policies or administration. Moreover, they could not foresee that the relationship of political parties and pressure groups to the government would profoundly affect its functioning from the standpoints both of democracy and of efficiency.

CHAPTER III

THE SITUATION NOW

The history of the United States is a record of rapid and radical transformation. Because conditions have changed, Americans now think differently. They expect more and different things of government; and they have given to the national government powers and responsibilities which the founding fathers, if they were to return, would find it difficult to grasp. In the light of these remarkable developments, many of us believe that our government, if it is to be successful, must operate in a different manner than it was intended originally to operate. The governmental organization was admirably adapted to the conditions, thinking, and needs of 1787. Since then, what alterations have taken place?

AMERICA AND THE WORLD

After 1787 we became first a nation, then a world power, and finally one of the world's two superpowers. The period since that date includes the industrial and technological revolutions. It probably witnessed more changes in the material environment and in the conditions of human living than had occurred in all the previous history of mankind. We are now passing the threshold of the atomic age.

An expanded empire and perfected nation. Continental United States today is more than three times greater in area than it was in 1790, and, with its outlying territories and possessions,[1] is more than four times larger. Its inhabitants number more than 140 millions,[2] 35 times the population in 1790. The bulk of the population and the balance of political power now lie in regions of which the founding fathers knew little or nothing.

The states have lost much of their peculiar significance. The 13 have become 48 and may soon become 49 or 50. Of the 35 admitted to the Union after 1789, only 2 had previously been independent.[3] A majority of the states may now be considered more or less artificial units. In place of the old sectionalism, we now have regions with distinctive needs and interests; but these regions overlap; they often cut through a state; and they assume different shapes and characteristics as circumstances change. By 1890 America had lost its frontier, and henceforward the country turned in on itself, developing intensively rather than extensively and rapidly diminishing the separateness and isolation of communities. Thus territorial decentralization no longer ranks as a basic condition in our national life.

Means of transportation and communication, unknown and unpredictable in 1787, have largely eliminated the obstacles created by distance, and, so far as concerns the transit of persons, goods, and ideas, have gone far to make the country one relatively compact community. Measured by railroad or automobile travel time, the United States, in spite of its expansion, is from a third to a half smaller now than it was in 1787; and measured by air-travel time, the country has shrunk to a small fraction of its eighteenth-century proportions.

Speedier and cheaper transportation resulted in a speedier and cheaper postal service, which with the telegraph and the telephone enables people to communicate and confer with each other quickly, and, in the case of the telegraph and telephone, almost instantly. The entire country can now read the same news at almost the same moment. The radio has made it possible for the whole population to attend one country-wide meeting and to hear the same speaker at the same time; while television also enables us to see the speaker.

Industry and urbanism. In striking contrast to the land of Washington and Jefferson, America has become predominantly industrial. That individualism which was once a primary political fact has almost entirely disappeared, along with the isolation and self-sufficiency that nourished it. The economic system by which we live is, at the least, national in scope; and its general characteristic is not the independence of individual or village, but the interrelationship of all the nation's parts and the interdependence of all its members.

The United States is no longer predominantly rural. It is a land of great cities; and in many ways the city overspreads the country, while the country shares in and imitates the life of the city. As a rule, one now finds in the cities, pretty much in proportion to their size, the highest and most extensive expressions of cultural life, the best newspapers, the foremost professional members and institutions, the seats of economic management, and the persons best qualified for public positions and informed leadership.

Economic interest and class division. The growth of the nation's territory and population, the altered position of the states, the passing of the frontier, the effect of modern transportation and communication, and in some directions the influence of industry and urbanism—have all contributed to unification. On the other hand, our history since 1787 has amply confirmed the truth of Madison's observations regarding economic interest. The conflict goes on between debtor and creditor classes; but the modern division and struggle between capital and labor had practically no counterpart in 1787.

International position. It is amusing to recall that the Indian tribes once figured in our international thinking and in our foreign policy, that the Spanish provinces in the New World once made the United States look puny in comparison, that we were annoyed by the infiltrations of the French Revolutionists, that our Great Plains belonged for a time to the Napoleonic Empire, and that we fought in a world war against the British. During our first quarter-century, we luckily escaped from foreign threats, and from 1815 to 1898 enjoyed remarkable security while holding aloof from the problems and quarrels of Europe and Asia. This happy situation resulted in part from the purchases of Florida and Louisiana and from the Latin-American revolutions. Afterward, we owed our security, not so much to our military power, our isolation, or the Monroe Doctrine, as to the friendliness of Great Britain, her naval supremacy in the Atlantic, and the balance of power that she maintained in Europe.

Despite our favored position, we became increasingly involved in the international system, not only of the New World but also of the Old. The First World War confirmed this involvement; and the second brought final and overwhelming proof, not merely of our involvement, but also of our insecurity and our power. No longer could one speak with much meaning, as the fathers did, of the Old World and the New. The factors that tended toward our domestic unity operated throughout the world to reduce distances, to weave nations together into a system characterized by interrelationships and interdependence. Politically, there is no longer a European system of power politics distinct from the Far Eastern and the American.

The United States, therefore, now occupies a position in world affairs somewhat similar to that which Britain occupied in the nineteenth century; but striking changes have occurred in the issues, methods, and tactics of international action. We have now formidable movements against free government itself, substantially new techniques of subversion and aggression, and the confusion, demoralization, and disintegration resulting therefrom.

Thus, the present situation of the United States resembles that which alarmed the founding fathers; but our present problem is bigger and more complex, while the tempo of international action has strikingly increased.

Modern war. Modern war comes without declaration and may come without warning; and no nation can any longer protect itself from attack behind fortifications, walls, mountains, straits, seas, oceans, or navies. Industry, science, and technology have supplied a bewildering variety of weapons and equipment, mechanization of the fighting forces, the airplane, electronics, the atomic bomb, and, finally, biological warfare. Either for its prosecution or in its effects, modern war engulfs the world, and, within the war-waging nations, it involves a practically universal mobilization of men and of industry, and the use of all conceivable instruments of offense and defense—military, political, economic, and psychological. Destruction or slaughter or both on a huge scale is a method, as well as an incident of war; and recovery from war, to the extent that recovery can be accomplished, is a long and painful process.

ATTITUDES, BELIEFS, AND EXPECTATIONS

Americans of today, compared with their eighteenth century ancestors, not only live differently in a different environment, but also feel and think differently. Some of the emotional and intellectual changes developed in the early years; others have only recently appeared.

Nationalism, isolationism, and internationalism. The feeling of nationalism now overshadows the local attachments and state loyalties that were potent in 1787 and persisted until after the Civil War.

The international outlook of the fathers, derived from geographical facts and from dislike of the European system, found reinforcement during the nineteenth century from a sense of security, preoccupation with internal development, and a large measure of national self-sufficiency. We seem now to have finally discarded isolationism in favor of a more realistic and more exacting conception of our international position and obligations.

Acceptance of democracy. The influence of the frontier farmers and industrial laborers soon swept away the philosophy of political privilege. In the Jacksonian era the word "democracy" lost it disrepute, and, at the time of the First World War, it had become a commonly accepted name for our system of government and way of life. During that war, we hoped and thought that victory over Germany would make the world "safe for democracy"; but afterward democracy met a new and determined challenge from the ideologies of fascism and communism. The outcome of the Second World War, like that of the first, seemed to buttress the democratic idea; but the challenge of totalitarianism continues both abroad and at home.

Constitutionalism and stability. Aided by the fame and wisdom of Washington, by the restoration of order and by a return of prosperity, the national government got off to a good start.

The Constitution became associated in American minds with the rising tide of nationalism and with the amazing growth of the country in territory, power, and wealth. Belief in American destiny and its apparent fulfillment reinforced the general feelings of respect and veneration. Thus, the Constitution, as a symbol of stability and ordered progress, quickly displaced the revolutionary idea.

Decline of individualism. In the complicated specialized society of today, the individual tends to lose his wholeness, his personal integration, and the sense of security that he once derived from his own self-sufficiency and the simplicity of his community.

The questions that now affect the citizen are both remote and complex. Observation, personal experience, and common sense are not enough for his guidance. The organized group and the expert have become necessary to the public functioning of Americans. The group gives us leadership, information, judgments, and prestige, as well as the power and the feeling of security that come from numbers and organization. The expert gives us a substantially new process of deliberation.

Freedom, security, and trust in political power. Distrust of political power, particularly of centralized political power, along with the original belief in individualism, localism, states' rights, and limited government, persisted with few essential modifications until after the Civil War. But at the present time, a majority of Americans apparently are not only unafraid of political power but look upon it as a refuge and a protection. What government should do is now determined not so much by a general theory of liberty as by changing social standards and accumulating group demands.

While these changes were taking place, the term "security" took on a new content. The founding fathers were concerned in the main with national safety and with the protection of property from lawlessness and disorder. In the twentieth century, security came to mean also the protection of wage earners against unemployment, accidents, and other hazards. Thus conceived, "social security" or "economic security" as an objective no longer allied itself with liberty or democracy, but largely over-shadowed these ideals and tended to be thought more valuable.

Rights and wants. During recent years and especially since 1929, economic conditions and "social consciousness" have altered the old conception of rights and stimulated the formulation of so-called new rights. Most of these have no fundamental character, but represent demands made on government by underprivileged groups. Instead of placing prohibitions or restrictions on public authority, the new rights impose affirmative obligations on government and assume the existence or creation of commensurate political power. They are concerned, not so much with the freedom of individuals as with their wants, privileges, and material well-being.

Economic expectations. The safety of the nation still takes precedence over all other popular expectations; but unless war is imminent or in progress, economic wants usually appear more immediate, concrete, and insistent. In the great economic-social contests that have marked American history, the masses have won successive triumphs; since 1900 they have fully understood their political power; and since the great depression of 1929, their view of the obligations of government has become the prevailing conception. Popular economic expectations at present can be stated as increasing production, rising standards of living, distributive justice, and economic security, with no disastrous interruptions or periods of serious unemployment.

Human nature. We agree today with the founding fathers that the power-seeking motive is one of the strongest, if not the strongest, of the elementary urges that make men act as they do. Most of us would admit that human institutions and agencies have a habit of expanding and encroaching. Contemporary thinking, however, is inclined to recognize the good in men, as well as the bad, and to give more weight than seemed expedient or possible in 1787 to the principle of responsibility as a means of attracting good men to public positions and as a safeguard against the dangers of concentrated power.

Americans probably still believe that military power is a danger to free government, that militarism is incompatible with the spirit and practices of democracy, and that the armed services must be under civilian control. In the existing international situation, however, a majority of Americans are willing to have a huge military establishment, along with a considerable degree of militarism and military control, in order that the country may be protected against despotism from abroad.

Efficiency and responsibility. Generally speaking, efficiency as an end or as a test is still considered to apply chiefly to executive and administrative matters. During the early years of the twentieth century, the study of administrative efficiency and the achievement of it—largely inspired by industry—took on the aspects of a new crusading cult. From 1910 on the municipalities, the states, and the federal government, pressed by taxpayers for reduction of public expenditure, joined in or subjected themselves to what was called the "efficiency and economy movement." To this movement came the "efficiency engineers," a growing number of researchers in government, and miscellaneous practitioners of applied political science, as well as many economy-minded politicians. They usually stressed the fixing of responsibility as an organizing principle; and this principle has become axiomatic almost everywhere except in the field of legislation.

Separation, checking, and balancing. The general theories advanced in the eighteenth century to justify the complexity of our government meet with little open opposition. The contemporary opinion of popular assemblies is similar in many respects to the views of the founding fathers, and on the whole no more flattering. It is still the executive department that tends to win and hold the greatest measure of public confidence and respect.

Parties, leadership, and good men. Parties have now won an assured place in governmental procedure, but in our own consciences we do not accept them steadily and unreservedly. In our politics, as in that of other countries, one can easily see what Ernest Barker calls "a new eruption of the personal,"[4] a tendency to put one's trust in a man, rather than a party or principles.

The triumph of democracy swept away the aristocratic leadership favored by the fathers, and we have not yet become again freely receptive to intellectual leadership in politics. By modern standards, we think of a "good man" in politics as one who is honest and, in a broad sense, popular. We have expended much of our reforming energy on the elimination of corruption, and we can feel pride justifiably in the progress that we have made. In administration we have also made great progress toward the recognition of merit and in the use of specialists, experts, and scientists. Through the administration, these intellectually qualified men have come to play an important part in the making of public policy.

EXPANDED SCOPE OF GOVERNMENT

With the growth and knitting together of America, an increasing number of conditions and problems called for governmental action, and these became interstate or national in scope, requiring national treatment. As a result, the scope of federal powers has become practically unlimited, and the multiplied activities of the national government are now predominantly concerned with positive economic, social, and international objectives. The attitudes, beliefs, and expectations of the people, which have just been outlined, have also tended to increase the work of government and to make it more complicated, more delicate, and more difficult.

Preservation of democracy. The first responsibility of a democratic government is to realize, implement, and maintain democracy. Fulfillment of this primary obligation requires (1) the exclusion of undemocratic features from the organization and procedures of government; (2) the safeguarding of the civil liberties; (3) maintenance of the machinery necessary for free elections; (4) attention to the effect of government on popular attitudes toward democracy; and (5) the combating of communism, fascism, and other subversive movements. It is primarily important, however, that government should operate efficiently: it must meet popular expectations; it cannot risk failure or a loss of public confidence.

Economic intervention. The national government from the

beginning has undertaken in various ways to promote and control economic activities. Promotion has applied to manufacturing, to agriculture, to highways, canals, railroads, the merchant marine, and air transport, to bituminous coal and petroleum, and to small businesses. Since the eighties, the idea that the federal government should be a regulating and reforming force in the field of private industry has spread over broad areas and has found a wide range of applications. In the development of its controls, the national government has advanced from prohibitions and a negative type of regulation to the stage of positive interference in the management of private industry.[5]

A land-owner from the beginning, the national government since the turn of the century not only has extended its holdings of land, forests, parks, and minerals, but also has acquired ownership of commercial and industrial enterprises.[6] One of the latest of these acquisitions, the control and development of atomic energy, is of incalculable importance. In regard to agriculture, the federal government passed in the thirties from promotion to "over-all planning and implemented activity designed to determine both the direction and the magnitude of agricultural enterprise."[7] In the field of labor, governmental powers and responsibilities involve a major control over the country's economy.

In selecting modes of intervention and the points where intervention should take place, the national government has not consistently followed any one philosophy, theory, or master plan. Our economic system is partly free and partly controlled, partly private and partly public; but the complex of governmental powers and responsibilities tends more or less rapidly to expand and as it expands, to curtail relatively the sphere of private enterprise.

Social guarantees. In addition to what is included in labor legislation, the social task of government relates to public relief, education, health, morals, recreation, housing, and social or economic security. These responsibilities still belong in large part to state and local governments; but the national government plays an increasingly influential role throughout the social welfare field.

Fiscal responsibilities. From 1816 to 1861 the average annual expenditure of the federal government was about 33 million dollars a year. In 1900 it amounted to 500 millions and in 1915 to 761 millions. During the period of the New Deal, federal spending reached unprecedented peacetime heights, coming close to 9 billion dollars in 1936. In 1948, however, President Truman presented to Congress a budget calling for expenditures of about 40 billions. The fiscal operations involved in finding and spending such a sum constitute a major task of government and an important influence on the economic system.

For a time about a hundred years ago we had no national debt at all. As late as 1915 the debt was less than one billion dollars;[8] but at the end of 1947 it stood at about 256 billion dollars. The annual interest on it is about ten times the total cost of government in 1900. The management of such a debt constitutes a substantially new responsibility and an important factor in the country's economic life.

International obligations. The international problems that confront the United States are political, economic, social, psychological, military, and strategic. Anything that affects appreciably the attitude of another nation may affect more or less vitally the position of the United States. In the changing world-pattern of power, the policies of another nation and its significance to us are determined by the internal conditions of that nation, as well as by its external relations.

Along with the interrelationship of nations and international problems, we have, so far as we alone are concerned, an intensified interrelationship and general similarity between foreign and domestic affairs. The necessity for military preparedness arises solely from the international situation, but it raises questions that relate to almost every phase of our domestic life. The success of economic action abroad depends on the maintenance of productivity and economic stability at home. The solution of our domestic economic problems is an essential means of meeting the competition of the Soviet Union.

Diplomacy today calls for the detailed execution throughout the world of what should be an extremely comprehensive and concrete program. For American responsibilities include the administration of occupied territories, the giving of loans and specialized assistance to countries having strategic importance, participation in international organizations, institutions, authorities and commissions, protection of American investments in strategic raw materials, the development and control of atomic energy, combating of antidemocratic ideologies, and attention to a multiplicity of matters incidental to the application under various conditions of military, economic, and political policies.

Though the immediate task is the safeguarding of our national security in a world where war is still a probability, we have, because of our international position, a responsibility for the political organization of the world.

"*To provide for the common defense.*" Modern war, preparedness for it, and recovery from it tend to obscure, if not to obliterate, the traditional distinctions between war and peace. The quickness with which an attack can be made and the possibly decisive nature of the first offensive emphasizes now as never before the necessity of peacetime military preparedness. Anything like complete preparedness against atomic attack would require the redistribution of industries, reconstruction of cities, and the provision of bombproof and radiation-proof shelters for a considerable proportion of the industrial plants and civilian population. With or without such a colossal undertaking, reasonable preparation under present conditions would seem to require an effort about as tense and about as total as war itself.

Preparedness for war is not merely military in the narrow sense. It calls for alliances, far-flung strategic outposts, organization and control of industry, and mobilization of technical and scientific resources. Preparedness involves also a worldwide diplomatic program, supported by and co-ordinated with the military. Furthermore, if military power is to be used for the prevention of war, the potential aggressor must know, as international issues arise, promptly and exactly where America stands.

MODERN OPERATING REQUIREMENTS AND NEW EMPHASES

Remarkable changes have occurred in America and the world, in the attitudes, beliefs, and expectations of Americans, and in the work of government. In the light of these changes, should our government act differently than the fathers designed it to act?

Reversed requirements. It is unnecessary now that government should be organized primarily to bring about a more perfect union, to placate the adherents of state sovereignty, or to protect one class or group of states against another. The nation the fathers imagined and worked for has become a reality. The concentration of power that the masses in 1787 feared has now become a fact, accepted and demanded by the masses of today. It is, therefore, now required of our government that it speak and act nationally, not as an alliance of states or a composite of localisms.

Furthermore, it is no longer a purpose or requirement of our national government that it curb democracy. On the contrary, it should realize democracy, express it, and stimulate the democratic spirit. To meet this basic need, we can no longer depend, as we could in earlier days, on the conditions of American life and on the vigorous functioning of local governments. Democracy is today a national ideal and a national problem, and we must consider the bearing of our national governmental organization on the ideal and the problem.

Requirements still valid. The framers of the Constitution had certain requirements in their minds which should be very much in our own. They wanted to prevent despotism; they wished to avoid violent revolution; they desired their legislators to deliberate and decide wisely; they intended that the executive department should act with vigor and promptitude; and they hoped to bring the best men into government. Of these requirements that remain essentially unchanged, three relate more especially to the efficiency of government. These are (1) deliberation and wise decision, (2) executive vigor and promptitude, and (3) the best men in government.

Deliberation. Whether deliberation occurs or does not occur, whether it is fruitful or unfruitful depend largely on the men who do the deliberating, on their mental qualities, their training and experience, the sense of responsibility that they feel, their ability to use experts, their willingness to consider various points of view, and the opportunity that they have for thinking and discussion. Sometimes, one man can deliberate better than a crowd. Deliberation takes time, but forced delay does not necessarily mean deliberation. This requirement of government cannot be met by formal or mechanical contrivances. That the founding fathers well knew. The devices that they contrived to compel delay were intended, not so much to produce deliberation, as to check the passions and impulses of the multitude and their representatives. The purpose was to prevent the nondeliberative part of government from making the decisions. Under modern conditions, however, the whole government must represent the people, and the whole government, therefore, if it is to be efficient, requires capacity and opportunity for deliberation.

Continuity. One of the modern marks of a wise governmental decision is continuity.

On certain matters of fundamental and crucial importance, it is necessary that government decide in what direction and how far it wants the country to go, and having made such a decision public policies should continuously and consistently conform to it. For example, in economic affairs, if the tendency toward more and more governmental intervention is to stop, if a real balance between private enterprise and public control is to be established and maintained, our national government will have to act quite differently than it has acted in the past. If we are to have a managed economy, the differences will be even more marked. To take another example, if government is to enforce social justice without undue paternalism and without sapping away the initiative and self-reliance of the people, government must be able to rise above demagoguery. In foreign affairs, similarly, we must be able to decide whether we shall indefinitely play the game of power politics and war, whether we shall fix on an objective consistent with our ideal of permanent peace, and, having done so, whether we shall proceed step by step toward that objective. Inconsistency and vacillation in foreign affairs mean weakness, failure, and possibly eventual disaster.

Integration. In this age a strong and wise government is equipped with maximum means of integration. Integration implies comprehension, co-ordination, and planning.

When we think of America and the world, as well as of contemporary beliefs, attitudes, and expectations, we are struck by the extraordinary variety of views and purposes that move the people, the many confusions and contradictions that exist, the conflicts of interest that press upon government, and the strength of different and often divergent trends. On the assumption that government is to lead and guide, it becomes evident that confusions must to some extent be removed, conflicts and contradictions appreciably reconciled, and so far as pressures and trends are concerned, a degree of independent mastery substituted for subservient drift.[9]

In the course of 160 years we have accumulated, largely in a piecemeal manner, an enormous mass of laws, judicial decisions, and executive orders. Our public authorities should be able, so far as humanly possible, to grasp the totality of adopted policies and foreseeable problems, to take comprehensive views, to keep policies in harmony with one another, and to carry on a continual revision of laws and policies, checking them against new standards and eliminating inconsistencies and contradictions. Our international position and responsibilities call particularly for unity.

Vigor and promptitude. We still want executive vigor and promptitude; but the legislative function today has become very much like the executive function as the latter was conceived in 1787. In large measure modern legislation provides not for the definition of rights and obligations, for the determination of large objectives, and for permanent organization, but for governmental action itself, for the specific means of reaching subordinate and transitory ends, and for repeated adjustments to meet situations as they arise. Consequently, economic control, distributive justice, and the conduct of foreign relations have come to depend largely on a step-by-step process of legislative policy-making, in which appropriations play a decisive part.

Government deals with an environment that rapidly changes and is in many respects delicate and sensitive. Along with continuity of action and integration of policies, we must have today quicker adjustments to changing situations. We can no longer look with complacency on a purposely slow government or on the possibility of deadlock. Since appropriate adjustment involves the anticipation of consequences, specialized information, technical advice, and advance planning become essential. In the presence of complexity and uncertainty, government will have to experiment, as it has often experimented in the past. To the extent that it experiments, it is all the more necessary that the results should be promptly appraised and corrective action promptly taken.

There is no reason to believe that emergencies and crises wil soon cease to plague us, or that time-limits on the effectiveness of action, domestic or international, will disappear. We are well aware that the prosecution of a war demands quick decisions; but today operations in peace impose similar requirements. In fact, there is no longer the old clear-cut distinction between peace and war. Alertness, flexibility, speed, and timing have become far more important than they were in the eighteenth century.[10]

It is not contended that government should always act quickly. The driver of the governmental machine should not keep his foot frozen to the accelerator. He should know how to use the brakes. At the same time, the machine should not be self-braking. It should not be liable to automatic stoppages. The driver should be able to speed up when he needs to. Statesmen should be free to decide urgently when urgency is called for. Prompt action does not necessarily prevent deliberation. What we now require from government is capacity for *both* deliberation and speed.

The best men in government. We still want the best men in government. We need more than we did in earlier years men of virtue, understanding, prudence, wisdom, energy, decisiveness, and courage. Without such men we cannot get deliberation and wise decision with continuity, integration, and promptitude. Furthermore, under present and future conditions an extraordinary quality of public leadership is required to make clear to Americans the complex and remote problems of today, while bringing other peoples to our side in the cause of an ordered world.

Responsibility and administrative supervision. To facilitate popular control as well as to keep leadership within proper bounds, democratic government calls for a much clearer fixing of responsibility than would be necessary in a government designed to be aristocratic. It is now a commonplace that administrators, specialists, experts, and technicians should be consulted regarding the content of public policy and should themselves engage in subordinate legislation. In a democratic government, however, the bureaucracy, through supervision and direction, must be made responsible to the political authorities. Moreover, since specialization and the elaboration of administration exert a disintegrative influence on policy-making, it is necessary that the political authorities have the capacity and the means to co-ordinate and unify the experts.

Government in modern America, therefore, reveals a new emphasis on responsibility, along with a substantially new requirement and a substantially new test of statesmanship: administrative supervision.

ALTERATIONS IN GOVERNMENT

In the light of the changes that we have noted, what alterations have occurred in the structure and mechanism of the national government?

Redistribution of power. In some respects, government in the

United States has reflected rather faithfully the growth of nationalism, of national unity, and of a closely-knit national economy. As already pointed out, a tremendous change has occurred with respect to the powers and responsibilities of the national government. With respect to power, major alterations have taken place within the national government. It now includes, in effect, two kinds of legislative authorities for which the original Constitution made no express provision: the Supreme Court itself[11] and the administrative agencies that possess legislative authority.[12]

Another phase of constitutional change has strengthened the president in relation to Congress. The balance between executive and legislature has not always been stable; but, up to the end of the nineteenth century, constitutional trends indicated to many observers the probability of a permanent shifting of power to Congress. When Woodrow Wilson wrote his *Congressional Government* in 1885, he thought that Congress was "unquestionably, the predominant and controlling force, the centre and source of all motive and of all regulative power."[13] Bryce in somewhat more measured terms agreed with Wilson.[14] On the other hand, Henry Jones Ford, writing in 1898, believed that the pattern of American government had been fixed by Andrew Jackson and remarked that Congress itself showed "an unconscious disposition to aggrandize the presidential office," while failing to use the legislative checks on the executive.[15] Woodrow Wilson took note in 1900 of "the new leadership of the executive," which he thought might bring about "an integration which will substitute statesmanship for government by mass meeting."[16] More recently, it has become the habit to view Theodore Roosevelt, Woodrow Wilson, and Franklin D. Roosevelt as exemplifications of a governmental change that had resulted, or would soon result, in presidential domination.[17]

As the responsibilities of the national government expanded, the federal administrative organization grew in size, complexity, and cost. At the present time, there are ten executive departments, each consisting of numerous subdivisions and enrolling thousands of officials and employees; but they represent only a part of the federal administrative organization. The Interstate Commerce Commission and other similar agencies have been held by the Supreme Court to be "arms" of Congress; and the Court has decided that the president's removal power, unless specifically provided for by law, does not extend to the members of these "independent" regulatory commissions. The so-called "executive branch" now includes three categories of administrative agencies: (1) the executive departments, (2) the "independent" agencies, which like the executive departments, are subject to presidential control, and (3) the "independent" regulatory commissions, over which the president has less control.

Power, as well as independence, comes to the administrator, wherever he may be located, from the authority delegated to him by Congress and the support that he receives from special interests. His position is greatly strengthened also by the expertness that he possesses or commands and by his exceptional, sometimes exclusive, knowledge of the results of legislation and the requirements of administration.

Popular control. Except for the growth of power and of administration, the most impressive change in government has come from extensions of popular control. These have occurred in various areas: the suffrage, the number of elective offices, the party system, the method of electing president and senators, and pressure groups.

Extensions of the suffrage after 1787 served both as cause and effect of democratization and helped to make the electorate a functioning part of government and its supreme controlling organ.

Frontier democracy left other marks on our political organization and procedure. In the states, counties, and townships, the people elected, not only the policy-making authorities, but also various and numerous administrative officials, ranging from the town constable up to the governor. The result was the "long ballot," which placed a heavy burden on the voter in national as well as local elections.

In 1787 parties were already in the making; and the party system, as it developed from then until 1840, represented a constructive political achievement of first importance. As the party perfected its organization to include the wards, townships, cities, counties, and states, it became a nationalizing influence and a co-ordinating instrumentality; and, as it functioned in the presidency, in the Senate, and in the House, the party became a means of unifying to an extent the constitutionally separated authorities, thus partially counteracting the effects of checks and balances.

The party system and the national convention made the Electoral College customarily merely a formal means of counting and weighing votes. From the time of Jackson, the parties have nominated and the people have elected, subject to certain mathematical rules and to several distinct hazards.[19]

In its attempt to create and maintain unity, strength, discipline, and loyalty, the party exploited the jobs and privileges that government dispensed, incidentally becoming identified with serious evils the spoils system, machine politics, and bossism. Partisanship and politicians fell into disrepute; and a movement developed after the Civil War to eradicate the spoils system. In the 1890's the democratizing movement then in full swing turned to the problems presented by the party organization; and most of the states established the direct primary method of making nominations.

The Seventeenth Amendment, ratified in 1913, provided for the direct election of senators by the people. The Twentieth Amendment, ratified in 1933, was designed in part to quicken the response of government to public opinion as expressed in elections and make periods of inaction less likely or at least shorter.[19]

The vast complex of groups and pressures, with which we are now familiar, represents a substantial and most significant part of the political organization of the electorate. The budding eighteenth-century republic also had its groups and pressures; but in this respect the situation now is vastly larger and more complicated. Among these groups, some are established frankly and solely for electoral action, others for the purpose of influencing legislation, and still others for propaganda and the shaping or manipulation of public opinion. Several of the more powerful pressure groups carry on all of these activities, along with many others, while numerous organizations perform incidental or occasional political functions. When the pressure group seeks to get something done, its effect is, like that of the political party, to bring a measure of unity into a government of separated departments. Moreover, the executive bureaus have their own peculiar relationships to regions and groups. To a large extent administration divides and subdivides into independent or semi-independent authorities, each with its special clientele or interested constituency. In some cases, as in the field of agricultural policy, the private group participates in the official administrative organization and in official activities.

Congress. Alterations with respect to Congress have affected chiefly (1) its relationship to the executive, (2) the method of choosing the senators, (3) the comparative power and prestige of Senate and House, and (4) the size of the two bodies and the number and size of their committees. The shift of power from Congress to the executive and the change in the method of electing senators have already been noted.

For various reasons, the Senate acquired a power and prestige greater than that of the House. According to the theories of 1787, the introduction of the same "spirit" into both houses would largely prevent one from acting as a desirable check on the other. Direct election of senators removed one source of difference between them. Before this change occurred, Senate and House with regard to the law-making function had become similar to one another. The Senate is an initiating as well as a revising body, practically so even in the passage of money bills. From the beginning, the Senate has never functioned, strictly speaking, as an executive council. With respect to the approval of appointments and treaties, the upper house acts more as an independent check on the president. Indeed, in practice, the political party and spoils system gave to both senators and representatives an important share in the initiation of appointments.

With the growth of the country, both assemblies increased

in size: the Senate from 26 to 96 and the House from 65 to 435. At the same time increases took place in the number and size of the committees.

How much and where? Despite the changes that have occurred since the birth of the Republic, most of the characteristic features of the original governmental organization remain intact. We have the four great institutions—the Senate, the House, the presidency, and the Supreme Court; and they reveal much the same partial separateness, blending of powers, and checks and balances that have always characterized their relationships. The theory and basis of representation in the presidency, the Senate, and the House show no essential alterations. Administration has become in effect a fifth institution or collection of institutions, possessing a measure of separateness, a mixing of powers, and a capacity to check and balance. These characteristics belong also to the administrative agencies in their relations with one another. With respect to the location and exercise of legislative power, trends and modifications have not produced any noticeable simplification. On the contrary, organization and procedure have become more complicated.

The flexibility that our Constitution is supposed to possess has been particularly apparent with respect to governmental powers, their division between the nation and the states, and their distribution within the national government. The remarkable changes that have occurred in this area may be attributed almost exclusively to the interpretations and decisions of the Supreme Court. Growth, change, and adjustments have occurred in that field of political organization which overlaps public and private domains. In this field, which includes the electorate, public opinion, parties, and pressure groups, the chief modifying forces have been practice, custom, and ordinary legislation. Judicial interpretation and constitutional amendment have played relatively minor parts. They have likewise made minor contributions to the expansion of administration, except that the Supreme Court has determined the limits and methods of legislative delegation and the peculiar status of the regulatory commissions.

A similar flexibility is not to be found in the great institutions of government, or, essentially, in their relations to one another. In this central and crucial area, relatively little essential change has taken place. In certain respects, therefore, the Constitution is not flexible: it is extremely rigid. Its rigidity relates mainly to structure and institutional relationships. From the viewpoint of distribution of power, Felix Frankfurter may have been justified in calling our fundamental law "a stream of history";[20] but with respect to structure and relationships, the Constitution bears more resemblance to a glacier.

CHAPTER IV

MATERIALS FOR A NEW DESIGN

In the late eighteenth century, the reformers of American government considered the conditions of their time and the needs and demands that those conditions presented. They analyzed the setup and operations of the existing government and decided that it did not and could not satisfy those needs and demands. Then they established certain principles and objectives which they believed should be embodied in or carried out by the government.

We have noted the changes that have occurred in America and in the responsibilities of government since the framing of the Constitution and the comparatively slight alterations that have taken place in the main structural or mechanical features of the governmental organization designed by the founding fathers. This fact does not mean that we have approximately the same governmental organization that came out of the eighteenth century. The growth of administration illustrates one of the striking modern developments. Furthermore, government does not now operate as it did in the early years, or in certain important respects as the fathers intended that it should operate. An expansion of one sort or another has occurred in each of the constitutional organs. Extra-constitutional organizations and forces have developed, such as political parties and direct-action pressure groups. Nevertheless, the general anatomy of our government has persisted; and its complications have become more complicated.

In the light of the responsibilities that modern government has assumed, some of the needs that the founding fathers recognized and some of the objectives and principles that they accepted have become irrelevant in this modern age and are in certain respects contrary to what we see and feel and wish for today. Is our government, in the form that it has come down to us, calculated to meet modern requirements? Is it as democratic and as efficient as it should be and might be? "After all," wrote William MacDonald some 25 years ago, "the proper test for the Constitution is not whether it was good when it was framed or whether it has worked less badly than might have been expected, but whether it is good and sufficient now."[1]

Our first concern in this chapter is with the operations of our government and especially with those operations that result from the peculiar pattern of organization. Part II of this book contains a somewhat detailed analysis of the organization and of the defects and tendencies that appear in its workings. At this point, we shall briefly summarize that analysis. Our summary is necessarily extremely generalized, and, if it does not seem sufficient, it is suggested that the reader turn at once to Part II and having read it come back to this chapter. Here we shall also examine the question of how to avoid despotism, one of the objectives held in view by the fathers that remains essentially unchanged. After this examination, we shall state the objectives and principles that one can deduce at the present time from our environment and experience.

DEFECTS OF GOVERNMENT

To understand our government, we must look at it as it actually is, not as it is supposed to be in theory or in the words of the Constitution. When we look at it in this way, we see that we have no clear separation of legislative and executive powers, no clear division of work, and no clear specialization of function. "Congress" means two practically independent assemblies, not one. The presidential veto is not the only veto; the Senate and the House of Representatives, each possesses and exercises the function of disapproval. So we have, at the least, three governments, none with the whole power of governing, but each able to obstruct action by the others. Governing power also resides in the administration; but the administration is not one authority: it is a collection of authorities. The presidency, apparently the simplest and most comprehensible of our several governments, is a multi-functional office and has become to a large extent a shifting and obscure assemblage of advisers and a complex of pressures.

But it is not enough to study the over-all legislative-executive organization by itself. We must consider not only the legislative and executive branches as they appear and operate in Washington, but also the country-wide plan of representation on which Congress rests and from which it comes, and the methods of election, through which we get president, senators, and representatives. Then, too, we cannot disregard the party system. We could have no democracy without it. And the pressure-groups also help for both good and ill to make our government what it is.

Restricted, frustrated, haphazard democracy. Democracy is today a necessary assumption, a first objective, and a general standard. It is not something that can be precisely measured and weighed. We use as testing devices six principles which, it is generally agreed, should find expression in a democratic government. These principles are: representation, majority rule, responsiveness to public opinion, leadership, responsibility, and voting equality.

The democracy that we boast of and sincerely wish to realize and perfect is "cribbed, cabined, and confined" by the organization and processes of government.

In practice, the constitutional plan of representation is approximately national only so far as the presidency is concerned. For the remainder, representation is localized, but not on a basis of equality. We expect interests to be represented; and in our system those elected to represent localities do represent interests; but in a wholly unsystematized and inevitably distorted fashion. Neither the Senate nor House nor the Electoral College produces a fair representation of regions or sections. Under this localized scheme, representation is artificial, arbitrary, and fractional. It is geometric, rather than organic. In practice, it is inequitable. In the formation and expression of opinion, a major role is played by localism, special interests, and personalities. The peculiar geography and arithmetic of our government produce an unequal distribution of voting power and preserve areas of political stagnation. Localized representation, fairly logical and probably unavoidable in 1787, has become in our age a clumsy and hampering anachronism.[2]

The governmental organization, built on the foundation of localities, denies in part and at times the principle of majority rule. As a result, we have hit-or-miss democracy, one subject to miscarriages. From the standpoint of those who fear the full implications and operations of popular control, much might be said for an organization that operates rationally, consistently, and continuously as a check upon the majority; but little can be said for one that does its checking haphazardly or accidentally. In May 1948 the Senate Committee on the Judiciary quoted approvingly a report from the same committee of the House: "The method through which we elect a President should be fair, honest, accurate, certain, and democratic. Our present system is not fair, honest, accurate, certain, or democratic."[3] The same words could be applied to the setup, election, and operation of the Senate or of the House. In the policy-making operations of government, the general interest too often yields to selfish pressures and the national interest to local demands. Such disintegrating minority influences get opportunity and aid from our policy-making organization and procedures, from the inherent weaknesses of our governmental authorities, and under the circumstances, from unavoidable maneuvering, manipulation, and excess of compromise.

One can readily admit the sensitiveness of our government and its measurable responsiveness to public opinion. But the state of opinion shows need for leadership. Except for the president, leadership is scattered and, on the whole, attached to localities and group-interests. In order to obtain national leadership, a larger measure of fixed responsibility, and a government capable of action, we turn at intervals to the "strong executive"; but in the process of making and keeping itself strong, the presidency becomes personalized, erratic, and unpredictable, and its incumbent partially irresponsible and possibly self-perpetuating.

While the administration grows in size, scope, and power, it becomes less answerable to the electorate as a whole. The reason is that it is not made practically accountable to a single authority which is itself responsible to the nation and qualified to control the administration.

A partially functioning two-party system. The party system seems to lie in the field of organic life or natural phenomena rather than in that of structure or mechanics. Many infer, often cynically, that no change can be made in the general workings of the system, that about all one can do is to explain it and to predict its results or developments. The author believes, however, that we should inquire not only how the party acts, but also how it ought to act.

The party system is an instrument and a very complex one, fashioned by political needs, that the electorate uses to control government. While parties are outside the Constitution, they are inside as well as outside of government. They figure in both political and governmental processes. They affect both the democracy and the efficiency of government. To what extent does the system form and focus public opinion? Is the electorate able to give clear directions to the elected authorities? In general, does the system tend to correct or to offset the questionable features of our government? Or does it tend to fit itself rather closely to the constitutional structure and mechanism? It is organized and it operates in close connection with the governmental organization. If that is changed, would not the party system also change or at least work differently?

Parties have not eliminated the inequities and accidents resulting from localized representation. As it operates nationally, the party system facilitates, but does not guarantee majority rule. The system tends toward the unification of government under the personal leadership of the president; but we still have from time to time a government divided against itself; and a state of governmental paralysis may result from the play of party rivalry or of factionalism within the check-and-balance mechanism. Nonpartisanship or bipartisanship is not a satisfactory general or long run remedy.

The customs and usages that accompanied the development of political parties did work some change in our governmental organization and adapted it in a measure to the requirements of democratic and efficient government. But the constitutional structure and mechanism have partially defeated the nationalizing, unifying, and integrating instincts of the party. An election ordinarily fails to bring into government a clear general mandate from the people, a consensus with respect to policies, a program of action, or even a general philosophy. The midterm congressional election is worse in this respect than a presidential election.

Each of the major parties is a loose alliance of factions. As an organization, it is disunited and without appropriate means of discipline. These phenomena are accompanied by and related to an intellectual undermining and moral weakening of the party. It lacks a logically developed, a sufficiently able, and a continuously effective leadership, and it is unable to maintain its solidarity. Consequently, we do not have clear party responsibility and definite party government.

Though we have accepted parties as natural and inevitable, we have retained the personal conception of politics, which holds that it is the man, not the party, that counts. The personal conception is now in the ascendancy and, on the whole and as a rule, operates strongly against that impulse to common majority action which democracy requires and the party originally reflected. Though we do not often get the capable men that we profess to prize, the tendency is to make indispensable a strong personal presidential leadership. Also the effect is to concentrate attention on the presidential campaign, even to a virtual stoppage of government, and to make the congressional election a reflection of apathy and an almost complete expression of disconnected localisms.

Because of its general inability to control government and to become really accountable to the people, the party performs satisfactorily and consistently only one function: that of filling offices. The means has become the end. An able political reporter wrote a few days before the 1946 election: "If it goes as expected, Tuesday's off-year election will demonstrate anew the vigor of America's two-party system."[4] Five months later an experienced political commentator observed: "So far as there is opposition between the two parties on important issues, it is a kind of token opposition, a going through the forms which are embedded in the mechanism of the two-party system. And it has the useful effect of preventing the line between the two parties from being obliterated, of preserving the two-party system."[5] One wonders wherein its vigor lies, and why it is worth preserving if it only keeps up appearances.

To point out the shortcomings of the party system is not to infer that it is in all respects bad, or that the bad in it outweighs the good. As it now is, with its weaknesses and defects, it represents a natural and on the whole a logical accommodation between democratic popular forces and the peculiarities of our governmental organization. The system falls short of correcting or offsetting the questionable features of our government. It tends for the most part to fit itself rather closely to the constitutional structure and mechanism. We cannot say that the system would change or work differently if the governmental organization were changed. But we can say that, without change in the governmental organization, we can expect little long-run change in the party system.

A design for inefficiency. It is often said that our national government has proved its effectiveness because of its survival and because of our national progress. As we have seen, certain important features have survived from 1789 to the present day; but the mere fact of survival under the conditions that have existed in the United States does not prove a great deal. As for national progress, that has been due primarily, it would seem, to three factors: (1) the unexampled natural resources of a once-virgin continent; (2) the initiative and enterprise of a gifted and self-reliant people; and (3) an international position that provided measurable isolation from complications and dangers. The governmental organization may be viewed as a secondary or incidental factor which, for about a century, left the economic development of the nation relatively unhampered, while expanding territorially the opportunities for economic enterprise. During this period, moreover, the wealth and security of the country concealed or minimized the short-comings of government. Sixty years ago James Bryce observed that, had the people of the United States not been extraordinarily favored by circumstances, they "could not indulge the easy optimism which makes them tolerate the faults of their government."[6]

From the viewpoint of *personal capabilities,* our governmental organization cannot be depended upon to place in positions of high authority the best qualified men in the country. At the same time, government in operation wastes energies, often excludes and usually weakens leadership, sometimes eliminates and normally discourages statesmanship. Upon those entrusted with the duty of governing the country the organization imposes an excessive burden of work, and subjects these men to petty and time-consuming distractions, to the wasting demands of intricate and duplicated procedures, and to the threat of paralyzing interruptions. While emphasizing the personal element, our political processes, in their normal working, give insufficient attention to personal capabilities.

From the viewpoint of *quantity,* our government appears unequal to its huge task. It is not designed to carry its load. Delegation relieves president and Congress to a considerable extent; but, with respect to the government as a whole, shifting and spreading the burden create dangers and enlarge the job of supervision and control.

The quantitative difficulty just mentioned is closely related to the *time element.* Time is both a precious resource and a driving compulsion. On the one hand, it must be saved and used, and on the other, it must be obeyed. Our government is not constructed to save it, to use it wisely, or to obey its critical commands. The system is predisposed to inaction, and even when inclined to act, it is set up to act slowly. Inherent in the system is the risk of complete or partial paralysis. At its best, the system operates by alternations of "coma and convulsion." Tested by the demands of time, it works fitfully and unpredictably. It is changeable but uncontrollable. It appears ill-adapted to meet the continuous and recurring crises of the present age.

Overburdened, handicapped by personal incapability, and bogged down by its own complexity and unwieldiness, our government is disposed to fall short with respect to the *quality* of its work. It is not equipped to review comprehensively the whole body of policy, examine relationships, avoid inconsistencies, establish co-ordination, and accomplish revision. Because it is divided and subdivided, specialized and compartmentalized, government fails to cope with the pressures to which it is subjected. Its structure is heterogeneous; its atmosphere, one of disunity. It is unable to integrate because it is itself organically unintegrated, and because in the absence of an intermediate integration by the party, the whole burden of integration falls on the government. Internationally, its internal lack of integration along with its slowness may prove a fatal defect. The fact is that we do not have strong government. Normally, it functions by the compounding of compromise, by evasion, or by surrender. Within the capacities of its personnel, our government deliberates in many ways, mostly in various isolated compartments; but, on the whole, the deliberation that it does is not in direct ratio to the time that it consumes. Our numerous assemblies do little real debating; but they are still constructed for debate, though most public debate now takes place outside.[7]

From the viewpoint of *administrative control,* the primary defect is divided and inadequate supervision, which hampers both co-ordination and reorganization, while dissipating responsibility. Administrative disintegration reflects legislative disintegration, while administrative conditions react unfavorably on Congress and on the presidency.

The shortcomings of Congress are pretty generally recognized. The presidency reveals a new design, but cannot escape from the old one. The administration is a truly modern development, but it fails to make a good enough showing when we apply to it modern criteria of over-all governmental efficiency. Of our several institutions, the House of Representatives seems the most open to criticism from the standpoint of efficiency; but the shortcomings are not confined to one part of government; they appear in all the parts and especially in the interworking of the parts.

We sometimes get good or moderately good results and even in the present critical age have escaped disaster thus far. But the disturbing point is that we have few reasons to expect efficiency. The organization of government makes it hard rather than easy to meet modern requirements. It is not designed to act in the way it ought to act. We want deliberation and wise decisions, continuity, integration, vigor, and promptitude. But to get them in a measure and at times, we have to subject government to superhuman effort, extraordinary expedients, and structural strains. We look for results not to the normal, but to the abnormal; and we recruit for the job of government men who are not quite up to the normal and much less so to the abnormal.

The criticisms just made do not add up to complete condemnation of our form of government. As no one would say that it is at all times 100 per cent efficient, so no one can claim that it is totally and always inefficient; but the degree of inefficiency that exists, especially if it is cumulative in effect, as it seems to be, should justify some serious thinking. Doctors may disagree whether it is a "teasing ailment" from which we suffer or a mortal disease; but the patient knows for sure that he needs all of his vitality. He wants no handicap in the race that he has to run.

Instability. In our government there is a long-run tendency toward one-man or bureaucratic dictatorship, along with the weakening of the popular supports of democracy. Then, there is a short-run changeability or unsteadiness that affects the predictability, continuity, and certainty of governmental action. Short-run changeability should not be taken as evidence of either adaptability or flexibility. It indicates just the opposite; for a completely adaptable and genuinely flexible system would maintain its self-control and operate smoothly and surely in the presence of varied and changing situations. Fickleness and vacillation are not signs of flexible strength. Nor do they show that an equilibrium is being maintained; but equilibrium, if it were possible, would not mean stability. A tug-of-war or a balancing act on a tight rope hardly offers an apt illustration of stability.

Short-run instability does not refer to the so-called "swing of the pendulum." Shifts from one party to the other are necessary and desirable in a healthy two-party democracy, and shifts of that kind, if the democracy and its party system are really healthy, should be not only meaningful but also stabilizing. The best examples of short-run instability are to be found in other connections.

First in the list would come the familiar and often uncalculated shift from congressional to presidential government and back again. Even the "strong executive," when we happen to get one, does not function continuously or always strongly. The personalizing of the presidency contributes to instability. If that office is what its occupant makes it, then our reliance upon the chief executive means a radical and largely unpredictable change in government when one president succeeds another. This uncontrolled variability is particularly evident when a vice-president becomes president. Changeability in the presidency is matched by changeability in Congress, for the character of Congress is determined basically by the play of economic interest, party allegiance, and personalities in four or five hundred territorial subdivisions. Then we have the instability resulting from, and indicated by, the frequent recurrence of a government divided between parties or between factions. In fact, "the kind of government this country may expect at any given time depends upon a number of variables."[8]

The absence of integration in and by the government illustrates and causes instability. The numerous and fickle forces that play upon government also exist within government. Parties and elections do not bring about an intermediate reconciliation or control of pressures. Lack of integrity in the party reflects and contributes to its essential instability, and lacking a clear electoral mandate, it carries its own lack of integration and consequent instability into the government. Accordingly, we have found it difficult to develop normally a statesmanlike leadership, a solid recognition of the deeper currents of opinion, or a definite responsibility in matters of principle. We see too often either a weather-vane sensitiveness or reckless attempts to stabilize the relations of government and people on a low moral basis.

The question of instability might be further explored; but it is believed that no additional illustrations are needed. It will be sufficient to emphasize the close relation between stability on the one hand and democracy and efficiency on the other. Democracy ultimately depends on governmental efficiency. In other words, efficiency stabilizes democracy.

Where are the defects? No one shortcoming of government presents a simple problem with regard to either causes or effects. The ramifications and interactions are numerous and complex. The setup and operations of one part of the system affect operations and tendencies in other parts. Such an interrelationship is natural and inevitable, because government is not divisible: the function of governing is one function. It seems practically impossible to make any substantial change in one feature without alterations in other features. Removal of any major defect requires a reconstruction of the entire policy-making organization and the plan of representation on which its rests, with constant attention to the system of parties, nominations, and elections.

AVOIDANCE OF DESPOTISM

It has been widely believed, and still is, that the scheme of separated authorities and checks and balances, as embodied in the legislative-executive setup of our government, safeguards the liberties of the people. If the system effectively serves that purpose, we might well afford to put up with a qualified democracy and with some inefficiency in both domestic and foreign affairs. So we must examine this question before we go any further.

Dogmas and devices. The complex mechanism set up in the Constitution was defended as an arrangement through which the ambitions and interests of a man or an institution would clash with and balk the ambitions and interests of other men or other institutions. Thus freedom would survive as a result of equilibrium in government. Even at the start, however, the system was not, and could not be, exclusively designed for this purpose and kind of action. The founding fathers were concerned also and primarily with creating a "more perfect union," and with the mechanisms and compromises required for the accomplishment of that objective.

Had the governmental organization been well adapted to the accomplishment of two quite different purposes, this organization did not, even in the beginning, constitute the only, or perhaps even the principal, means of protecting liberty. The placing of limits on the scope of government as a whole was looked upon as an essential and effective safeguard. Division of power between the central government and the states was held an important feature of the tyranny-preventing apparatus; and down to our own time Americans have viewed local self-government as one of the main bulwarks of democracy. The Bill of Rights appeared to be a prime defense; and an independent judiciary figured as the ultimate institutional protection. To guard against military despotism, it was thought that the standing army should be small and that the militia, placed partly under state control, should be the main military reliance. It was intended that civilian control, along with the check-and-balance system, would mitigate the danger of armed usurpation.

At no time, however, have Americans relied solely on organization, on constitutional guarantees and provisions, or on the courts. In *The Federalist,* governmental devices were viewed as necessary "auxiliary precautions." "A dependence on the people is, no doubt, the primary control on the government."[9]

To the original doctrines and arrangements, political developments have brought certain additions, subtractions, and revisions. The political party aimed with general assent to unify government; and the party system introduced new checks largely unforeseen by the founding fathers. The ballot, once greatly restricted, is now viewed, not only as a universal right, but as a means of symbolizing, expressing, and maintaining individual liberty. Freedom of elections has become one of our fundamental freedoms and is generally viewed as an essential political means of forestalling dictatorship. We now attach more importance to civil rights, to judicial processes, to free and competing political parties, and to free elections than we do to the separation and balancing of departments within the government.

The power of public opinion has led us to look upon government, not as an isolated, self-contained and self-acting mechanism, but as an instrument to be controlled in all its parts by the people. While many still defend the traditional doctrine of checks and balances, the more common disposition at present is to emphasize the importance of forces outside the formal governmental organization, particularly the popular character and mass feelings.

The doubtful value of the check-and-balance system as a way to avoid despotism will become clearer if we take a few examples of modern trends and modern sources of danger.

Executive encroachment. Our governmental organization is pressed by powerful forces to adopt another operational pattern. The emerging pattern is one of concentrated power; and the concentration is in the presidency. The trend, reflected by presidential leadership and the "strong executive," is in the direction of an elective dictatorship. Such a dictatorship probably would be periodically answerable to the people; but a president, favorably circumstanced, can through the power and resources of his office manipulate and possibly control the electorate, while perpetuating himself in office. Paternalism and demagoguery, aiding in the management of opinion, serve also to sap from the public character that sense of responsibility which is necessary to the assertion of real, rather than nominal, popular control. Such an insidious and involved process of usurpation wears, whether sincerely or not, a "mask of zeal for the rights of the people" and constantly pays "obsequious court to the people." The resulting absolutism, as Bryce suggested, would be "not against the masses, but with the masses."[10]

This trend has gone its way, not in spite of our governmental organization, but largely because of it. Probably the main reason for the present power and primacy of the president lies in the fact that government must not only avoid subversion; it must also govern. The inability to prevent executive encroachment stems from the incapacity and inefficiency of the check-and-balance system and of our legislative assemblies in the job of governing the country.

The president has the veto to protect himself; but he has rarely needed to use it for that purpose.[11] On the side of Congress, the last determined effort to subordinate the presidency occurred in the administration of Andrew Johnson and culminated in his impeachment. Since then, the weapon of impeachment has never been used or seriously threatened against a president; and it has been resorted to only once against an executive officer. There have been frequent displays of jealousy on the part of Congress and numerous congressional and partisan attacks on the alleged dictatorial tendencies of presidents;[12] but the net result has been that Congress by its own acts of commission and omission has steadily increased the power of the president.

It is argued, however, that the "strong executive" is a cyclical phenomenon, and that political forces periodically restore the governmental equilibrium.[13] It is true that weak presidents have succeeded strong ones; and a certain alternation has occurred in the relationship between president and Congress; but the alternation never fully restores the pre-existing balance.

Administrative aggrandizement. One hears a good deal today of the threat of bureaucratic tyranny. Whether the threat is real or imaginary, the tendency has been to accentuate administrative irresponsibility. It results from division and fragmentation of supervisory authority and from an inherent incapability in each of the supervisory institutions.

Speaker Rayburn has capably argued that delegation of power to administrative agencies "enables the Congress to know and understand the nature of the legislation upon which it votes. And it does not take from the Congress the power to amend or supplement legislation of this character at any time that it finds that legislation is not being applied and enforced in accordance with Congress' own understanding of its declared policy."[14] As a matter of fact, when an administrative agency opposes amendatory legislation, and when the president supports the agency with his veto, Congress can act only when it musters a two-thirds majority in both houses. Speaker Rayburn goes on to say:

Far from undermining the constitutional authority of the Congress, delegation of authority to administrative agencies is one of the surest safeguards. It is a procedure which conserves the vital powers of the Congress for vital matters. It removes rather than creates the danger of dictatorship by providing the means of making democracy work under the complex conditions of modern life.[15]

The necessity of delegation is undeniable; but, even in the "vital matters," for which the legislators supposedly conserve their energies, Congress is to an increasing extent dependent on the administrators.

Administration not only is largely beyond control because of its vastness, complexity, and expertness, but its expanding activities also affect the initiative and self-reliance of the people in political as well as in economic and social affairs. For when administration enters economic and social fields, it becomes increasingly paternalistic. Paternalism, as De Tocqueville pointed out more than a century ago, "does not tyrannize, but it compresses, enervates, extinguishes, and stupefies a people, till each nation is reduced to be nothing better than a flock of timid and industrious animals, of which the government is the shepherd." He went on to say:

It is indeed difficult to conceive how men who have entirely given up the habit of self-government should succeed in making a proper choice of those by whom they are to be governed; and no one will ever believe that a liberal, wise, and energetic government can spring from the suffrages of a subservient people.[16]

The system of separated departments and checks and balances appears to expose us to the danger of administrative absolutism or of paternalism, instead of shielding us against the danger. For better protection one should look to a simpler governmental system, arranged to provide constant and effective supervision, fixing and enforcing responsibility.[17]

Economic control. Extension of governmental controls over economic life poses the much-discussed issue of authority vs. liberty. Government has assumed responsibility for the economic well-being of the people; and this responsibility, along with definite trends during the last sixty years, makes it highly probable that we shall have more, rather than less, governmental control in the future. Our policy-making institutions are improperly designed to review, co-ordinate, and integrate policy, to resist pressures, to establish a balance between freedom and control, and to reorganize and supervise the agencies that exercise control. It seems fair to place on our check-and-balance system a part of the blame for the trend toward a controlled economy.

Communism and fascism. The three-sided conflict of democracy, communism, and fascism aims to resolve in the domestic sphere the issue of liberty vs. authority. This conflict represents also an aspect of the international struggle. The immediate threat, such as it is, comes from communism. The techniques of subversion include obstruction and the spreading of confusion. A system of separated departments and of checks and balances seems hardly appropriate to counteract such techniques, for the system itself obstructs and confuses.

Foreign-inspired antidemocratic movements depend also on infiltration. Our electoral scheme, party composition and party strategy, along with the direct primary and the growing strength of political-action groups, appears to facilitate infiltration. Under the existing setup, the subversive process can proceed unit by unit, while avoiding the full light of national publicity.[18]

Antidemocratic ideologies and practices profit from four conditions: (1) the economic inefficiency and failures of democratic government; (2) contradictions and weaknesses in its foreign policies; (3) inconsistency and hypocrisy in the organization and processes of democracy; and (4) decline of popular faith in parliamentary institutions. The manner in which our government is organized and operates hardly serves to reinforce these weak points in the armor of democracy.

The new bossism. The old bossism was a kind of localized informal dictatorship. Bryce pointed out that rings and bosses were "the product not of democracy, but of a particular form of democratic government, acting under certain peculiar conditions."[19] The particular feature of government in the United States, on which he laid most stress, was the complex electoral machinery, and the multiplication of offices and procedures which imposes an unbearable burden on the citizen. It appears also that complexity of government and diffusion of responsibility within it contributed to "machine" politics, for the great merit of the boss lay in his concentrated authority and his ability to get things done.

Certain it is that the check-and-balance system did not hamper the development of this type of autocrat; for he appeared repeatedly in states and cities possessing the traditional checks and balances and in many cases additional ones. Behind an intricate and bewildering front, the boss functioned as the real but generally invisible power. The Louisiana of Huey Long, whose domination was exceptionally visible, could boast all the separations, checks, and balances that characterize our national government. The old type of bossism waned whenever and wherever it lost its opportunities for gain and "good citizens" became intelligently interested in government.

The recent tendency seems to be toward a kind of national bossism, based on presidential leadership and on the dispensing of material benefits to individuals and groups. To this tendency, many conditions have contributed; and the check-and-balance system has figured less as a preventive than as a contributing factor.

Militarism. It is not contended that America has become militaristic or is in any danger of an overt military seizure of power. It is believed, however, that the chances of military domination of American life and politics are considerably greater now than ever before in our constitutional history. Nothing in the Constitution prevents the election of a military president, the appointment of military cabinet members, or the exercise of military influence over a civilian president and civilian congressional committees. The best, if not the only, safeguards in our time against militarism and military supremacy lie first in the people and second in a government controlled by and responsible to the people.

Weakening popular supports. The ultimate and only dependable protection against any type of usurpation is to be found in the people themselves; and the real protection lies much deeper than in the formality of voting. Popular control is now inadequate, because of inadequacies in the electorate and in the machinery through which the electorate functions. This machinery is so intricate and burdensome and its operations so uncertain and in some respects so undemocratic, that it renders popular interest in politics an artificial and fitful phenomenon. At the same time, it tends to destroy in the citizen the sense either of political power or of civic responsibility.

This is not, of course, all of the story; for a truly living democracy is rooted in personal qualities deeper than those just mentioned. These include "a capacity and a passion for the enjoyment of liberty,"[20] a devotion to the ideal of democracy, an appreciation of the general good, and enough intellectual equipment to know what liberty, democracy, and the general good mean in practical situations. There can be little doubt that America suffers from a weakening of these basic supports. Such a weakening may be checked, if free government can do three things: (1) make possible a genuine and stimulating exercise of popular control; (2) provide leadership; and (3) operate efficiently. Our governmental organization is not designed to do these things.

Concluding observations. The idea that in the modern age a system of separations, checks, and balances can save free government or help in its salvation rests on an oversimplification and misunderstanding of the problem. Something could be said for the theory in 1787, because the issue then was between aristocracy and autocracy, not between democracy and dictatorship, and the purpose of government, as then conceived, was restricted and negative, not comprehensive and positive. Moreover, the threat to freedom does not appear all at once, openly, and in a concrete form; it develops gradually, insidiously, and in most deceptive guises. It comes, as a fatal disease often does, without recognizable symptoms during its curable stage.

In view of the deep-seated and complicated nature of the disease, it is futile to rely for protection on an ancient fixed distribution of governmental prerogatives and on the spontaneous generation of reciprocal antagonisms. It is not merely futile; it may be fatal; because an organization so constructed falls short of both democracy and efficiency and induces or aggravates the condition that it is designed to prevent. For real stability we must look to the foundation, to the people themselves. We cannot afford, however, to neglect the superstructure and the machinery, because these react on the people.

It is not to be inferred that all limitations and checks are unnecessary or undesirable. Some are indispensable. Can government be organized in such a way as to operate safely, democratically, efficiently, and with tonic effect on the people? What checks and limitations should be maintained or restored?

OBJECTIVES AND PRINCIPLES FOR THE FUTURE

"In disquisitions of every kind, there are certain primary truths, or first principles, upon which all subsequent reasonings must depend."[21] These truths or principles, however, are not eternal, and they should not be purely theoretical. Since principles should go hand-in-hand with facts, rules that are valid for one age become obsolete in another.

An objective, as distinguished from a principle, represents an end, to which the frame of government is a means. In 1787 the principal objective was to form a more perfect union. We have long since attained that goal. So far as governmental organization is concerned, our immediate objectives now are democracy and efficiency. There is no necessary contradiction between these two present-day objectives. Restrictions on democracy are usually obstacles to efficiency; and the things that make government inefficient endanger democracy. It would appear, therefore, within the reach of human ingenuity to set up and maintain a government both free and effective.

Adaptability. Adaptability means, not only that the Constitution should lend itself to formal revision, but also that the constitutional organization of government should possess considerable elasticity. It should never be rigidly fixed to one set of conditions or assumptions. It should adapt itself to the needs of the day as well as to those of the age; but the adaptation should be visible. Political opportunism will continue to play its part in governmental adjustment, but the role of opportunism should not be a primary or an unduly glorified one. Few would question the application of the principle of adaptability to the administrative organization. It is not so generally realized, however, that, unless the same principle is intelligently applied to the over-all authorities, it cannot be applied to the subordinate agencies.[22]

Majority rule. According to what they feel and say, the American people have unqualifiedly accepted the ideal of democracy. It seems about time to embody this ideal, without qualifications or inhibitions, in the organization and operations of government. We should, therefore, remove so far as we can in an instrument of government the many obstacles that now block the path of majority rule; and we should, if we are to be sincerely democratic, apply the principle of majority rule to the process of constitutional amendment. Giving full sweep to democracy is one way to create or restore an active, intelligent, and continued public interest in government.

The principle of majority rule implies the political equality of individuals. All voters in the nation should possess equal voting power; and no vote should be wasted.

It is true that classes, groups, interests, and sections cannot be excluded from the exercise of influence in and on government; but a truly democratic government, controlled by a voting majority, cannot directly or proportionately represent subdivisions of the population. On the contrary, democracy requires a decrease, rather than an increase, in the power of groups, a subordination of special minority interests to the general or national interest, and a renewed emphasis on the rights of the individual, as distinguished from the rights of classes.

Minority participation. While the majority should be in a position to control government, the minority should participate. It should have full opportunity to know what the government does or proposes and to criticize the government's policies and plans. This opportunity to participate, to know, and to criticize establishes an essential check on government, a protection for individual rights, and a means of compelling wholesome compromises. It is also indispensable to public debate, to popular enlightenment, and to genuine stable democratic control. Majority and minority representation in government does not necessarily mean parliamentarism, at least not in the traditional sense of the word.

Effective leadership. The governmental organization should be such as to provide clarifying, statesmanlike leadership. Only through such leadership can democracy function with vitality and intelligence. Governmental leadership, if it represents both majority and minority, promotes public discussion and public enlightenment. It is required for the inspiration and education of the people, as well as for channeling their expectations and moderating their demands.[23] What we want is governmental leadership, competitive in make-up, general and national in origin and impact, speaking for the whole government, and continuously available. Leadership *within* government is also necessary; but it should be sharply distinguished from the maneuvering, pressure, and rationalized bribery that now pass for leadership in too many instances.

Fixed responsibility. Democratic leadership means responsible leadership; and democratic government means responsible government. Fixed and enforced responsibility provides a primary and an indispensable check on the use of governmental power. Possession of power is not in itself dangerous. The danger comes from power without commensurate responsibility. To divide, confuse, or scatter responsibility is to destroy it. A public servant who can evade or escape responsibility is in effect irresponsible.

The principle of fixed responsibility applies to government as a whole. It applies also to each institution within government and to the men who control it. It applies likewise to whichever political party we "put in power." Finally, the principle extends to men and organizations outside the formal structure and processes of government who use their economic or voting strength to dictate public policies. The principle implies that whoever exercises decisive power over government should be an accredited member of government and answerable to the nation; or, if a controlling group is not made responsible in this manner, then government must become strong enough to keep the group in definite subordination to the general interest.

Fixed and enforced responsibility demands a hierarchy of authorities, each answerable for the acts of his subordinates and each accountable for his own acts to his immediate superior. In a democracy, the electorate stands at the top of the hierarchy, with the function of electrifying the ramifying chains of authority and responsibility.

National representation. Localized representation is incompatible with principles already stated—majority rule, effective leadership, and fixed responsibility; and, as we come to other principles, we shall see that these also assume that we want and should have a truly and completely *national* government.

The popular attitude toward the presidency and the interest taken in presidential elections, compared with the indifference shown in congressional elections, illustrate both the merits and the general acceptability of national representation. The electoral college system, however, introduces into party strategy and into the selection and functioning of the president some of the complications and disadvantages of localism. To realize democracy, as well as to promote and express national unity, the national electorate should control the national government by means of simple, unconfused, and unqualified national elections. When the whole government stands on such a broad foundation, we shall have an institutional reason for its members to take a national point of view and give priority to the general interest. Then government will have met one of the essential conditions for the performance of its integrating function.

Of course government will always have to deal with local, state, and regional influences; but it can best deal with them when it is itself national. The government of the world's greatest power cannot risk remaining in large part a mosaic of local peculiarities and special pressures.

National representation would eliminate federalism, along with localism, from the structure and mechanism of government; but it would not necessarily affect division of powers between the nation and the states, and it would not necessarily mean further centralization or a further decline of local self-government. On the contrary, the effect should be to promote an intelligent and controlled division of work between the national government and the states.

Concentration of power. Various efforts have been made to bring about a working unity in our system of separated, checked, and balanced authorities. These efforts, as well as the general concern felt over evidences of disunity and possibilities of deadlock, may be construed as a tacit acceptance of the principle of concentration of power. Few now argue that disunity in government is preferable to unity. Most of those who still defend checks and balances or accept the system as unchangeable nevertheless search and hope for the painless introduction of unifying practices, in order to make the system act in contradiction to its own character.

The principle of concentration means in practice a single governmental organ, possessing all the powers entrusted to government, along with an inherent capacity to think intelligently and to act effectively. This organ cannot be one man, for it must represent both the national majority and the national minority; and it should not be many men, for a numerous assembly dissipates its power and loses capacity for deliberation and decision. Concentration of power means one indivisible and unobstructed government built for co-operation, instead of three or four governments set up for reciprocal antagonism.

Concentration of power supports the principle of effective leadership and makes possible fixed responsibility. As Woodrow Wilson observed: "The more power is divided the more irresponsible it becomes."[24] Power responsibly held and responsibly exercised, present no danger to democracy. It is, on the contrary, essential to the realization of democracy.[25]

The principle of concentration is opposed to any constitutional separation of policy-making powers, branches, or departments; but we should keep in mind that the kind of constitutional separation with which we are familiar is not the same thing as division of work. The present system precludes any logical division of work. It makes each of the over-all authorities multifunctional and duplicating. Concentration would in no way prevent delegation of power to executive and administrative authorities; but concentrated government would give greater assurance than we now have that delegation will be intelligently controlled and that delegated powers will be responsibly supervised, continuously reorganized, and responsibly exercised.[26]

Concentration of power would facilitate mobilization of experts and conduct of research; and a government which is itself integrated is best calculated to integrate policy. Concentration should give strength to government and make it "definitely superior to any and all special-interest groups."[27]

Concentrated government, finally, is simplified government; and relative simplicity facilitates public understanding. Because of its strength and simplicity, concentrated government would possess at all times that flexibility which we attribute to our present system in time of war, when we largely discard the doctrine of checks and balances.

Party government. In spite of the low estimate commonly placed on politicians and on partisanship, Americans generally accept in principle the party system as an essential instrument of democracy. The system is necessary to provide leadership, to form and focus public opinion, to carry on public debate, to fill elective offices, and to make elections meaningful. From the viewpoint of efficiency, the party system is equally necessary, for only through parties, campaigns, and elections is it possible to achieve an intermediate integration of opinion. In principle, the party should announce its policies and program before it comes to power. Only as it does so can a party contest become a clarifying and determining stage in the policy-making process.[28] If the whole task of integration falls on government, we shall have, as we do now, incoherent policy-making with delay and strain.

We no longer confuse parties with factions, and we must reject factionalism now as the fathers rejected it in 1787. Our parties are now loosely joined leagues of factions. The remedy for factionalism in its present forms lies not in the weakening of the party: it lies in the strengthening of both government and party.

The principle of party government requires that the party should be more than a mere vehicle for riding into office. The majority party should control government and, as a party, should take full responsibility for governing the country.[29] The principles of majority rule, minority participation, effective leadership, and fixed responsibility all imply that, in the policy-making operations of government, the party should act as a party with appropriate discipline and with a large measure of solidarity. It is evident also that the principle of concentration of power, along with the requirements of party responsibility, calls for a fusion of party control with party representation in the government. This fusion we do not now have, except in the presidency. The principle of national representation goes hand in hand with the principle of party government; for localism, along with the system of separation, checks, and balances, has made a major contribution to the disintegration of parties.

It should be clearly understood, however, that modern principles of government are not determined by the situation of the party system; and it is difficult to subject that system to any principles of its own. It would be futile and probably damaging to formulate principles of government with the sole aim of checking anti-party influences. To do so would be to repeat in reverse the error of the founding fathers, who signally failed to prevent what we now seek to preserve. If it should happen that personal rather than party government is inevitable under modern conditions, the governmental organization should be so arranged as to fix responsibility on persons, as well as on parties. Moreover, we are not now seeking directly any moral regeneration of party politics. Politics is the essence of democratic government, and it is vain to try to eliminate it. We are right in denouncing corrupt politics and petty politics; but, when parties and politicians are unable to function on a high plane, they must act on a lower plane if they act at all. The principles already stated embody the ideal of government on a high plane.

Personal capability. The ideal of government on a high plane will be attainable to the extent that government normally attracts, holds, and efficiently uses the best talents of the country. Government is not a matter purely of institutions and parties. It cannot be anonymous. A succeeding chapter will show more concretely how the application of the principles already stated may be expected to prevent waste of leadership, of ability, and of energy. At this point, we are concerned with general principles only; and it will be sufficient to draw attention to the three principles of fixed responsibility, national representation, and concentration of power. The qualitative working of these three principles finds illustration in the presidency compared with either house of Congress and in the Senate compared with the House of Representatives.

If we had a truly national government, we might avoid some

of those distasteful aspects of politics and of political apprenticeship which are most evident at the local level and which have kept many of our ablest men out of politics and outside of the elected part of government. Furthermore, as will appear more clearly in a later chapter, concentration of power would permit the selection of a qualified administrator as chief executive. When we cannot find a man big enough for that position, we should have a way to cut the job to the dimensions of a small man.

We cannot expect any type of organization to bring out a wisdom beyond the maximum capacity of human beings; but we can hope and aim for a type which will enlist a considerable proportion of the best brains, encourage deliberate and constructive thinking, and prevent the stupid from obstructing the wise. Nor should we look for a government purged of politicians. What we may hope for is to create a better balance between followership and leadership, between politics and statemanship, reducing the premium that the present system puts on tactics and raising the premium on statesmanship to the standards fixed by our exacting age.

Secondary principles. There are two secondary principles of government: the principle of *publicity,* which refers mainly to democracy, and the principle of *continuity,* which refers mainly to efficiency.

The principle of publicity calls for a government that works in the open, so that the spot light of public attention can be brought to bear on each participant and step in the process of government. Fixed responsibility and concentration of power would go far to ensure open, visible, and comprehensible government. In the present state of the world, secrecy on some matters, or at least a temporary postponement of publicity, may be vital. Concentrated government is the one best calculated to know and guard its secrets. At present, how many of our 532 elected policy-makers can be fully informed about foreign and military affairs or be trusted with secret information?

Continuity in the government should come from stability of party leadership, with a resulting low turnover among the makers of policy. The principles of national representation and personal capability would also do much to ensure continuity.

It hardly needs saying that, while we are questioning some of the tenets of 1787, we must be no less critical of several later maxims. Among these, we should place in the discard the principle of rotation in office and the idea of discontinuous legislative sessions, along with such panaceas as the direct primary, the initiative, and the referendum.

Needed limitations and checks. To discard the doctrines of separation of powers and mechanistic checks and balances is not at all to argue for an unlimited and unchecked government. Checks are inherent in the principles just listed—in fixed responsibility and concentration of power which mean a single strong control of the executive and the administration; in responsible party government or, if that is impossible, responsible personal government; in minority participation, which is lacking in the much-vaunted "strong executive;" in the increase of the government's strength, compared with the strength of specialized and special-interest groups; in the capability, including character, morals, and ideals, of members of the government; in the simplification of organization and operations; in the expectation of publicity; and in the probability of a better informed, more interested, and politically conscious electorate.

We certainly should retain our constitutional guarantees of individual rights and fundamental liberties, and would do well to add an explicit guarantee of the freedom of elections. For the enforcement of these constitutional safeguards, we must in the first instance depend as we have in the past on independent, impartial, and courageous courts. The principles above mentioned are not intended to apply to the judicial branch or necessarily to effect it.[30]

Supplementary and incidental aims. Those who search for means to realize democracy and achieve efficiency in the national government are compelled to consider conditions outside the sphere of that government, as well as many matters which can only be dealt with indirectly or incidentally.

Most students agree that we are asking too much of the American voter. Yet, the simplifying of the voter's task requires far-reaching and difficult reorganizations in state and local governments. A reorganization of the national government, particularly the stimulation of political discussion which would precede and follow such an accomplishment, might gain enough momentum to produce results on all the lower levels of government. If we could obtain in the national government the kind of leadership that we need nationally, it might be possible for such a leadership to deal in a comprehensive way with all the interrelated problems of government in the United States.

Whether the terms of elected members of the government shall be long or short is not, it would seem, a question of principle. It is one rather of practice or procedure; and the test of the rightness or wrongness of the choice lies in its consistency with accepted principles and its effect of their application. A similar stand may be taken on the question of fixed elections, such as we have in the United States.

CHAPTER V

PROPOSALS ALREADY MADE

Having stated the objectives and principles that modern government should embody, we shall now examine various concrete proposals already made.[1] Would these, if adopted, attain the objectives and carry out the principles?

A RESTORED AND IMPROVED BALANCE OF POWER

We shall first notice proposals that aim at no basic or overall alteration of the ancient design. Some of those who make these proposals deny the desirability of concentrating authority and responsibility. Others may favor the principle of concentration, but think that it would be inexpedient or impracticable to attempt any radical change. They would restore the balance of power and make it more efficient.

Correction of the two-chamber system. From 1787 down to the present day, proposals have been made at different levels of government that one legislative assembly should replace the dual system. The idea has made most progress in the municipalities and in other local governments, though it has been strongly advocated for the states and constitutionally established in one of them (Nebraska). Obviously, the two-house system is incompatible with several of the principles stated in the preceding chapter. In practice, however, if one of the existing assemblies were to be abolished, leaving the other unchanged, or if we combined the two into one,[2] we would be closer to some of our objectives, but more distant from others. To establish a single authority, embodying and harmonizing all essential principles would require a reconstruction of both the foundation and superstructure of government. Few have had the boldness to propose such action,[3] and the general disposition is to seek other remedies for the ills that spring from the two-chamber system. One suggestion is for a constitutional amendment "forcing the Senate to sit jointly with the House in case of a deadlock on revenue or appropriations."[4]

The conference committee is an established and unavoidable, though unsatisfactory, expedient for bringing the two houses into agreement at the final stage of passing a bill; but, in the words of Arthur N. Holcombe, "What is needed in order to present a united front most effectively to the Executive is some effective means of coordinating leadership in the initial stages of the legislative process instead of in the final stage of that process."[5]

To bring the two assemblies together into a better co-ordinated and more fruitful relationship, certain familiar suggestions have been made and to an extent tried; for example, that the committee systems of the two houses should parallel each other, that joint committees should be used, and that duplicate committees should hold joint hearings. Other recommendations include the strengthening of the party caucus[6] and the setting up of joint steering committees[7] or joint policy committees.[8] Such proposals imply party solidarity, party responsibility, and the centering in Congress of party leadership; but none of these implications correspond to present-day realities.[9]

Making the two Houses more efficient. The movement that culminated in the Congressional Reorganization Act of 1946 aimed to strengthen, improve, and modernize the two assemblies and thus restore the balance between Congress at one end of the scale and the president and bureaucracy at the other. The act provided for reduction of committees and definition of their jurisdictions, staffing of committees, supplying of administrative assistants to individual members, expansion of the Legislative Reference Service of the Library of Congress, restriction of the normal length of sessions, and provision of larger salaries and a pension system for members. In Part II when discussing problems of integration and acceleration in Congress, we call attention to the proposal for policy committees, not yet fully or durably provided for. We also note the Employment Act of 1946, which established a Council of Economic Advisers, along with a committee of Congress for the study of the President's Economic Report.

Another proposal not yet accepted in practice is for the abolition of filibustering.[10] Solutions have been advanced, but not yet adopted, for the problem of seniority.[11] Various other suggestions have been made. One is for the installation of electric voting,[12] (a time-saving device) and another for the broadcasting of congressional debates (the merits of which are debatable).

Other proposals aim to make Congress more efficient by unifying and strengthening congressional leadership and by supplying the committees and individual members with unbiased information and expert assistance. The finding of a practical substitute for seniority and means of preventing obstruction would evidently help toward effective leadership and majority rule. Increased compensation, along with retirement pensions, is expected to attract abler men to Congress and keep them there. Registration of lobbyists, along with staffing of the committees and strengthening of the Legislative Reference Service, was designed to reduce the pressure of special-interest groups and enable congressmen to give more attention to the general and national interest. One suggestion is that an Office of Public Counsel should be created for the representation and protection of the public interest.[13] It has been suggested also that each candidate for Congress should present verified credentials to the voters, that he should have had previous experience in public positions, that he should submit to psychological and aptitude tests, and that Congress should provide in-service training for its members.[14]

Another set of proposals has to do with additions to the membership of one house or the other or both. Thus, it is often suggested that ex-presidents should have membership for life in the Senate, either with or without the right to vote. To this end, bills have been introduced, but thus far without result.[15] Galloway suggests an amendment providing "a nucleus of national representation in the two houses of Congress" through the election by the people of the whole country of about 10 senators and 24 representatives.[16]

Others have suggested means of widening the field of selection or broadening the basis of representation. Some have favored a drastic reduction of the membership of the House. It has been proposed to abolish the constitutional requirement that senators and representatives must reside in the states from which they are chosen. Some would have the representatives from each state elected at large instead of by districts. Elliott proposes multi-member districts and election by proportional representation.[17] He would also do away with the states and divide the country into twelve "commonwealths," each of which would choose 8 senators. To the 96 senators so chosen, the president would have the right to add 15.[18]

Lightening of the load. It is proposed to reduce the congressional burden of work by decentralization and delegation, and by eliminating the errand-boy work of congressmen.[19] Many believe that Congress should frankly adopt the view that it can be and should be exclusively an enacting or revisionary organ and an over-all controlling authority, and should not attempt to legislate in the traditional sense or manner.

For the job of initiation and preparation, it has been suggested that a legislative council be established, that legislation should be initiated by the executive branch, or that plans prepared in the administration should be fed to Congress through the legislative council. If the legislative council were to be separate from Congress, it would constitute another governmental institution, an additional wheel or set of wheels in an already over-complicated mechanism. If the council were to be drawn from the membership of Congress, it would be merely a joint policy committee under another name. If the executive branch were made the sole initiating authority, we would be confronted with a problem which as a matter of fact has already become acute; for, with Congress dependent in this way on the president and the bureaucracy, the legislative-executive balance could be maintained only by making congressional control of administration a continuous and effective process.

Improvement of administrative supervision. Concrete recommendations for the improvement of administrative supervision aim for the most part at more effective control of expenditures through a strengthening of the budgetary process and of the

General Accounting Office,[20] as well as through a lightening of the legislative task and a general increase of congressional efficiency. It has been proposed that the committees of each house should conform as closely as possible to the organization of the executive branch.[21] Along a similar line it is suggested that Congress "break itself into a series of small groups, each of which has its own supervisory domain."[22] If either of these ideas were acted upon, the probable effect would be to make administrative reorganization more difficult than it already is and to induce further legislative and administrative disintegration.

In general, the proposals in regard to administrative supervision recognize that the relationship of individual congressmen with administrative agencies must be greatly changed; and there seems to be a consensus that Congress can hardly make a start at supervision without special instruments and expert assistance. Congress, however, is ill-fitted to supervise and direct its own accessory organs and experts. Nevertheless, it has been suggested that Congress "recapture its legislative power by the creation of its own bureau of legislation, under the immediate direction, supervision, and control of Congress and its committees, to investigate and draft all subordinate rules and regulations needed to supplement any acts of Congress."[23]

Another recommendation that has come from high quarters and has gathered many endorsements is that members of the Cabinet should have seats in Congress, submit to questioning, and participate in debate. So far as congressional supervision is concerned, such a practice would probably do more harm than good.[24]

Curbing of the Executive. Few of those who stand for the restoration and maintenance of the constitutional balance favor any calculated or definite weakening of the president. It is expected, however, that a strengthened Congress will more efficiently control the administration, and it is considered desirable that the legislature should keep to itself the means of withdrawing delegated powers and checking the exercise of such powers. It has been proposed that, while the president should retain his veto, Congress should have power to override it by a simple majority vote in both houses.[25] The proposed two-term amendment, which is now before the state legislatures, was intended not so much to curb the executive as to prevent presidential aggrandizement through self-perpetuation in office.

GOVERNMENT BY CO-OPERATION

Some of those who want to keep the ancient mechanism would do a thorough cylinder-cleaning and tune-up job; and they would add a number of special contrivances, though there is a considerable difference of opinion about the usefulness of particular gadgets. But others would do more. They would get the gears meshed and the brakes unlocked, synchronize the several clashing motors, and apply to the work that the machine has to do the full power that it has available. They would have the engines working together, rather than against one another.

Prevention of divided government. One fairly obvious step toward the harmonizing of government is to prevent division of control between the two political parties. It has been suggested, therefore, that the Constitution should be amended to provide for terms of the same length and elections at the same time for president, senators, and representatives.[26] Such a scheme would make the two-chamber system more illogical than ever; and divided government, though less likely, would still be possible.

When the Republicans won the mid-term election of 1946, Senator Fulbright suggested that President Truman appoint a Republican Secretary of State and then resign. Thereupon, under the presidential succession law as it was at that time, the Secretary of State would have become president and the Republicans would have come into control of all three branches of government. A similar procedure has been proposed to do away with the interregnum between the election and the inauguration of a new president.[27]

In the case of divided government, much could be said for

such procedure if it were based on established and binding custom. Were usage to require the resignation of the president when his party loses a mid-term election, the people and politicians would know what to expect, the minority party would nominate its candidate for president, and the mid-term election would tend to resemble the quadrennial presidential election. The chief difference would be that the Electoral College would not figure in the off-year proceedings, and, when the outs won, their candidate for president would take an official position in which he would immediately succeed to the presidency on the resignation of the incumbent. Under the present law of succession, however, the mid-term presidential candidate nominated by the outs would have to be a candidate for Congress in some congressional district. Upon his election to the House, he would be chosen speaker, and would thus be next in line for the presidency.

To harmonize government in the manner suggested by Senator Fulbright is a highly complicated matter. It would mean biennial presidential elections and, even then, would not guarantee governmental unity, because the Senate and House, separately elected, might be controlled by different parties.[28] A more minute examination of the proposal would disclose other difficulties and shortcomings.

The system of separation, checks and balances, along with the territorial basis of representation and election, is a major cause of divided and disintegrated government. Until this cause is dealt with, no equalization of terms and no established understanding about mid-term elections will solve the problem. Another cause lies in the weakness, disintegration, and malfunctioning of the political party. Under present conditions, government may be, and often is, divided and subdivided when one party completely controls its three political authorities; and another type of division comes from the power possessed by minorities. To prevent the division of government by parties or minorities, we rely largely on nonpartisanship and bipartisanship; but, by doing so, we tend to reduce or eliminate the unifying possibilities of the party.

Co-operation through party leadership. In spite of the attitude just mentioned, it is generally recognized that party leadership plays an essential role in bringing about co-operation within government; but there seems to be little disposition to state the price that must be paid for effective party leadership. Such leadership calls for strong, cohesive, homogeneous, and disciplined parties; and it calls for concentration of leadership.[29] But such developments would bring about co-operation only when one party controlled all three independent governmental authorities. In the event of a division of governmental control, stronger parties would simply make disagreements and deadlocks more probable.

A triple alliance. In many minds the strengthening of Congress is a means rather than an end. The end is balanced co-operation between the two houses and the president, an imposition of unity upon a disunited government. Those who work toward this end accept the principle of concentration of power, though perhaps with some reservations. They would make as easy as possible the carrying out of the principle, but without any undue disturbance of things as they are. For the most part, the development of unity would be voluntary, or enforced by public opinion. The hope seems to be that co-operation so induced will in the end crystallize into a more or less compelling custom.[30]

There is nothing in the Constitution which prevents voluntary and informal co-operation between the president and the two houses. On the contrary, the Constitution expressly provides for certain forms or fields of co-operation.[31] Collaboration of different sorts and degrees has always been desired and has always gone on to an extent.

To bring about a more constant and stable interworking, some would rely chiefly on exhortation. They urge frequent consultation between the president and congressional leaders, a full interchange of information, and a sparing constructive use of the presidential veto. Many attach great value to bipartisanship; and, at times of divided government or crisis, a coalition Cabinet is often recommended and gestures in that direction are sometimes made. But in this country the Cabinet is not the government. It is not even the executive. Consequently, a bipartisan cabinet, while it may serve in some degree to placate the opposition party, can never mean a genuine coalition government or an effective concentration of governmental power.

Accordingly, a number of those who see dangers in divided government would take a step beyond any of the proposals previously discussed. They would organize and formalize legislative-executive co-operation. Disregarding variations in detail, these plans assume a majority policy or steering committee in each house. These committees, with the addition of the president and his Cabinet, would constitute a legislative-executive council or cabinet.[32]

There have also been a number of proposals for better working relations between the president and Congress in the making of foreign policy.

In some of the thinking on co-operation, one finds the idea that the internal working of our government can be made to resemble that of a corporation.[33] Under the existing governmental setup, however, the relations between president and Congress can never even remotely resemble those of a corporation executive with his board of directors. The latter is a single and relatively small body. It elects the executive, and it is itself more or less chosen by the executive. Thus the government of a corporation represents, not a tripartite separation, but a fairly complete fusion. It would be more apt to compare the proposed co-operative devices with the Security Council of the United Nations. The purpose is essentially the same, to bring together independent authorities, each retaining its veto, in the expectation that contact and discussion will, with the help of public opinion, resolve differences and make possible unanimous decisions.

Back of the plans for a formalized conference lies the hope that most of the members of Senate and House will act as rubber-stamps and thus admit that they are superfluous, as most of them are. But none of the proposed legislative-executive get-togethers would actually possess power to reach a final decision. The proposed super-steering committee would bring no real concentration of authority. It would force the leaders into contact; but they would still be the kind of leaders that are consistently produced by our governmental system and by congressional seniority. They would be neither nationally representative nor nationally responsible. The scheme would add another complication and another source of public confusion.

Seats in Congress for the Cabinet. The proposal has frequently been made that members of the Cabinet should have seats in Congress, should take part in congressional debates, and submit to questioning regarding their administrative policies and acts. Endorsements of this plan have come from those who favor better legislative supervision of the administration, those who would like more executive control of the legislature, and those who want a closer relationship between the two branches.[34]

Harold Laski, a British political scientist, believes that the proposed change "is not a superficial one. Its ramifications are, in fact, so wide that they might easily change the whole balance of power in the American system." He adds: "The real result, in a word, of the adoption of such a scheme as Senator Pendleton proposed would be very rapidly to transform the president into a person more akin to the president of the French Republic than to that of the United States."

The writer is inclined to agree with Colegrove when he says:

The proposal for granting Congressional seats to cabinet officers is a superficial answer to an old problem. So long as the presidential system is retained, cabinet seats in Congress are a futile gesture. The reason is plain. The Secretary of State owes no responsibility to Congress. If, in the course of debate, members of Congress seek to wring commitments from him, the legislature encroaches upon the rights of the Chief Executive. If he speaks merely as an agent, his participation in Congress tends to decline to routine announcements.[35]

GOVERNMENT BY CONGRESS

The plan of Cabinet participation in Congress may have originated in a somewhat thoughtless admiration for one of the features of responsible government in Great Britain; but it should be recalled that over there the members of the Cabinet are also members of Parliament. The cabinet system of government, as it developed in England, represented a high concentration of legislative and executive power, and, as the system operated during the nineteenth century, gave the Cabinet parliamentary and party leadership and made it directly responsible to the majority in the House of Commons. The Cabinet resigned when it lost its majority. The system achieved in large measure and with considerable continuity a fixed responsibility of the government through the Parliament to the electorate. The responsibility, moreover, was party responsibility; and the government was party government. While it exemplified a thorough concentration of the legislative-executive power, it illustrated also a clear division of work or of function.[36] American political scientists, as they observed the British system in the latter part of the nineteenth century, naturally found much to admire, especially when they contrasted its theory and practice with those of our own system.

During the period of academic emphasis on concentrated responsible government, a second strong influence came into play, derived from the example of the industrial corporation. Here, as in the British government, one could observe concentration of power and responsibility in the board of directors, along with division of work or of function; and it appeared that this corporate type of organization operated with a high degree of efficiency within its special and limited sphere.

Legislative supremacy and cabinet government might have developed in this country if a deep-seated antagonism had existed between the president and the House of Representatives, if the House had consistently shown determination to subject the president to its will, if it had used the "power of the purse" to reach its goal, and if public opinion had taken the side of the legislators. Had these conditions been present, the heads of the executive departments might have become truly political officers responsible to Congress, and the president transformed into a figurehead. The president, however, became a party and national leader, with greater prestige and popularity than Congress; and the Senate, unlike the House of Lords in Britain, increased its influence and its popular character. Before either house of Congress could impose responsibility on the executive, one body would first have to assert its primacy over the other. Two houses, both popularly chosen, each standing on its prerogatives, each armed with a veto over the other, and neither controlled by a strong national party system, along with the popular and national character of the presidency, have interposed in this country insurmountable obstacles to the kind of responsible government that developed in Britain. Accordingly, there have been many expressions of regret that we do not have the Cabinet system, but relatively few specific proposals for its formal and effective establishment.[37]

GOVERNMENT BY THE PRESIDENT

A number of the proposals already mentioned aim, not only to strengthen Congress or to encourage co-operation, but also to implement presidential leadership. According to Corwin, "agreement is general among technical students of government that the retention of democratic institutions depends today largely upon the capacity of these to afford a matrix for strong executive leadership."[38] But the modern idea of presidential government did not come from any deliberate plan of governmental reorganization. It came rather from recognition and acceptance of what has appeared to be an established and popular trend.[39]

Reinforcements. A number of recommendations are primarily designed to remove the handicaps and defects of the presidential office, make it more efficient, and give it greater strength. A major proposal, which has been discussed for many years, is to amend the Constitution so as to eliminate the requirement that treaties be concluded with the advice and consent of two thirds of the Senate. Instead, it is usually suggested that treaties be approved, like other laws, by a majority vote of both houses. It has been suggested that the initiation of legislation should become pre-eminently an executive function,[40] that the right of Congress to increase the appropriations provided for in the executive budget should be restricted,[41] that the president should have power to veto items in appropriation bills,[42] that he should be authorized to veto parts of any bill,[43] and that "riders" on bills should be prohibited. With more particular reference to administration, it has been suggested that assistant presidents be provided,[44] and also that the vice-president should be made an operating vice-president,[45] or that a second vice-president for executive work should be elected.[46] It has been proposed that senatorial confirmation of executive appointments should be abolished. Other recommendations designed to improve the presidency include: the familiar suggestion frequently made for a single six-year term, the plan for a special election following the death of a president, and solutions for the still unsolved problem of the presidential succession.[47]

Introduction of responsibility. The discussion in Part II of the trend toward one-man rule points out the dangers presented by the trend and the shortcomings of the "strong executive" from the standpoints of democracy and efficiency. Presidential domination of Congress does, in a way, bring about a concentration of governmental power along with a measurable national representation. Many students of government, however, including those who accept presidential government as the answer, turn to the problem of how to make the president truly responsible. Some feel that he should be balanced and checked by a stronger and better adjusted Congress.[48] To aid in the enforcement of executive responsibility to Congress, as well as to stabilize and improve presidential leadership, proposals have been advanced for a new kind of cabinet headed or controlled by congressional leaders.[49]

DISSOLUTION

Dissolution, as it operates in certain other countries, means the termination of the life of a legislative assembly, followed by the calling of a new election. While members of the assembly may be elected for a maximum term (five years in Great Britain), it is neither necessary nor customary that they serve out their full terms. For the practice of dissolution we can find no antecedents and no precise analogies in our own constitutional history. The procedure involved is in marked contrast with our system of fixed terms and fixed elections. Some have proposed, however, that the practice, or at least constitutional provision for it, be adopted in this country; and others, who make no precise recommendations on the subject, feel that our government would function better if it were adapted to the principle of dissolution.

Purposes. The main purpose of those who would introduce the dissolution procedure into our governmental organization is to prevent divided government. The idea is that when conflict or deadlock materializes, a new election would place one party in control of all governmental institutions and thus ensure unity, with the required capacity for decision and action. It is also argued that, were an election held when a major controversy develops, the contest would revolve around a major issue or group of closely related issues. Consequently, the election would mean a definite and understandable expression of public opinion. Once able to impose a clear mandate on government and thus to control it and hold it responsible, the people also would feel their power and their responsibility.[50]

While some advocates of dissolution seem to view it chiefly as a way to attain harmony or co-operation within government, others make the proposal for the purpose of strengthening presidential control of Congress. Those who favor the scheme contend that it would introduce greater promptitude and flexibility into our political processes, thereby correcting the faults inherent in our rigid system of fixed terms and fixed elections.[51] It has been argued that dissolution procedure would strengthen the resistance of the president, and through him the whole government, to pressure groups,[52] and that localism would largely disappear.[53] It has been urged also that the power of dissolution in the hands of the president would give him a means of party control superior to patronage,[54] the inference being that the president would either be doubly armed or would abandon his present method of bribing the legislators.

Mechanics. Is it necessary to change our governmental organization in order to introduce the dissolution procedure and give it a fair chance to accomplish its purposes? The general opinion seems to be, that certain major changes must first be made. Some advocates of dissolution have suggested that members of the House of Representatives, all senators, and the president should be elected at one time for six-year terms.[55] William Macdonald, who aimed at a responsible cabinet system and wished to make the president a mere head of state like the British King, thought that the president should have a five-year term and that senators and representatives should all be elected for a maximum term of four years.[56] One exponent of the plan has proposed (1) that the Senate should have power to delay (for a month) but not to reject revenue and appropriation bills, and (2) that the term of representatives should be four years.[57]

Which of our elected authorities should be dissolved? Who should do the dissolving? On these questions the dissolutionists fall into two classes: those who would attach the procedure to our present system, and those who would adopt something like the British type of cabinet government. Among the proposals that assume the retention of the existing setup, the following appear fairly illustrative:

(1) When President and Congress are of different political faiths, Congress by concurrent resolution could call for a new election of President, Senate and House;[58]
(2) The President would have power to dissolve the House of Representatives;[59]
(3) The President would have the right to dissolve all three authorities—the presidency, Senate and House—whenever a deadlock arises between Congress and the Joint Cabinet; and Congress could force the President to order a dissolution "by refusing to enact any of the proposals of the Joint Cabinet."[60]

Those who would adopt in this country something like the British system of cabinet government would favor also a transplanting of the British dissolution procedure; that is, the order to dissolve and the call for a new election would issue nominally from the president, but actually from the prime minister.

When and how often should dissolution occur? All would presumably say, whenever the executive lost the confidence and co-operation of the legislature; and most would place no limitation on the number of dissolutions, since they would not be likely to occur frequently, and the mere threat of dissolution would itself serve to bring executive or legislature into agreement.[61]

Importance and usefulness.[62] In the British government, the dissolution procedure is an accessory, rather than a central or principal feature; and, like the cabinet system as a whole, the practice and the results corresponded more closely to the theory a half century ago than they do now. At present, prime minister and cabinet have become directly responsible to the electorate rather than to the House of Commons; and, because of party solidarity and party discipline, there is no longer the possibility that there once was of a cabinet's losing its majority in the House of Commons.[63] Consequently, a prime minister is more likely than formerly to decide on dissolution for purely tactical reasons. An election in Britain does not always produce responsible party government.[64] Nor does an election necessarily decide a major issue or produce a clear mandate.

Neither can we say with any certainty that the dissolution procedure in Britain contributes to the political education of the people and creates a sustained public interest in government. If these desirable ends have been attained, other factors have probably had a hand in their attainment—cabinet government itself, along with effective leadership and fixed responsibility, to say nothing of the short ballot, which makes voting a much simpler and easier task than it is here. Great Britain is a quite different country from ours, smaller, more homogeneous, highly centralized, and with a virtually one-chamber legislature.

In this country, to make the terms of president, senators, and representatives uniform is not sufficient to ensure the effectiveness of dissolution procedure; for the principal causes of conflict in our government lie in localized representation, in the character of the party system, and in the institutional setup of government. Our institutions work at cross-purposes not only when they are controlled by different parties, but also when one party controls the entire government. When an election puts one party in complete control, unity is by no means assured. Dissolution procedure would have little if any effect on nonpartisan or bipartisan government. It would be unlikely to produce the requisite party solidarity or, in other respects, to rejuvenate the party system. This procedure, if introduced into our governmental organization, would not materially diminish the power of pressure groups; for the pressure-group system has its roots in localism and thrives on a localized or sectional party strategy.

An election following dissolution would not necessarily bring government into line with a changed public opinion, for our governmental organization makes the president responsible to one public opinion and each senator or representative to another. Conflicts between the president and one house or the other seldom arise from disagreements on clear-cut issues. Even if a disagreement were sharply defined, there is no reason to suppose that a special election for president, Senate, and House would decide the issue and bring about co-operation. It would take six months at the least to make nominations and carry on the campaign. The result would be pretty much as it is now. Issues, as well as responsibility, would become confused, personalities would intrude, local influences would play their customary role. During this time, government would be practically at a standstill and soon afterward, changing conditions would produce new opinions, new policies, and new disputes.

Hazlitt[65] takes the case of Franklin D. Roosevelt's plan for packing the Supreme Court as an example of the advocacy by the president of something that neither public opinion nor his own party favored. Under a system like the British, Hazlitt argues, the President's plan would have gone to the country, been defeated in a national election, and Roosevelt would have resigned. In our governmental organization, however, a special election would almost certainly have produced an exactly contrary result. Had Roosevelt appealed in this way to the country, he himself and the New Deal, not his Supreme Court plan, would have been the paramount issue; and doubtless he would have been triumphantly though somewhat confusedly vindicated. It is a far-fetched assumption that the people in 1937 would have put the Republicans back into power solely to reject the Supreme Court plan. If power to dissolve had belonged to Congress, Congress in that case would not have exercised the power; and it did not need to exercise it, because it could safely defeat the President's plan without any dissolution.

To import the dissolution procedure into American politics without a far-reaching reorganization of government would, in the writer's opinion, produce little if any improvement. It would probably increase maneuvering and compromise. It would complicate and probably further professionalize politics. It would not correct the inherent deficiencies in the presidency or in our dual assemblies. It would fail to reach the various individual and isolated sources of obstruction. It would add another set of wheels to an already over-intricate mechanism.

PEOPLE, PARTIES, POLITICS, AND ELECTIONS

Those interested in the improvement of government are naturally concerned about the people. Suggestions with regard to education are numerous. Other and related proposals range through the fields of expertness, research, and scientific leadership. Local government, the "nursery of democracy," frequently attracts attention. W. F. Willoughby has pointed out the bearing of direct taxation on the problem of civic interest and civic responsibility.[66]

It seems to be generally desired that the political party should develop greater solidarity, a more coherent program, and more effective legislative leadership. Many have hoped for a realignment of parties, and some for more political assertiveness in the middle classes.[67] Some would encourage minor parties. A fairly familiar proposal is for federal payment of party campaign expenses. A few have argued for proportional or functional representation.[68] It has been recommended that officeholders should be deprived of the voting privilege. Practically everybody endorses the idea of a "short ballot."

A number of proposals concern the times and methods of election. These reveal a mixture of purposes related to both democracy and efficiency. The most common aims are to improve leadership and in general the quality of elected officials, to bring government nearer to the objectives of majority rule and national representation, to reduce the likelihood of uncertainties and accidents, to mitigate the influence of localism and special interests, and to promote co-operation within government. Some of the proposed changes in terms of office have already been mentioned.

Various suggestions reflect dissatisfaction with the convention system of nominating candidates for president and vice-president. Some would establish the presidential primary in all states and allow the members of each party to express an unrestricted choice of candidates.[69] According to another view, the national convention would select several men. The names of these men would be placed on the party ballot in the order in which they are favored by the convention. There would then be a "uniform primary in which the people of every state would vote for their candidates for President and Vice-President, the nomination going to the candidate with the majority of votes cast by the voters in his party."[70] Woodrow Wilson approved the nationwide presidential primary and recommended that the national conventions be deprived of their nominating function. He suggested a new setup for the national convention and a new way to draw up the party platform.[71]

Many major proposals have been made for changing the method of electing president and vice-president. The most usual of these and also the latest, contained in a joint resolution for a constitutional amendment,[72] would "(1) abolish our fictitious electoral college, (2) abolish electors, (3) provide for direct voting for President and Vice-President, and (4) retain the electoral vote of each State as at present, but provide that such electoral vote be divided in exact ratio with the popular vote."[73]

PROVISION FOR AN ATOMIC EMERGENCY

Representative Trimble of Arkansas introduced a resolution in the Seventy-ninth Congress calling for a constitutional amendment to provide an emergency government in the event an atomic bomb should wipe out the president, vice-president, Cabinet, Congress, and the Supreme Court. The high military officers would first select a civilian interim president, who would call a meeting of state governors, who would choose from their own number a president and a vice-president to serve until the next regular presidential election.[74] Another proposal for emergency government has been advanced by Senator Wiley.[75]

GENERAL EVALUATION

Many of the proposals already made endorse, expressly or tacitly, the objectives and principles stated in the preceding chapter. This cannot be said of those recommendations which aim deliberately to restore and maintain separation and checks and balances in anything like their original form. Nor does it seem sound to establish government by Congress unless at the same time we transform Congress into a unified, democratic, and truly national organ, capable of assuming full responsibility for governing the country. With regard to proposals for bringing about co-operative government in a formal manner, a legislative-executive cabinet or council, if it did not prove utterly futile, would introduce another institution into our complex of institutions, an additional means of confusing and diffusing responsibility, without removing inherent defects or basic maladjustments. So long as the over-all organization keeps its present form, the possibility will remain of deadlocked, divided, or excessively *compromised* government.[76]

Many of the suggestions for strengthening the president *as chief of administration* appear well taken; but they could have only limited effect so long as responsibility for administration remains divided and subdivided, and so long as the president's qualifications for administration are left to the accidents of politics. The writer cannot agree with one-man government either as a deliberate aim or as something to be surreptitiously contrived. Executive responsibility should accompany executive power. Little merit can be seen in proposals to give an inadequate executive a new club to swing over an inadequate legislature.

In this country, dissolution procedure would have slight usefulness and importance without substantial changes in governmental organization. Those changes should be made on their own merits. When we propose them for the purpose of implementing dissolution, are we not putting the cart before the horse? Fixed terms and fixed elections do not seem to be fundamental defects. Would we not do better to keep our eyes steadily on the main objectives and basic principles? If in the process of reorganization we finally reach these objectives and fulfill these principles, we shall then find ourselves in a better position to decide whether terms of office should be long or short, and whether we should make provision for the calling of elections to bring government into accord with public opinion.

It seems fair to say that no one of the proposals and no selected combination of them would, in any comprehensive or satisfactory manner, attain modern objectives or carry out modern principles. Some would remedy one evil while aggravating another. For example, to set up a legislative-executive cabinet or to give the present cabinet members seats in Congress would further tax our leadership without improving its capabilities. The proposed amendment to abolish the electoral college and to change the method of counting electoral votes looks in the right direction and would remove some existing defects and dangers, but there is good reason to think that such an amendment would further weaken the two-party system. Such also, apparently, would be the effect of nominating presidential candidates in a national party primary.

It seems idle to discuss substitutes for seniority, when seniority is merely one of a number of symptoms which are practically certain to persist so long as the underlying causes remain. To make the vice-president an operating officer or to elect another vice-president as the president's administrative assistant is a clumsy, unnecessary, and probably injurious method of solving a problem that would solve itself if we had a proper over-all organization of government. With such an organization, many of the secondary difficulties, would automatically disappear.

In fact, until we are ready to go to fundamentals we shall be forced, as we have been, to content ourselves with the treatment of symptoms, with haphazard patchwork, and with piecemeal alterations of doubtful value, or to expend prodigious energy in efforts to add more gadgets, gears, and accessories to a cumbrous and complicated machine.

CHAPTER VI

A PLAN FOR DISCUSSION

You may think that our government works reasonably well as it is. You may not agree with the objectives and principles stated in Chapter IV. You may agree with them but believe that these goals can be reached without any great change in the ancient design. Or you may look upon any plan for fundamental reorganization as academic and impractical. If you hold such views, you will not be interested in this chapter. But, before skipping it, you should know exactly what its purpose is.

Put yourself in the place of a research engineer. You are asked to devise a machine that will meet certain general tests. Having given thought to your problem, you put a rough sketch on paper. Then you draw a blueprint. From this you make a model and, finally, an experimental machine. You probably have no idea that this will be the final one, but you will have something that you can observe and study and something for other engineers to appraise. Observation, study, and criticism may lead you to change some parts and scrap others, or perhaps to give up the whole design and to try another.

Or take the method that is often followed in what is termed pure science. Here the student often finds himself in the presence of facts that call for orderly arrangement, for explanation, or for the revealing of cause-and-effect relationships. The scientist may not be sure that he has found all of the answers. He may know that he lacks absolute proof. So he makes a guess, as well informed and intelligent as he can make it, and calls it an hypothesis. An hypothesis is provisional. It is something to be attacked and defended, to be proved or disproved. Even if it is shown to be false, it has served a useful purpose. It has helped understanding.

It is always easier to discuss the concrete than the abstract.

It is only when we reduce the abstract to the concrete, that we can really know what the abstract means. People often readily agree on something in principle, but disagree violently when practical applications are proposed. Often there can be no discussion at all of an objective, but discussion becomes lively and fruitful when someone spells out a way to reach the objective.

The plan proposed in this chapter should be viewed as a rough sketch, something in the nature of an hypothesis, or a statement of the abstract in concrete terms. One purpose is to show that the objectives and principles stated in Chapter IV can be applied, exactly as were the objectives and principles that the founding fathers had in mind; but, assuming that the stated goals are desirable, the author is under no illusion that this is the best way to reach them.

Certainly, no one individual can or should make the final plan. It will take form presumably only after much co-operative research, representative conferences, and compromising of views. Nevertheless, individual thinking must precede and accompany group effort. There are different methods of applying a set of principles; and a final choice of methods can only be made after many and wide exchanges of views. Perhaps you feel that basic change is needed but, because of the obstacles in the way, it can come only from the pressure of some future crisis. If you are right in this feeling, it seems all the more needful that we should have in advance broad analyses of our governmental needs and prepared plans for meeting those needs.

Like the founding fathers, we should approach the task of reorganization as practical men interested, not only in the design of a new government, but also in the way Americans— more specifically American politicians—are likely to operate and develop it. Organizations often act in contradiction to the principles on which they are founded; and, conversely, it may be true, as Sait remarked, that governments "decline and fall as often by carrying their principles to excess as by neglecting them altogether."[1] The trends and workings of government are more important than its form, and when change is proposed, it is necessary to forecast for the future as best one can, the complicated and formative play of human motives and social forces. The question is not, What kind of government is it? but rather, What kind of government will men make of it? No effort is here made to explore fully all the possibilities and probabilities.

As we develop our hypothetical form of government, we should keep constantly in mind the primary objectives and principles that we are trying to reach or carry out. These are: adaptability, majority rule, minority participation, effective leadership, fixed responsibility, national representation, concentration of power, party government, and personal capability. Secondarily or incidentally, we aim at publicity and continuity in government. In general, we want a simpler government, not only that it may work better, but also to arouse and hold the interest of the people and to make their task easier. We must abandon the complex mechanistic system of separated authorities checking and balancing one another, but we intend to keep various needed limitations and checks.

ONE WAY TO SIMPLIFY GOVERNMENT

The first step in applying our objectives and principles is to work out a general outline of the over-all legislative-executive organization.

We suggest: (1) a single governmental authority, called for ease of reference, the National Council, to possess supreme legislative and executive powers; (2) a Senate, with reviewing and delaying functions, but no veto; and (3) a chief executive charged with the conduct of administration, appointed by and responsible to the National Council.

A National Council. The general conception back of the proposed National Council amounts to a rejection on the one hand of the numerous assembly and on the other hand of executive or one-man government. The Council is to offer a substitute for dictatorship, as well as for traditional parliamentarism.

We shall give the Council 21 members. Perhaps any odd

number between 15 and 25 would meet modern needs equally well; but, as we shall see later, the number suggested is an especially convenient one. The purpose is to establish a body small enough to deliberate as a good committee, a good commission or a good board customarily deliberates; small enough also to take a broad view of policy, to plan, co-ordinate, integrate, and supervise, and to reach reasonably quick decisions. Because such a body is simple, visible, and understandable, its effect should be to fix the personal responsibility of its members. In a face-to-face business-like group of this kind, intricate procedures would go, along with much of our present maneuvering and manipulation; obstructive individuals would find themselves at a great disadvantage; compromises would be limited to those that are inherent and desirable in a democracy; and either seniority or filibustering would be unlikely to persist.

While small size is essential for the achievement of concentration, the Council should be large enough to ensure adequate representation of regions, interests, and points of view. A membership of from 15 to 25 would, it is believed, permit sufficient diversity.[2]

Government is not a part-time job; and the Council should be in continuous session. As we shall see later, we are going to provide a number of alternates or substitutes for the members of the Council. Thus, it would be feasible for that body to function continuously, and at the same time a number of its members could take vacations, go on speaking tours or inspection trips, and even make visits to foreign countries. With unending sessions, there would no longer be any adjournments *sine die* or any question of special sessions. The election and organization of a new Council may be expected to occasion some interruption, but it should be less pronounced and prolonged than the interruptions that now occur either in Congress or in the presidency.

Any plan for war in the atomic age should include some such an arrangement for uninterrupted constitutional government. Under this plan, no atomic attack or other foreseeable crisis would be likely to paralyze the government; because, like a football team, the Council would have sufficient substitutes to carry on. We are assuming, of course, that we shall have sense enough to keep the homes of the councillors and alternate councillors fairly well scattered about the suburbs of Washington.

The Council would have to work through committees. Experience has shown that when a small body attempts to do the work of a large body and to do that work in the same way, the members of the small body will be more over-burdened than those of the large. The Council could not do all of its research and investigation with committees of its own members. It would presumably set up permanent commissions for permanent fields of policy, special commissions for the study of special problems, and a general commission for co-ordination and review of policies. The Council could develop a corps of trained investigators. It could arm its commissions with full power to hold hearings, subpoena witnesses and cite for contempt. Because this auxiliary organization could be flexibly adapted to its purposes, the results should be considerably better than those which have come from the committees of Congress. If the Council believed that two or more commissions should study the same subject or aspects of it, nothing would prevent the establishment of duplicating or overlapping bodies.

The Council supplants the House of Representatives. The establishment of the Council would make the House of Representatives unnecessary. It seems impossible, in any event, to reconcile an assembly like the House with the principles that we are trying to carry out.

The Senate. The Senate with limited powers could continue to serve certain important and useful purposes without contravening the principle of concentration.[3] No suggestion is made for any change with respect to the number of Senators, their qualifications, their terms or the manner of their election; but a change is later recommended in the times of election.

It is proposed that every bill that has passed the Council

shall, before it becomes a law, be presented to the Senate. A treaty would be handled in the same way. But the Senate would have no power of absolute veto. It could only suspend the passage of a law or the ratification of a treaty. The period of suspension might be sixty days for an ordinary act and forty-eight hours in case of an emergency declared by the Council.[4]

It is believed that something approximating these periods of time would be sufficient for the purposes that are held in view. These purposes are three: first, to provide a check against hasty action by the Council; second, to ensure that no law will be passed without public notice and opportunity for public discussion; and, third, to bring into government decentralizing influences, to counteract, or at least to criticize, any centralizing trend that the Council might reveal.

While the Senate today is no more opposed to centralization than is the House of Representatives, it is likely that the senators, if they were restricted to functions of delay, criticism, and advice, would become more nearly what they were originally intended to be, representatives of the states as states. They would be able to do what no one in the government is now well-equipped to do; that is, speak for the interests and values involved in decentralization. Thus, the Senate might become a better guardian than it now is of that aspect of federalism which has lost vitality but retains validity. We might imagine a further development that would make the senators true liaison officers of the states, equipped with adequate staffs to assist their constituents.

The functions left to the Senate would not be inconsistent with the principles that we are trying to carry out. They are all that an institution so undemocratically constituted can reasonably claim.

The proposed provision would eliminate all the varieties of minority rule that now find sanctuary in the Senate, including the minority power to block or indefinitely delay the conclusion of a treaty. The provision would partially prevent divided government. It would absolutely prevent deadlocks between the two legislative bodies. The conference committee would become unnecessary. Filibustering might continue, if the Senators wished it to, but it would have no effect beyond the constitutional limits on delay.

Conceivably, the emergency clause might be abused, depriving the Senate of opportunity for debate and for the arousing of public opinion. The fact is that formal and informal declarations of emergency are pretty common under the present setup. We have developed crisis government because of the speed with which conditions change, because of governmental lag, and because real crises do arise. The declaration or pretension of an emergency, however, is also at present a useful technique of presidential leadership, one of the means of accelerating the legislative machine. Such a technique would be unnecessary if the machine were geared to action; and the leaders of the Council would have comparatively little reason to exploit or to fabricate emergencies, since the proposed plan of government would eliminate most of the present sources of delay and centers of obstruction. Furthermore, the Supreme Court would remain as a check on any unconstitutional use of the emergency clause.

Some may feel that additional checks would be needed on hasty action by the Council. It may appear that a bill, disapproved by the Senate, should not only be re-passed by the Council, but should require re-passage by two thirds of that body. Such a provision might be desirable as a compromise, but it would open the way to obstruction and would contravene the principles of majority rule and party government.

The chief executive. The National Council would choose the chief executive and would be empowered to remove him at any time. His function would be the immediate direction and control of all executive departments and agencies. In this manner we complete the concentration of power in the National Council, placing full responsibility on the Council, as well as personal responsibility on its members. Such an arrangement does not diminish executive jurisdiction, but seeks to make the executive fully accountable to a body capable of enforcing accountability.

The present power of the Senate to confirm executive appointments would disappear. The Council would become the final and single authority for administrative supervision, as it would be actually for legislation and policy-making.

Divided government in its present familiar form would thus become impossible. So far as the legislative and executive are concerned, separation of powers, branches, or departments would vanish. Yet, the union of the two branches would facilitate a logical division of work and of function. There would be no executive veto. Co-operation should come as a matter of course, for there would no longer be much reason or opportunity for jealousy or for the magnification of prerogatives. The Council could really act as a national board of trustees. As a policy-making body, it would be in the best possible position to obtain information and assistance from administrative agencies.

Since the executive could be removed at any time, the cumbrous method of impeachment, already obsolescent, would become superfluous.[5] When a chief executive incurred some disability, demonstrated unfitness, or lost the confidence of a country or of his party, the Council could, and presumably would, dismiss him. When conditions radically changed, as from prosperity to depression or from peace to war, the Council could, if necessary, change the chief executive, selecting a man with appropriate qualifications. In general, this scheme would obviate the embarrassing situations that may now arise in the election of a president,[6] and it provides satisfactorily for the succession, something that the present system has not yet done.

Vice-presidents. Under this plan, the vice-president, as he now is, would disappear. The Senate, therefore, would regularly choose its presiding officer, as it now frequently does its president *pro tempore*, except that the Senate should be permitted, if it so desires, to select a presiding officer from outside its own membership. The Council would be authorized to provide by law for an assistant chief executive or for not more than five such officials. One of them could be designated to act as chief executive in case of a vacancy in the office. Thus, an immediate successor would be at hand for the chief executive in the event of a sudden vacancy in his office; and we would have added insurance against the chaos that might result from an atomic attack on Washington.

The chief executive and the administration. This plan would, it is believed, simplify the functions of the chief executive and, in general, bring about a desirable deflation of his office. The new office would call primarily for broad administrative qualifications and grasp of the policy problems that lie back of administration. If the provision should work according to expectations, the Council would choose a man distinguished for these qualifications.

The existence of real executive vice-presidents would lighten the chief executive's burden of work, organize the top control of the executive branch as it should be organized, and establish an authoritative and effective means of administrative co-ordination and integration. Each assistant chief executive would probably hold frequent conferences with top officials; while the chief executive himself would work on matters of policy chiefly, if not exclusively, through the assistant chief executives. The Cabinet as it now is would disappear. The new cabinet or executive conference would cover, not a part of the administration, but the whole of it.

The Council and the administration. The intent is to do away with all limits on the delegation of legislative power, and thus further concentrate authority and responsibility in the National Council. What we seem to need is not a judicial check on legislative functioning in this particular, but a legislature able to delegate with intelligence and self-control, as well as to supervise properly the agencies that exercise delegated powers. The author can see no reason why in this setup any administrative agency should be treated as "independent" or semi-independent, since the chief executive himself would be directly responsible to and controlled by the Council. Nevertheless, the regulatory commissions, if it were thought desirable, could still be treated as "arms" of the legislature and kept partially exempt from executive control. The Council could, if it so desired, retain the power to approve administrative regulations, and it could even initiate and issue them. Nothing in this type of organization would prevent judicial control of the administration to ensure the constitutionality and legality of administrative acts.

A NEW POLITICAL PROCESS

The question now arises, How can we make concentrated government democratic? How will it be controlled by and responsible to a popular majority? How can it embody national representation?

Nominations and elections. The Council must be chosen by direct vote of the people so that a true majority may control the government. No states, districts, or other arbitrary subdivisions should figure in the election, except for the administration of the casting and counting of the ballots. The Electoral College, already largely discarded, would have no place in elections. We would say farewell to much of our political geography and arithmetic, with their peculiar, complicated, and disconcerting aspects.

A national popular election would give to all eligible citizens equal voting power. Any number of voters, wherever they might be, would have no more and no less importance than the same number anywhere else. The slogan "Let the people rule" would mean a certain, not an accidental, practice.

We would use the present nominating system, with a hope that eventually it might become a better one. Instead of nominating candidates for president and vice-president, the national convention would nominate twenty-one candidates for the Council. Their names would go on the ballot in the order determined by the convention, presumably in the order of their nomination.

It is anticipated that the delegation thus named would include all of the demonstrated national leaders of the party. There would be room also for regional and group leaders and other men and women of special distinction whose presence on the ticket would give it strength and popular appeal. A "dark horse," a mere "favorite son" or a "military hero" could never win, as he can now, exclusive leadership of party and government through a deadlock or a stampede in the convention. On the other hand, "dark horses," "favorite sons," and "military heroes," if they had wide popularity, could be included in the delegation.

The candidates would evidently be drawn from all parts of the country and from the principal classes and occupational groups. Party strategy, as well as a desire to conciliate factions within the party, might be expected to produce a broadly representative ticket. A purely sectional delegation or one drawn from a single economic group would be unlikely to win a national election, unless the opposing parties were equally tactless. Yet, one may believe that this plan would exploit much more fairly than does our present organization the rich sources of leadership and statesmanship that are now so largely neglected. One would expect the delegation to include the principal political leaders, such as those who, under the present system, are mentioned for the presidential nomination. There would be places for former chief-executives and others experienced in administration. There would be opportunity, too, for a consideration of the claims of university presidents and professors, scientists, newspaper editors, publicists, philanthropists, industrialists, and labor leaders.

It is difficult to give a concrete illustration of how the plan would work in practice because the situation with regard to leadership would change at the instant the plan is adopted. Many able men and women would become available who now have no chance and know that they have none. Others who are now active aspirants would cease their self-advertising because it would no longer be worth while. The professional politician would by no means lose his importance or his influence; but the amateur would have a better chance to become professional or at least to work side by side with the professional.[7]

The party program. In the ordinary course of events, the delegation would in practice prepare the party program, as the presidential candidate does now; but the delegation's program would probably be more comprehensive, better integrated, and less opportunistic than the statements of policy that we now get from presidential candidates. For the delegation would embody collective, not one-man, leadership. A delegation would have to agree at the very beginning of a campaign on a broad program; and the program would have to be reasonably precise in order to prevent one candidate's contradicting another.

It is anticipated, therefore, that the campaign would come closer than our national campaigns now do to the realities of a national debate. The party in power would sum up its record and state its purposes for the future. The opposition would attack the record at its vulnerable points and submit alternative policies. Thus, the issues would be clearly stated and, to a greater extent than now, the election would produce a popular decision and a popular mandate. The tendency, it is hoped would be gradually to develop a real philosophical integrity in each major party, a real philosophical difference between the parties, and, consequently, an opportunity for a real choice by the people. For only when men are fundamentally like-minded is it possible for them to agree on a concrete program.

Stronger party government or better personal government. Let us assume first that we wish to strengthen the party system, prevent factionalism and disintegration, and check the trend toward personal government. If so, the proposed plan might be helpful. We could probably put most hope in the disciplinary power which the members of each delegation would possess. The nomination of legislators would no longer be scattered among states and districts without national co-ordination and control. The national party convention would alone exercise the nominating function, and the leaders of the party representation in the Council would exercise great influence in the national convention, if not full control over it. They could and probably would prevent the naming of any member of the Council who had persistently refused or failed to co-operate with his party colleagues. In fact, we would provide expressly that the delegation should serve as the national governing body of its party. Probably without any express provision, control over the national committee of the party would gravitate to the delegation, for the same reason that presidential candidates and presidents now exercise such control. Effective leadership, fixed responsibility, and concentration of power require as perfect a union as possible between party and government.

The kind of national election here proposed would eventually exclude irreconcilable extremists from the delegation and likewise from the party. An exchange of extremists would no doubt take place between the major parties, resulting in a considerable realignment. In this process, direct popular elections would play a part, especially in the South. In that section, the growing differences of political outlook could more easily find expression in different party affiliations. The South would in fact become a major political battle-ground, for it contains at present the largest number of nonvoters.

The proposed plan is intended to encourage party government and realignment, but it would not exclude personal, nonpartisan, bipartisan, or factional government, or any other type except multiple-party government. The disadvantage of the present governmental organization is that it makes nonpartisan and personal government well-nigh inevitable, without providing for it appropriate governmental and electoral machinery. The merit of the plan here discussed is that it fixes the responsibility both of parties and of persons and permits a development in either direction—toward strong party control or toward individual independence.

Two-party government. It is proposed that only two parties shall be represented in the Council. The head of the majority party delegation would be president of the Council. The remaining twenty seats would be divided between the two parties in proportion to the share of each party in the total vote cast for the two parties. If twenty seats were to be distributed between the two parties, each party would obtain one seat for each 5 per cent of the total vote for the two parties, or for a major fraction of the vote. The members of a delegation would become councillors in the order of their appearance on the ballot, presumably in the order of their nomination by the convention. If a party were entitled to twelve councillors, the first twelve candidates would be declared elected. If it were entitled to eight councillors, the first eight would be chosen. The majority party would have an additional seat, that occupied by the president of the Council, thus assuring the majority party a clear majority in the Council, even were the election as close as the presidential election was in 1916.[8]

Members of a delegation who were not elected councillors would become the alternate councillors. An alternate councillor would become a councillor when a seat belonging to his party became vacant because of death, resignation, disability, disqualification, or absence.

Thus the plan would produce and maintain within the government a party in power and an opposition; and the campaign leaders of the two parties, continuing as party leaders, would become members and leaders of the government. Each group would become responsible: the majority for carrying out its program and the minority for constructive criticism. The national debate would continue, with resulting popular enlightenment.

No seat in the Council would go to any independent candidate or minor party. Their exclusion would seem necessary to ensure party responsibility and party government. The intention is to maintain and to strengthen the *two*-party system.[9] To introduce proportional representation of all parties might produce a situation comparable to that which exists in certain European countries where government can be carried on only by coalitions. In such a situation, deadlocks become possible, and a minority party holding the balance of power may bargain itself into a controlling position.

Since 1900, minor parties in the United States have cast a negligible percentage of the vote in presidential elections, except in 1912 and 1924. In no other of the last thirteen presidential elections have such parties polled more than 6 per cent of the total vote. In 1940 they accounted for only 0.5 per cent of the total, and in 1944 for only 0.7 per cent.

The method of voting. The voter would cast his vote for the delegation as a whole; that is, for the party. Any other method of voting would undermine the unity of the delegation and of the party. If, for example, the voter were to split his ticket and vote for, say, ten candidates of one party and eleven of another, the result would be strongly to emphasize the personalities and the particular claims of individual candidates. In consequence, each candidate would tend to conduct his own campaign independently; and party responsibility would be unattainable. We would be transferring to the national sphere the situation that now exists in congressional elections. As a possible alternative, the voter might be permitted to vote for a party, but also to express his preference among his party's candidates. The effect would be, however, to carry intraparty contests into the national elections. The candidates of a party, while fighting the opposition, would also fight one another. Under such circumstances, no delegation could adopt and collectively advocate a unified party program.

What voting for a delegation would do is precisely what we now aim to do in a presidential election; that is, to put a party in control of the government. Those citizens who might complain of having to vote for a "hand-picked slate" would doubtless be admonished to join a party and participate actively in the nominating process.

We are going to suggest that each qualified voter shall have two votes: one first-choice and the other second-choice. If no delegation receives a majority of the first-choice votes, the second-choice votes would then be counted, beginning with those cast by voters for the party having the least number of first-choice votes. The purpose is three-fold: first, to ensure that the successful party shall obtain a majority instead of a minority or a mere plurality; second, to prevent the wasting of votes cast by minor parties; and, third, to preserve the useful functions of minor parties as means of protest and of realignment.[10]

Effect on third and minor parties. In general, the effect of preferential voting should be to encourage the formation of minor parties and thus to counteract any discouragement that might be caused by their exclusion from the National Council. Under present circumstances, we are told that if we vote a minor-party ticket we shall waste our votes. This argument, which is usually well-founded, is also an argument against the organizing of a minor party in the first place. Preferential voting would prevent waste of votes.

As things are now, a third party may not merely waste votes but it may actually help its worst enemy. A third party of the Left draws votes from the Center and the Left, rather than from the Right, thus relatively strengthening the Right. A third party of the Right weakens the Right and the Center, not the Left.

Preferential voting would leave the minor party free, not only to act as a vehicle of protest, but also to influence the philosophies and programs of the major parties and thus bring about a realignment of those parties. While neither major party would have to make stultifying concessions to prevent the formation of a third party, each of the major parties would, as a matter of strategy, shape its nominations and its program to attract as many second-choice votes as possible. This realigning tendency would be most evident in a close election or when, as in 1924 and 1948, a third party seemed to present a real threat. It may be expected, therefore, that the governmental organization and the plan of election here proposed would strengthen the major parties and the two-party system, while facilitating party realignments.

Certainly, not all voters would take the trouble to indicate their second-choice. At present, a qualified elector may influence an election in any one of three ways: by voting for one of the major parties, by voting for a minor party, or by staying away from the polls. The proposed plan gives him a fourth means of expression, the second-choice vote. He would not need to avail himself of this privilege. If no second-choice votes at all were cast, a considerable number of votes might be wasted, but no procedural difficulty would arise.

Election every three years. No one can absolutely prove the correctness of any specified term of office. It would doubtless be agreed, however, that, unless provision is made for dissolution and the calling of a special election, some danger may lie in long terms. The writer does not recommend any dissolution procedure. In his opinion, a two-year term would not necessarily be too short. In fact, more frequent national elections, with more continuity of political discussion, might serve very useful purposes. No objection is seen to a constant "playing of politics," when the politics are truly national and on a high plane. In that event, frequent elections might actually promote stability, as well as realize the responsibility of government to the people.[11]

In the writer's opinion, a three-year term is long enough and short enough. If it were found unsatisfactory it could be lengthened or shortened by constitutional amendment. Any change in terms is now a complicated matter, because the governmental organization is complicated. Once simplified, it would lend itself more readily to adjustments in detail.

In any event, it would seem that one half of the senators should be elected at the same time as the members of the Council. The senators would still have six-year terms of office; but, at each triennial election, every state would regularly choose one of its two senators. Thus, *all* the states, not two thirds of them as now, would at each general election impress their opinions on the Senate. Furthermore, this change would reduce the number of general elections in a six-year period from *three* to *two;* and we would no longer have any mid-term or off-year elections.

During a twelve-year period, a voter is now called upon to participate in six elections to fill national offices. During the same period under the proposed plan, there would be four national elections. At the six elections, the voter now marks his ballot a maximum of thirteen times: six for representative, four for senator, and three for president. Under the proposed plan the voter would mark his ballot not more than twelve times: four for his first-choice delegation, four for his second-choice delegation, and four for senator. So far as attendance at elections and balloting are concerned, the proposed system is the simpler.

QUESTIONABLE POINTS

The plan of government just described leaves many points untouched and many questions unanswered. It invites criticism and it is open to many objections. We can expect sweeping objection from those who do not admit that the defects of government are fundamental, who believe that the present general design is sound, and who disagree with our statement of modern objectives and principles. We shall not repeat here the argument set forth in other chapters. But, without going back to fundamentals or undertaking an elaborate defense of our hypothesis, we may usefully anticipate certain criticisms and objections.

Nothing like it in American experience. Perhaps the most obvious criticism is that the plan has never been tried in the field of government and has no analogy or precedent in American political experience. It is true that this type of organization has never been used for the government of the Nation. Neither had the Constitution when it was adopted. It is also true that the plan has had no trial by any of the states. But it is, nevertheless, a logical outgrowth of American experience with the existing organization, its results, and its trends. We have had considerable experience with each of the principles on which the proposed organization is based, as well as with contrary principles. Concentration of power in a National Council is less novel than presidential government, to the idea of which we have become accustomed. Experience has amply demonstrated the merits of a policy-making and supervisory body of a size intermediate between the single individual and the mass meeting. Experience has shown with equal clearness the injurious results of divided responsibility.

On the whole, the plan here submitted for discussion appears more closely related to American experience than was the constitutional plan of federal union at the time of its adoption; and we may well recall what Madison said during the great debate:

Hearken not to the voice which petulantly tells you that the form of government recommended for your adoption is a novelty in the political world; that it has never yet had a place in the theories of the wildest projectors; that it rashly attempts what it is impossible to accomplish. . . . Is it not the glory of the people of America, that, whilst they have paid a decent regard to the opinions of former times and other nations, they have not suffered a blind veneration for antiquity, for custom, or for names, to overrule the suggestions of their own good sense, the knowledge of their own situation, and the lessons of their own experience? To this manly spirit, posterity will be indebted for the possession, and the world for the example, of the numerous innovations displayed on the American theatre, in favor of private rights and public happiness. Had no important step been taken by the leaders of the Revolution for which a precedent could not be discovered, no government established of which an exact model did not present itself, the people of the United States might, at this moment, have been numbered among the melancholy victims of misguided councils, must at best have been laboring under the weight of some of those forms which have crushed the liberties of the rest of mankind. Happily for America, happily, we trust, for the whole human race, they pursued a new and more noble course.[12]

The fact is that Americans, at the lower levels of government and in the private sphere, have had a long, a varied, and on the whole a satisfactory contact with the proposed type of organization. It is found in any administrative agency controlled and supervised by a board or commission which appoints an administrative director or executive officer. This type of organization is illustrated by the council-manager plan in cities and counties, by the setup of industrial corporations, and by the organization of many private associations and institutions. The American people, wherever they have been reasonably free of constitutional restrictions and political vested interests, have generally adopted and retained this simple type of concentrated government.

It can be said, of course, that the government of a city, a county, an administrative agency, a corporation, or an association is not comparable to the government of the United States. It is true that the proposed plan of organization has appeared only in comparatively small enterprises; it is joined to the political process only in the cities and counties; and it has nowhere been exposed to the full sweep of party politics. American experience supplies no absolute proof that such a plan could be used to govern a great democratic nation with its divergent interests and sections, with its comprehensive and complex responsibilities, domestic and foreign, and with its elaborate and intricate political processes. One can argue with much truth that government is not business and is not like business.[13]

We shall never find an undertaking precisely analogous to the national government; for the nation is unique. It must, to a large extent, suggest its own model and use its own experience. Nevertheless, counties, cities, administrative agencies, business enterprises and private associations are comparable to the United States government in one important respect: they all perform three functions—policy-making, supervision, and execution. Modern government more and more resembles business management.

No one would deny the significant differences between a small job and a big one. Our present organization, however, seems to be better fitted for a simple and easy job than for the enormously complicated and difficult task that it is now attempting to perform. The characteristics of the nation, which are said to make it different from all other units and undertakings, seem to be the very things which make the existing governmental organization difficult to operate. Our eighteenth-century nation was a comparatively small enterprise and government was comparatively simple. At present, it is the very diversity of interests and sections, with their competing pressures and clashing claims, which calls for strong, integrated government. It is the growth of responsibilities which makes checks and balances inappropriate. It is the elaborateness and intricacy of the political processes which discredit the existing system.

The present organization does something that the proposed one could not do. A contemporary student of constitutional history and law says: "It is not generally questioned that in a rough way the functions of government fall logically into categories of legislative, executive, and judicial characteristics."[14] This is true; but we have in our national government today a separation of authorities, of institutions, of departments, or of branches without proper regard for "logical categories" of functions or "characteristics." We do not get a clear division of work or real functional specialization.

The same writer recognizes that president and Congress must both operate in the field of policy; but he goes on to say:

The relationship ought not to be one of principal and subordinate but one of equals struggling toward creative compromise. Only in terms of such a relationship can we be assured of the continued evolution of inchoate bodies of public sentiment into clear statements of public policy and into harmonious governmental programs operative in terms of the principles of the Constitution.[15]

The fact is that we more and more demand co-operation within the government. Of course we want "creative compromise" rather than obstruction and log-rolling. We want also "harmonious governmental programs." But if we want these desirable things, why not organize to make their accomplishment easy, rather than difficult? If we hope for co-operation, we should build it into the government. We should not make express and careful provision for obstruction and conflict. The proposed plan is designed to make possible division of labor, in the form of specialization of function, without excluding co-operation. The division and specialization which thus become possible seem to be the only kind that reconciles democracy and efficiency.

Another quotation from the same author:

The fact remains . . . that on no important occasion of intergovernmental conflict thus far in our history would the complete elimination or subordination of the restraining branch or branches of government have left us with an entirely satisfactory solution even of the problems immediately at hand. As for the effect of such elimination upon the solution of other problems as they arose, it would have deprived us of the instruments needed to correct the distorted perspective of aggressive individuals and agencies.[16]

What is thus stated as a fact may or may not be one. Suppose we think of some important occasion of conflict within the government, for example, the conflict between Congress and

Andrew Johnson. If at that time one authority could have been over-ruled or subordinated, the conflict probably would not have arisen and it certainly would have been shorter-lived and less bitter. It seems idle to conjecture what the effect might have been on problems as they arose in the past, if one or two of our governmental authorities had been eliminated. The organization can only be treated and conjectured about as a whole. We can hardly assume, however, that in our government as it is the "distorted perspective" of the president will correct or neutralize the "distorted perspective" of Congress; or vice versa. President and Congress may suffer from the same sort of distortion, as they frequently do. Instead of attempting in complicated ways to correct "distorted perspectives," would it not be wiser to get a government less afflicted with astigmatism?

"Domination is not the answer." Along somewhat the same line, another student has written: "The only kind of relationship which in fact constitutes true government is harmony. Domination is not the answer; if it were, realities might be better observed . . . by the abolition of one part or the other."[17] No one, so far as the author knows, has ever proposed to abolish either the legislative or the executive branch. But it should be understood that government means domination. We should have no illusions on that score. The power of action within government involves domination of somebody by somebody else. The above quotation implies that to prevent domination we must maintain the conditions that invite domination and make it necessary. It is implied also that to get "harmony" in government we must preserve the kind of organization that causes disharmony. In the present setup the getting of harmony is so complicated and difficult as to present a critical danger. Under the proposed plan, we shall have to obtain agreement among eleven members of the Council. When they agree, harmony results and government functions.

Of course no reorganization of government can eliminate all internal conflict and friction or should try to do so. So far as possible, however, artificially induced jealousies and suspicions should be eliminated, along with conflicts that are irrelevant to the making of public policy. Government, if it is to be continuously capable of governing, should be equipped to resolve conflicts, terminate obstruction, and break deadlocks. Under the plan here proposed, if an unwholesome rivalry should arise between the president of the Council and the chief executive, the Council can intervene. If the Senate is controlled by one party and the Council by another, the worst that the Senate could do would be to delay legislation. A short passage of time would end the deadlock and permit government to go on.

It is not quite true, however, that the plan sets up a legislature unchecked by the executive. The proposal would eliminate the executive veto; but, in all probability, the chief executive would exercise great influence over the majority members of the Council. At the same time, his check on the Council or his leadership of it would not involve loss of his responsibility to the Council, the danger of deadlocks, or an excessive compromising of differences.

Division of work would vanish. There can be no absolute guarantee that the Council would not unduly interfere in administrative matters or make the chief executive a puppet. But he would have a constitutionally defined jurisdiction and, presumably, would be a man of considerable stature. If he were not big enough, strong enough or tactful enough to maintain his proper sphere of action and prevent damaging interferences, he would become a political liability for the party in power. If the members of the majority chose to overstep the proper limits of over-all administrative supervision, the minority would hardly fail to give publicity to the administrative ineptitude of the party in power. Correction of the situation would then become the responsibility of the electorate; and the people would enjoy a better opportunity than at present to understand legislative-executive relationships.

We cannot make the administration responsible, without vesting in some authority the power to control administration. The best protection against the abuse of that power is to make it comprehensive and its operations visible and to make the authority which holds and exercises the supervisory power genuinely and effectively responsible to the people.

Another possible objection, the opposite of that just mentioned, is that the chief executive would dominate the Council, producing one-man government, an elective dictatorship. This development, it may be argued, would result from the action of political forces similar to those that nullified the neat scheme of the founding fathers and made the president the leader of his party and a popularly elected leader of the nation. People and party, it may be said, demand a single personal leadership and would see in the office of chief executive, as they see now in the presidency, the prizes and the opportunities in which politicians are chiefly interested. The party managers would therefore insist that the party candidates for the Council pledge themselves to the appointment of a particular man as chief executive. Candidates for chief executive would be nominated by the national conventions, as they are now, and the Council would become another Electoral College, a collection of figureheads. As such, the Council would never remove a chief executive until control of the Council had passed from one party to the other.

What we are here warned against is pretty much what we are getting under the present organization. If one-man government develops under the proposed plan, it would at least come in a clear and simple form. The "strong executive" would be free to govern with a minimum of manipulation and demagoguery and with a maximum of responsibility to the people.

It should be kept in mind, however, that the National Council would differ from the Electoral College in several important ways. The Electoral College has only one function, to choose the president and vice-president. The electors meet by states; they do not assemble as a national body; they have no continuing institutional character. They have no power or responsibility and, customarily, no opportunity for an exercise of judgment.

In contrast, the Council would possess the supreme governing power, and, constitutionally, would meet and continuously

function. Even if the majority members were willing or compelled to be figureheads, the minority members would not be;
and, presumably, they would contest executive domination and
carry their protests to the people. On the whole, it would seem
that one-man government as an ultimate development would be
considerably less likely under the proposed plan than under the
present system. Unlike the two houses of Congress, the National Council could operate effectively without executive leadership, if it were necessary to do so.

Government might oscillate, as it does at present, between
executive government and legislative government; but there
would be a chance to impose intelligent control over the oscil-
lation. The fact is, of course, that we want and must have governmental flexibility, an organic adaptability to different situations. The proposed plan would provide more flexibility with
greater assurance of efficiency, wherever power might be located. Since the Council would be better able than Congress
to deal with an emergency, the Council would not need to
abdicate, but it could delegate freely, retaining, as Congress
cannot, an effective supervision of the delegated powers.

We would have too much secrecy. It may be objected that a
small body like the Council would operate in secret. The Constitutional Convention of 1787 was itself a small body and held
no public sessions. Few realize to what an extent the government
now operates in secret. Nothing in the Constitution requires
Congress to hold public sittings, although "each House shall
keep a journal of its proceedings, and from time to time publish
the same, except such parts as may in their judgment require
secrecy."[18] The president, who is said to move in the bright
glare of publicity, does not think out loud in front of a micro-
phone and does not hold his official talks in an auditorium. His
Cabinet meetings are not open to the public and what goes on
there is seldom divulged. As a practical matter, little of the
work of government can be carried on in the public eye; most
of the process of reaching decisions is and ought to be secret;
and many of the decisions must be kept confidential until an
appropriate time arrives to announce them. The merit of the

proposed Council is that it can operate secretly, when secrecy is necessary, possess itself of all information, as Congress cannot now do, and keep its legitimate secrets, as Congress at present does not always do.

Practically speaking, there is no way to compel publicity, except on certain matters and at certain stages. The best way to ensure publicity, so far as it can be ensured, is to fix responsibility, eliminate the dark corners and devious by-ways, and arouse that keen public interest which will demand the information to which the public is entitled.

The Council would not give us legislative unity. It might be argued that there would be less unity in the Council and less capacity to decide and to act than there is now in the Senate or the House. Unity, it can be said, is more easily obtained in a large body, because mediocre men will follow leadership while the Council will consist of nothing but leaders—prima donnas—each responsible in reality to the section or the pressure group which has forced his nomination. But our present leaders—those for example who compete for the presidential nomination—are compelled to diverge from one another and to become in appearance prima donnas, because the present political process puts a premium on competition among personalities, rather than on co-operation and teamwork. Change the emphasis, and political advantage will lie with those who can work together without undue personal publicity-seeking. It is the mosaic of separate local constituencies which produces disunity in Congress and makes its members peculiarly vulnerable to special-interest pressures. The members of the Council will have a common constituency in which the general interest has opportunity to make itself felt.

To be sure, the fact that the majority-party delegation had stood on the same platform during the campaign might not prevent a split after the election. One can argue that conditions would soon change, creating new issues.

To discuss the question of unity in the government we have to consider the party system and the political process. It is expected that the proposed plan would contribute to party solidarity. The party would still have to satisfy its factions and attract the independent vote; but the pressure groups would perforce act nationally; and, in a national election, local influences would tend to cancel one another. The plan would lessen prenomination contests within the party, particularly those contests that revolve around personalities rather than policies. It is hardly likely that a delegation would include men with contradictory opinions or irreconcilable philosophies, for the delegation would have to present a solid front to the opposition. Lack of fundamental harmony within the delegation would seriously jeopardize the party's success at the polls. The tendency would be, apparently, to emphasize policies and de-emphasize personalities. Ample opportunity would exist for the recognition of outstanding men and women; and national attention during the campaign would no longer focus on two personalities. Accordingly, one could expect a more intelligent discussion of issues and policies.

In the process of naming its candidates, the party could go far to achieve that intermediate integration of opinion which should be one of the party's essential functions. This integration, furthermore, would not be a superficial and transitory thing, confined largely to the appearances of harmony and to the period of the national campaign. The integrated opinion represented by the delegation would be carried into the government and would unite government, for the successful delegation would be the government.

The suggested plan would promise greater continuity and stability in the leadership of the party. Unless a sudden and radical realignment took place, a party's delegation would change only gradually from election to election. In fact, the plan would make sudden and radical realignments less likely than they are now; but deliberate and gradual realignment would become easier, since a party, by dropping its unpopular extremists either of the Right or the Left, could shift its ground without repudiating its past and without serious danger of an outright split. On the other hand, it would be easier than it is now to introduce new blood, new faces, and new names into the party leadership and into the government, should public opinion call for a thorough "housecleaning."

On the other hand, the view may reasonably be taken that the two-party system cannot be rehabilitated, that no change in organization will have much effect on the party, and that the theory of the party as an instrument for the formation and focusing of opinion has no application under modern conditions. Let us admit for the sake of argument that the party can only fill offices, and that those who are chosen for the offices will act as individuals, moved not by partisan but by factional and nonpartisan considerations. What is evidently needed, to enable these individuals to reach decisions, is personal and responsible contact as individuals at the moment of decision. One important reason why legislative-executive conferences are helpful and unifying now is that the participants are forced to talk as man to man. In a small conference they cannot orate to the galleries: they must speak on the question.

This is a poor time to give up federalism. Another general criticism might be that the government of the United States as organized in 1787 is an example to the rest of the world of how federation can be achieved, and it would be bad for us to reject federal government at home while advocating it abroad. The plan here submitted does not reject the idea of decentralized government or a constitutional division of powers between the central government and the states. The plan does reject a government based in large part on out-dated theories of representation, of separated departments, and of checks and balances. Such a government could be justified when the prime objective was union among the states. It lost its logic when American nationalism became an accomplished fact. In a world or a part-world federation, the United States must become one of the states.

For the larger federation, our government as set up in 1787 may provide an appropriate model, particularly if the central government of the federation possesses strictly limited powers. To accomplish its first and indispensable purpose, that of union, the organization would necessarily embody compromises. An unobstructed democracy or complete operating efficiency could not be the exclusive or primary objective. If the function of world or part-world government were solely to maintain the peace, a complicated and somewhat negative government might stand a good chance of success.

What our own governmental organization shall be, so long as it maintains its democratic character, has no more direct bearing on the question of world organization than the form of government in a state has on the form of government at Washington. Our national governmental organization, however, has considerable indirect bearing on the problem of world or regional federation. The United States can hardly be expected to exercise successful leadership in the organization of the world or of the West unless the government of the United States operates both democratically and efficiently, unless it is so built and equipped as to meet courageously and responsibly the supreme and ultimate challenge of this modern age.

The new political process would be impracticable and dangerous. It cannot be denied that the suggested plan would create difficult political problems. A preferential system of nationwide voting would make ballot-counting and determination of election results a task that would truly challenge the organizing ability and self-control of Americans. It is hard to see how under this plan we could leave the states in control of the suffrage. The choosing of a national government by direct popular vote would put a premium everywhere in the country on "getting out the vote." Likewise, in a state that is "safe" for one party or the other, the state legislature would be strongly tempted to lower the voting age, to make voting compulsory, or to give special inducements for going to the polls. Similarly, the enormous electoral prize at stake might encourage a lax administration of the election laws and stimulate corrupt practices, such as "repeating," fraudulent counting, etc. Furthermore, it might be unwise to give to the National Council, as we now give to Congress, the right to judge the election, returns, and qualifications of its members.[19]

Some would probably see in the plan and in the political

process connected with it a danger of national bossism. It may be argued that if the president now can perpetuate himself in office, the chief executive would do likewise if he were to become party leader, and the members of the Council could do the same if they were to run the government. The majority of the Council or the chief executive or both would have complete control over the dispensing of patronage as well as over the general distribution of material benefits through paternalistic legislation. It could be said further that, with elimination of localism from representation, the local bosses would lose their power, thus opening the way for the establishment of a national machine.

The direct popular election of the Council would make strong local party organization more generally necessary than it is now. Machine politics, in its older form, implies a breaking-down of merit systems and of controls designed to ensure honesty in public finance and public purchasing. At present a greater danger lies in demagogic and paternalistic legislation; but the existing governmental organization promotes that kind of party strategy, electoral bribery, and opinion management. In the proposed Council few changes would occur from term to term. The abrupt and decisive changes would be in party control, not in personnel. Thus, except for possibly a few misfits or extremists, none of the members of the Council would have to worry much about perpetuation in office. They would need no national "machine."

It can be objected that the plan would increase the power of the national party convention, an institution which has shown many faults. But no other nominating device is consistent with party solidarity and a two-party system. The party must have a representative and authoritative organ through which to make its strategic decisions. If nominations were left to direct primaries, the party would lose its power to enforce either unity or discipline, the party would become weaker and more disintegrated than it is today, and the National Council would reflect both the weakness and the disintegration. It seems essential, therefore, to preserve the convention, removing its faults so far as may be possible and putting it under the control of the party rank and file. To fit the convention for its more responsible task, perhaps a more difficult task procedurally, would be a considerable undertaking, it may be admitted.

Let us assume, however, that the national convention would remain a somewhat defective instrument. We now entrust to it the nomination of the party candidate for the presidency. To the large number who depend on the "strong executive" for democratic and efficient government, all their political eggs are in one basket. Under the proposed plan, the convention would make a diversified investment. One error would not be necessarily fatal.

The arrangement would at first put considerable strain on American politics. But in the past we have been strongest and most resourceful in this field. What we have done to purify politics and make elections free represents, perhaps, our greatest political success. It does not seem likely that we shall be unable to protect ourselves against dangers from this quarter, provided the governmental organization permits a direct and effective expression of public opinion. The plan here outlined rests on a hope that, if adopted, it would tend, more than the present organization, to focus public attention on government and raise political leadership to a higher moral plane. It seems designed also to develop in the people that comprehension of government, that political awareness and watchfulness, that feeling of civic responsibility, and that general participation on which an enduring and efficient democracy depends.

The author desires at this point to emphasize once more that his primary purpose in this study is to realize more fully the political democracy to which Americans are dedicated, to make popular control more effective. The intention is to maintain completely the constitutional guarantees of individual rights and judicial, as well as legislative and administrative, protection of them.

CHAPTER VII

CAN WE PREPARE FOR CHANGE?

At the beginning of this book, we considered the circumstances that produced our constitutional organization of government, the requirements that people then had in mind and the goals that they had in view. During the last 160 years, conditions have radically changed; and we now expect government to meet quite different requirements. But no comparable alteration has taken place in the legislative-executive organization. We have, therefore, analyzed the operations of government in some detail (Part II) and have summarized in Chapter IV the defects and shortcomings as we have seen them. In the same chapter, we noted the objectives and principles which, in the author's opinion, must be followed if the defects and shortcomings are to be removed and if modern requirements are to be met. In Chapter V we showed that proposals already made do not satisfy the new objectives and principles. So in Chapter VI we outlined a hypothetical plan of organization and cited some objections, minor and major, that might be advanced against the plan. It remains to consider whether any plan for comprehensive change can be discussed with a view to its adoption or appropriate modification.

The genius of the founding fathers consisted not only in reaching agreement among themselves, but in bringing about the adoption of what they had agreed upon. They suffered from few inhibitions. On the question whether or not to reorganize, they were radicals. Since the Confederation had been founded on fallacious principles, it appeared to them logical and practicable to "change this first foundation, and with it the superstructure resting upon it."[1] Thinking in the late eighteenth century about governmental change bore little resemblance to the attitudes of our own day.

If we should now agree that fundamental reorganization is needed and decide what form it should take, we should still find enormous obstacles in the path of practical accomplishment. A number of writers and speakers have expressed skepticism regarding the fitness of our institutions. Some have proposed drastic alterations. Yet no movement has developed even to achieve a consensus among social scientists, much less to convince the people and the politicians that substantial change may be desirable. One who sets out on such a bold adventure faces an almost universal indifference, a mountainous inertia, a conservatism unparalleled in other fields of public interest, and a general defeatism as un-American as it is unscientific. How to engineer change seems to be the most important of all political problems.

This book does not advocate the immediate adoption of any plan. The purpose has been to urge discussion of the problem and to help in the making of an agenda. The idea has been to sketch the outlines of a visible goal toward which we may advance steadily without too many detours or too much backtracking.

As Winston Churchill said on May 14, 1947, in his speech on European union:

In my experience of large enterprises, it is often a mistake to try to settle everything at once. Far off, on the skyline, we can see the peaks of the delectable mountains. But we cannot tell what lies between us and them.

We know where we want to go, but we cannot foresee all the stages of the journey or plan our marches as in a military operation. We are not acting in the field of forces, but in the domain of opinion. We cannot give orders. We can only persuade.

We must go forward step by step.[2]

Here at home we can take the first step with assurance only when we "know where we want to go." We must first make the distant goal visible. This we can do only through research and discussion. Unluckily, the obstacles to reorganization are also obstacles to discussion. We shall now take a look at these obstacles.

CONSTITUTIONAL AMENDMENT

The most tangible of our difficulties lies in the method of constitutional amendment.

The founding fathers recognized the imperfections of their handiwork and the probability that it would require modification. To them, the Constitution was a vast and promising experiment; but, in view of "the novelty of the undertaking," they wished "to provide a convenient mode of rectifying their own errors, as future experience may unfold them."[3] Their "convenient mode" was not intended to be too convenient; for an easy and quick method of amendment would have been inconsistent with the dominant purposes. The amending process that they devised aimed to protect federalism and to check popular impulsiveness. No bare majority could bring about a change.

Article V of the Constitution provides two methods of proposing amendments: (1) by a two thirds vote in each of the two houses of Congress; or, (2) by a convention called on the application of the legislatures of two thirds of the states. For amendments so proposed, there are two methods of approval or ratification: (1) by the legislatures of three fourths of the states; or, (2) by conventions in three fourths of the states.

This amending process has become a fundamental defect in our government. The check-and-balance system, as worked into the process, prevents constitutional adaptations, conscious, timely, and well co-ordinated. It does so, in the first place, because of the opportunities that it offers for obstruction, and, in the second place, because it puts the initiation of amendments in the hands of those who have a vested interest in the perpetuation of the system.[4]

During a period of 160 years only twenty-six amendments have been proposed and only twenty-one approved.[5] Of these, only four relate to the governmental structure. In contrast to the small number of proposals that have issued from Congress, some four thousand resolutions for constitutional amendment have been introduced into the two houses.[6] The state legislatures have never called a national constitutional convention for the initiation of amendments.

These facts may merely indicate that our governmental organization, on the whole, has been a sound one or, at least, has satisfied the people. It is noticeable, however, that our use of the amending procedure has been about the same, whether we are dealing with debatable features or with generally recognized absurdities. As a president of the American Political Science Association remarked in 1933:

The absurdity of having the first regular session of a Congress postponed until thirteen months after the election of representatives and the danger involved in having the old Congress legislate for three months after its successor has been chosen were recognized at an early period. Inertia and traditional adherence to established forms, however, were able to prevent a realistic solution for more than a century.[7]

Popular election of senators had been proposed as early as 1826. From 1870 on, demands for this change become fairly frequent and after 1892 a growing public opinion supported it. Between 1893 and 1902 the House of Representatives five times passed a resolution for such a constitutional amendment. Yet, the Senate did not produce the requisite two-thirds majority until 1912. Once submitted to the people, the amendment won speedy ratification.

Edward S. Corwin calls attention to the constitutional method of choosing a president when no candidate has received a majority of the electoral vote, and expresses the opinion that "no feature of the Constitution has raised more difficulties in the past, or remains at this moment a graver menace to our domestic peace."[8] Nevertheless, no proposal designed to correct this "preposterous arrangement," as Professor Corwin calls it, has received the approval of Senate or House.

One must note, as among the most disturbing features of the situation, the unwillingness of Congress to examine the problem of government in all its aspects, including fundamentals.[9] Such unwillingness is matched by the tardiness and hesitance with which Congress approaches even the simplest and most superficial reforms. Reforms have taken place, but almost invariably after long delay. One cannot doubt that the proponents

of the Congressional Reorganization Act of 1946 were sincere
in their expressed desire to improve the functioning of Congress; but it appears that the principle motive for the improvement was to "reassert the power and independence" of Congress,[10] and "to redress the balance of power between the
legislative and executive branches."[11] Congress itself had, for at
least sixty years, been contributing to that unbalance.

Franklin D. Roosevelt's court-packing proposal in 1937
brought the situation into clear relief. When the Supreme Court
had declared certain New Deal legislation unconstitutional,
the Republican candidate in 1936 declared himself in favor of
amending the Constitution. The Democratic convention stated
in its platform that many national problems could not be settled
by state action. An attempt would be made, it was promised, to
meet these problems through legislation within the Constitution; but, if this should prove to be impossible,

. . . we shall seek such clarifying amendment as will assure to the
legislatures of the several States and the Congress of the United
States, each within its proper jurisdiction, the power to enact those
laws which the State and Federal legislatures, within their respective
spheres, shall find necessary, in order adequately to regulate commerce, protect public health and safety and safeguard economic
security.

Shortly after his second inauguration, President Roosevelt
found other means which he thought would attain this end;
and he rejected the idea of amendment for the following announced reasons:

There are many types of amendment proposed. Each one is radically different from the other. There is no substantial group within
the Congress or outside it who are agreed on any single amendment.

It would take months or years to get substantial agreement upon
the type and language of an amendment. It would take months and
years thereafter to get a two-thirds majority in favor of that amendment in *both* Houses of the Congress.

Then would come the long course of ratification by three-fourths
of the States. No amendment which any powerful economic interests
or the leaders of any powerful political party have had reason to
oppose has ever been ratified within anything like a reasonable time.
And thirteen States, which contain only five per cent of the voting

population can block ratification even though the thirty-five States with ninety-five per cent of the population are in favor of it.

. . . .

And remember one thing more. Even if an amendment were passed, and even if in the years to come it were to be ratified, its meaning would depend upon the kind of Justices who would be sitting on the Supreme Court bench. An amendment like the rest of the Constitution is what the Justices say it is rather than what its framers or you might hope it is.[12]

After a fashion, Mr. Roosevelt accomplished his immediate purpose through the appointment of new justices; but, in doing so, he discouraged popular discussion of constitutional questions and lost a rare opportunity to rally public opinion behind an effort to simplify and democratize the amending procedure.

The first step toward fruitful discussion of reorganization should be to change our undemocratic and cumbrous process of amendment. Proposals have been advanced to make constitutional amendment easier and more speedy. For example, Hazlitt suggests the following procedure: amendments to be proposed by (1) a majority vote in each of the two houses of Congress, or (2) one fourth or more of the state legislatures; and such proposals to be approved by (1) a majority vote in a popular referendum, or (2) two thirds of the state legislatures.[13]

These suggestions seem worth thinking about. The author believes that amendments might be proposed, not only by Congress, but also by the legislatures or by the chief executives of any number of states that contain a majority of those voting in the preceding national election. It is suggested that a proposed amendment might be submitted to popular vote, not in a special referendum but at the next general election.

Such a method of amendment, if adopted, would go far to remove one obstacle. It would introduce democracy through majority rule into the formal process of constitutional adjustment.

INHIBITING FACTORS

Other obstacles are less tangible. These lie in the general complexity, the confusions, and the burdens that mark Ameri-

can politics. They arise in part from the organization and procedures of government. They have tended to make us a superficial people in matters of politics, interested in immediate ends
to the neglect of deeper meanings and causations.

One result of the formal amending procedure along with
these other factors has been largely to shift to the Supreme
Court the function of constitutional amendment. The part
played by the Court created an illusion of constitutional flexibility and adaptation; while the emphasis given by political
science to the exposition of constitutional law led many to look
upon the justices as the anointed shapers of the Constitution.
Between those who are preoccupied with the Supreme Court
and those who are obsessed with administration, the core of
government has been largely ignored or left to the academic
philosophers and descriptive historians. With the accumulation
of judicial decisions, the Constitution, so far as much of its
meaning is concerned, became voluminous, technical, and obscure. The people, apparently assured of constitutional adjustment without thought or effort on their part, naturally lost much
of their interest in fundamental change and their feeling of
responsibility for it. In sum, we have put a premium on inertia
and have encouraged drift rather than mastery; and, as pointed
out in Chapter III, judicial amendment has not been sufficient,
and it cannot be.

Adjustment by judicial interpretation has gone on side by side
with another type of attempted adjustment—by usage, delegation, and encroachment—with much the same effect on the
popular mind.[14]

Conditions. Indifference and opposition to constitutional
change have grown, in large part, from historical conditions. At
the end of the eighteenth century, the spirit of inquiry, of criticism, and of skepticism was in the air; and in a revolutionary age
men are compelled to think constructively as well as imagina-
tively and idealistically. In 1787 America possessed a remarkable combination of statesmanship and political philosophy. A
period of prosperity followed the establishment of the Constitution; and, according to Woodrow Wilson, "opposition to the

Constitution as a Constitution, and even hostile criticism of its provisions, ceased almost immediately upon its adoption; and not only ceased, but gave place to an undiscriminating and blind worship of its provisions. . . ."[15] Thereafter, in the presence of economic opportunity, a steadily rising standard of living, and general sense of security, one could perceive little cause or reason for popular discontent,[16] or for the discussion of fundamental political questions.[17]

To a large extent, especially from the Civil War to 1900, industry attracted much of our best constructive talent;[18] while recently the physical sciences and the professions have offered increasingly strong inducements. Since the eighties, a growing interest in economic and social policies has tended to divert leadership and attention from basic problems.[19] Because of national progress and the sanctity of the Constitution, the minds that might have challenged our constitutional arrangements turned in most instances to pursuits that were socially more acceptable or personally more profitable. Political science became largely an academic avocation, divorced from the art of government; and when in the twentieth century students of government aimed once more to develop an applied science, they too often adopted the standards of "practicality" set by the politicians and derived from a narrow and shortsighted expediency.

The growing power of mass opinion also discouraged fundamental changes. These could not take place without bold political leadership; but those who engaged in politics found it safer and more profitable to follow and register opinion than to oppose or create it. We have had, to be sure, much public dissatisfaction, but it has been directed in most cases, not at the structure, but at the action or inaction of government; and for unsatisfactory government the people have tended to seek for scapegoats in persons, parties, and economic groups, or for relief in more checks and more machinery.

As the responsibilities of government become more extensive and more intimately concerned with the lives of the people, the interest of the public and of specialists shifted to the content of policies and to the political maneuvering incidental to their adoption. At the same time, the lag in political action, the accumulation of unsolved problems, and the pressure of day-to-day demands forced leadership and attention from the basic and the long-run to the immediate and the routine. So we became engrossed in what government *does*, and less concerned about what government *is*—emphasizing ends and neglecting means.[20]

Our protracted constitutional lag left us with so much to be done that we seem now to have no time for the task, pressed as we are by day-to-day operational demands. To a great extent, therefore, opportunism determines our thinking. When circumstances are such as to make a government defect appear dangerous, we feverishly occupy ourselves with the idea of repair. Before any substantial repairs can be made, the circumstances change. When a new crisis comes, we forget the previous one and busy ourselves in a new direction and with meager results. So we intermittently tinker with the machine and attach new contrivances to it, but never try with forethought and persistence to get a really up-to-date model. There is a general disinclination or seeming inability to face realistically the whole situation and to grapple courageously with its wide and deep meanings. The disinclination or the seeming inability serves, in turn, not merely to conceal and confuse the problem, but also to postpone and impede its solution. The often demonstrated disposition to accommodate oneself to political expediency, to refrain from any break with vested interests or custom, and to avoid anything that might appear radical or revolutionary, leaves us in many instances with proposals that are anything but constructive.

Ideas. Out of this situation have come various ideas that are employed to rationalize the existing system or to oppose plans for fundamental and comprehensive change. Of these ideas, four appear to call for comment.

One favorite device for dodging the fundamental issue is to declare that the people do not want a change. However desirable an ambitious reform may be, it just can't be done, because the people "are not prepared" to accept it.[21] Accordingly, those who indulge in basic criticism or propose fundamental changes are "impractical," "academic," or "utopian." This name-calling is nothing new. Bryce noted in the eighties that in America, "Persons who propose comprehensive reforms are suspected as theorists or faddists."[22] One writer has recently asserted that if proposals, "however sound in theory," are "incompatible with public opinion and prevailing political conditions in the United States," such proposals "have no practical value whatever."[23] It may be true that the people do not now want a fundamental change in the form of government. It would be surprising if they did, for there has been no leadership for a change or influential advocacy of it. When the idea finds organized support and intelligent persistent propagation, it will be time to say whether or not a majority of the people can be converted to it.

But whether the people want it or not does not define the duty of social scientists. They cannot safely abandon the skeptical attitude, the steady search for truth in its complete and ultimate meanings. Applied political science in a democracy carries an obligation to provide leadership. A purely theoretical or utopian approach is inadmissible; but one person may term theoretical what another considers practical, and some may call utopian what others believe to be realistic. In the author's view, those are most impractical who refuse to face all the facts, who make a religion of expediency, who rationalize evidences of misgovernment, and who serve the *status quo* as glorified yes-men.

According to a second view, it is undesirable to discuss basic reorganization, because such discussion would make it more difficult to effect minor reforms, the only kind, it is alleged, that can be carried out. That it would be enormously difficult to bring about a basic reorganization of our government is perfectly apparent; but it does not follow that one should keep silent about fundamental needs on the ground that discussion of them will hamper the small reforms that have a chance of success. It would seem that a greater danger arises from concentration on superficial adjustments, the raising of false hopes regarding their efficacy, and the postponement of the major problems that condition the minor ones. If the foundation of a building is crumbling, little will be gained and much may be lost by redesigning two or three apartments on an upper floor. Diseases are not cured by treating symptoms only. We can count it lucky that the founding fathers concerned themselves with fundamentals and challenged the difficult. If they had not, they would never have discussed the more perfect union and naturally would not have achieved it.

Thirdly, much stress is laid on the assumption that our political institutions have become deeply rooted in our experience, traditions, folkways, and habits, and for that reason no radical departures should be considered. We are told that "our form of government has been adapted to our character and circumstances."[24] It is declared that our governmental organization is a feature of the American "way of life."[25] "The fact is," says a recent book, "that the presidential system is as much a part of our civilization as is the English language."[26]

One may doubt that our form of government, as distinguished from its spirit and purpose, is really deeply rooted in the habits and emotions of the people, although it certainly is stubbornly fixed in the folkways and vested interests of politicians and others. The idea that any form of government "must be adapted to the traditions, political experience and habits" of the people can easily be turned to the support of an eternally unchanged *status quo.* For political institutions tend to gather traditions around them and become encrusted in custom; and, so long as one form of government exists, there can be no political experience with any other form.

In any event, because tradition and habit may be opposed to change is not an argument against change. It is the task of rational men, when convinced that change is necessary, to overcome popular inertia. Federation, the prime objective of the founding fathers, was alien to their experience.[27]

A form of government may be a discovery; but to be at all durable it cannot be a pure invention. Any governmental organization, if is to lay claim to any great measure of success or long life, must result from a series of adaptations, as in the case of the British government. Or it must represent the work of flexible minds, equipped to evaluate and use experience, make concessions to contemporary conditions and ideas, and compromise the more stubborn differences. It was in this second way that our own government came into being. Those who stress experience and habit, however, should admit that, if government must be adapted to the conditions of its age, it follows that in a later age, when these conditions have changed, government should also change.

The fourth inhibiting idea is that sound governmental change results only from evolution. Some compare government to an organism. One or two have said that it is an organism. In any case, writers on government frequently represent political evolution to be not only an unconscious process, but also an inevitable and always a desirable one. Thus represented, the idea of evolution discourages movements for planned reform and gives its specious blessing to do-nothing attitudes.[28]

Political evolution is not the same as biological. Political change is never unconscious to everybody. It is always willed by individuals who often know precisely what they are doing and the probable effect of their action.[29] Moreover, enduring institutions have come and can come into being as a result of conscious design and preconceived plan, provided the design or plan is based on experience and adjusted to realities. Our own form of government came into being in this way.

Governments do not inevitably "evolve." If evolution or "muddling through" had worked as infallibly as some appear to think it does, Britain would not have lost the thirteen colonies. Had the Bourbon kings been willing to make concessions and accept relatively small changes in 1789, or preferably earlier, the swelling discontent in France would probably have been allayed; but the kings, that is, the government, resisted change, and revolution followed. The same resistance with the same result happened in Czarist Russia. Our own government did not evolve a solution for the slavery question. Institutional rigidity and reactionary attitudes exist everywhere; and when strong enough they prevent gradual adjustments and invite revolution.

It is absurd to suppose that governments become what they ought to be when no thought is given to the process of change. While despotisms evolve into democracies, free governments also evolve into autocracies. We cannot afford to depend exclusively on "evolution" or understandings, at least not until we know that these "unconscious" movements are in their actual operation of good effect and in the right direction.

A STEP-BY-STEP METHOD

The term evolution, when applied to government, can have only one rational meaning—gradual, piecemeal, or step-by-step change. Such a process will be sound and desirable in proportion to the thought that goes into it, the desirability of the ultimate goal, and the depth, breadth, and farsightedness of the agreed plan. Discussion of a basic solution should facilitate, rather than handicap, the step-by-step method. Unless we first "know where we want to go," we are likely to go in all directions and end by getting nowhere.

"It has been frequently remarked," wrote Hamilton, "that it seems to have been reserved to the people of this country, by their conduct and example, to decide the important question, whether societies of men are really capable or not of establishing good government from reflection and choice, or whether they are forever destined to depend for their political constitutions on accident and force."[30] Can we decide this question for our age as our forefathers did for theirs?

PART II

A SUPPORTING ANALYSIS

The three chapters that follow present the facts, interpretations, and analysis of organization and operations on which are largely based the summary and statement of principles in Chapter IV.

CHAPTER VIII

DEMOCRACY IN GOVERNMENT

Is our national government set up in such a way as to realize, implement, and preserve democracy to the greatest possible extent? To answer this question we shall use as testing devices six principles which, it is generally agreed, should find expression in a democratic government. These principles are: representation, majority rule, responsiveness to public opinion, leadership, responsibility, and voting equality. The analysis in this chapter will necessarily be preliminary, and certain points will receive further attention in succeeding chapters.

REPRESENTATION

Our national government is and must be a *representative* government. As such, is it in accord with the ideal of democracy? If it were, the government as a whole would represent, or reflect on a reduced scale, the nation as a whole; that is, the opinions and feelings of the nation as a whole. We can take this view now more easily than our ancestors could in 1787 because the unified nation is an accomplished fact. Yet, when we look at our government, we see that in theory and in form only one authority, the president, is chosen by and from the nation as a whole. The senators are conceived to represent the states, and the representatives, for the most part, congressional districts.[1]

In the Senate. In 1787 equal representation of the states in the Senate clearly accorded with the facts and requirements that confronted the makers of the Constitution.

When the state legislatures chose them, the senators, like ambassadors, could claim to be accredited by the governments of sovereign states; and the Senate, in many respects, has behaved like an international conference. Direct election by the people, however, discarded the idea of a select upper chamber

155

and aimed to make the senators direct representatives of the people, like the members of the lower house. Equal representation of the states in the Senate was originally designed also to protect the small states and to maintain the federal system. The small states no longer need this protection. Neither American politics nor the legislative process has turned on any antagonism between small and large states; and state feeling has been no more pronounced in the Senate than in the House.[2]

The development of the party system has frequently produced the incongruity of two senators posing as representatives of the same state, but attached to different parties and taking opposite sides on legislative issues.[3] Some of the states are in effect divided by custom. In such states, there is a down-state senator and an up-state senator or the metropolis claims one and the rural part of the state the other.

In the case of the senators, equality of states produces an extreme inequality of voting power among the citizens of different states. As a result, a majority of the senators may represent a minority of the people.[4]

In support of the foundation on which the Senate stands, some would probably say that the small states still need protection against the large or that the farmers and rural residents should outvote the industrial and urban centers. Whatever merit there may be in such a view, it fails to square with the standards of democratic representation and voting equality. It may be further argued that equal representation of the states keeps the Senate small, that the smallness of the body permits freedom of debate, and that senators do in practice represent the nation, rather than their respective states, the reason being that, because of their long terms, the smallness of the Senate, and its powers with respect to foreign policy and administrative appointments, the members of the upper house develop a truly national viewpoint. This contention has a good deal of merit, but it is well to note that the fathers used much the same argument to support the electoral-college method of choosing the president, as well as election of senators by the state legislatures. Much the same argument was used in England more than a hundred years ago to defend the rotten-borough system.

In the House of Representatives. District representation in the lower house resulted in part from the same facts and requirements that fixed the plan of representation for the Senate; but it was also felt that the members of the popular chamber should be able to keep in close touch with their constituents. Local communities had reality at that time. The people were scattered; transportation and communication slow. It was intended that the House of Representatives should be a comparatively numerous body. It seemed logical, therefore, that its members should be apportioned according to population, distributed among localities, and elected locally. It was believed that when the representatives came together in Congress, each would speak with special knowledge of the interests and views of his constituents. Thus, the House as a whole would be informed, extensively and intensively, and would be truly popular.

Since the congressional district must be constructed to include a specified number of people, it was bound to lose any identity that it might conceivably have had with a natural community, a unified interest, or a particular aspect of public opinion. The district became arbitrary and artificial, delimited usually by county lines or in the cities by streets or ward boundaries. To make matters worse, custom and usage, operating within an artificial unit, tend in many cases to divide the district itself. "The county in which the representative may happen to reside 'has had the nomination,' and that is a reason why another county or part of the district should have the nomination next time."[5]

If we take the word representation in its literal sense, it is hard to see how any one could *represent* a congressional district. It could not be done unless by some means the interests and opinions of the people of the district could first be integrated or unless the mind of the representative were a composite of the minds of his constituents.

The district system introduces practical difficulties and voting inequalities. Constitutionally, the members of the lower house are apportioned according to population and a reapportionment takes place after each decennial census. Each state has at least one representative. The general rule, according to custom and usage, is that a state having more than one representative shall be divided into as many congressional districts as there are representatives. The division of a state into districts is done by the state legislature.[6]

In practice, it has been found extremely difficult to maintain an equitable apportionment either among the states or among the districts within a state. Popular representation on a district basis would have been more logical and considerably easier if state boundaries could have been disregarded; but, under the Constitution, no district can overlap two or more states. Because of the difficulties involved, along with legislative lethargy and political influences, Congress and the state legislatures have sometimes neglected reapportionment altogether. This neglect, along with growth and shifting of population and political manipulations produce in some areas wide differences in the population of different districts, as well as frequent overrepresentation of the rural population.[7]

Of localities in general. There are, it appears, four main arguments for a geographical or localized plan of representation.

The first is that so many and marked differences exist throughout the vast expanse of our country that the government cannot be representative unless it is itself geographically distributed, unless each difference has its spokesman. It is true that all significant aspects of our national life are not uniformly distributed over the country. If they were, we would have a better case for the representation of localities, since each locality would then be a fair sample of the nation and would be in a position to integrate its opinions on national questions.[8]

At the present time none of the states or congressional districts can be viewed as having an identity which is economically or socially either like the nation or entirely distinct from that of other states and districts.[9] Each is somewhat different economically from the others, and each has some predominant interest or combination of interests. Our national legislators should be qualified to understand and balance the various interests and opinions that are identified with different sections and regions. It is, however, quite another matter to assume that localized representation is necessary or desirable for the recognition and fair treatment of sectional and regional interests. It should be noted, too, that we say sectional and regional interests. A state or a congressional district is not a section or a region.

The Constitution, reinforced and amplified by custom and usage, decrees that a member of the Senate and House not only shall be elected by a territorial unit, but also shall reside in the unit which he is chosen to represent.[10] This residential requirement has in practice contributed to the perpetuation of an exaggerated localism. Those who hold a vested interest in such a localism foster the prejudice against participation of "outsiders" in their electoral contests, very much as a sovereign nation insists that no other nation shall "interfere" in its internal affairs, even for a friendly purpose or in the general world interest.

With respect to the conduct of foreign relations, the founding fathers evidently had no idea that the nation could act except as a nation. They assigned the conduct of foreign relations to the central government. Within the central government, this function went to the president, who was expected to represent the whole nation. He was to be checked only by the Senate, and by that body only in the making of treaties. So far as the Constitution goes, the House of Representatives was to participate only in the establishment and maintenance of the armed forces and in declarations of war.

The conduct of foreign relations, however, has gone far beyond the kind of diplomatic intercourse with which the founding fathers were familiar; and treaties are no longer as inclusive, as vital, or as essential as they once were, or as binding. The adoption, implementation, and execution of foreign policy today generally involves the Senate and the House as authorities co-ordinate with each other and with the president; and the whole governmental organization operates in the international sphere on practically the same basis as in the domestic field. In view of the obvious need of a united front, we must question at once the appropriateness of a scheme of congressional representation which seems calculated to carry localism, provincialism, and parochialism into the operations of the national government.

A second argument for our plan of representation is that we "can symbolize our national unity in the presidency, our sectional interests in the Senate, and our localisms in the House."[11] The answer to this seems to be that we are concerned, not with symbolism, but with what our scheme of representation purports to do and what it actually does.

A third view, which appears to be a defense, is that government should be so constructed as to bring its facts and problems close to the people geographically and that this can be done by arranging a fairly uniform distribution of persons equipped to interpret government to the people. What is argued for here is not representation, but leadership or liaison.

The fourth argument is that no other plan of representation would be as democratic or as practicable. This argument has been answered in Part I of this book.

By the president. The intent of the Constitution and the early democratizing changes went far to make the president a representative, an embodiment, and the chief instrument of a nation functioning as a political unit. The presidency, in fact, offers a standing refutation of the argument that numerous men elected by localities are necessary for purposes of representation.

The electoral college, however, still operates as a final means of counting votes for presidential candidates. The vote is taken by states; and the result of the popular majority in each state is weighted according to the number of electoral votes that the state possesses. Since a state has as many electoral votes as it has senators and representatives, its voting power is not proportionate to its population. In other words, the electoral college, resting on a combination of the localized schemes of Senate and House, is not accurately representative, nor does it reflect voting equality. In proportion to their populations, the voters in the small states have greater power in the electoral college than those in the large states.[12]

When no candidate for president receives a majority of the electoral votes, the House of Representatives chooses the president from the three candidates who have the highest number of votes; but, in exercising this function, the members of the House vote by states, the congressional delegation from each state having one vote. Twice in the past a president has been chosen in this manner. The procedure is anything but representative. Furthermore, it would not necessarily result in the election of the leading candidate; and if the state delegations should be divided, like the electoral votes, among three parties, no election whatever might ensue. In fact, a deadlock might occur within some of the delegations.[13]

The vice-president, elected in the same manner as the president,[14] is in theory equally representative of the whole people; and, so long as these two are the only ones chosen in a national election, no one in the line of succession after the vice-president can have the same representative character. The Speaker of the House, whom pending legislation puts next in line, is elected by the people of a single congressional district.

In the administration. Administrative agencies are not intended or set up to be formally representative; but usage, strategy, and legislation have made the agencies and their personnel rough reflections of the country's geography and of its different interests and groups. The regional or special-interest character of some administrative activities contributes to the same result. Moreover, senators and representatives have a concern in and power over the distribution of federal patronage; and, therefore, if there were no civil service apportionments, administrative appointments would tend to follow the pattern of localized representation.

MAJORITY RULE

It is an essential and a practical rule of democratic government that it shall function by majority vote; and a government is procedurally democratic to the extent that it operates on this principle.

The function, right, and duty of the minority is to criticize those who represent the majority, to persuade the people of the soundness of the minority view, and thus to become a majority. To provide opportunity for criticism and legitimate opposition, the governmental organization should permit minority representation. In addition, successful popular government requires, on the part of the majority, tolerance of minority opinions, along with scrupulous respect for the general principles and processes of democracy.

But when a government permits control by a minority, it is not at that time acting as a free government. Our national elections, whether for president, Senate, or House, proceed on a localized basis. Such elections do not guarantee that a national popular majority will win. Whether it wins or loses depends on the territorial distribution of the vote.

Through the president. The electoral-college system of voting by states does not assure that any candidate will actually be the majority choice or, in close elections, that the candidate who receives a majority will be elected. The system does not even guarantee that a candidate who obtains a plurality will be elected. Under this system, the vote cast for minor parties may be totally wasted, though in certain states a relatively small vote for such parties may swing the total electoral vote of the state from one major party to the other and thus decide the election.[15]

So far as actually determining the result, the size of a majority or plurality in any state is of no consequence. In the casting of New York's 47 electoral votes, a majority or plurality of 500 has the same effect as one of 500,000.[16] Furthermore, the voting power of a state in the electoral college bears no necessary relation to its actual popular vote.[17] It makes no difference how many people vote in a particular state. Whether the number is a few thousand or several hundred thousand, they cast no less and no more than the state's full electoral vote.[18] The result is gross voting inequality.

Through the Senate. Direct election of senators by the people was intended to make the upper house more democratic and more responsive to public opinion, but left it with characteristics that are scarcely consistent with the principle of majority rule. A majority of the senators may represent a minority, perhaps a small minority, of the people; and even a party majority in the Senate may represent a minority of the country's population.[19] Because of staggered terms, it is difficult to find out whether a majority or a minority of the voters have chosen a majority of the Senate. If we compare the results of presidential elections since 1880 with the composition of the Senate following such elections, we find that, with the exception of the years 1881 and 1885, the same party at the beginning of the presidential term has controlled the presidency and the Senate. This result appeared even in 1889, when the incoming president, Harrison, had failed to obtain a majority of the popular vote.[20]

It is generally assumed that in the mid-term elections the will of the majority is indicated by the result of the congressional vote, which means the vote for members of the House of Representatives. Four of the 17 mid-term elections since 1880 have produced a different party control in the Senate than in the House.[21] In general, it can be said that the Senate is slower than the House to respond to changes in the electorate and that an absolute tie in the Senate is not unlikely. A tie actually occurred in 1881; and in 1918, 1926, and 1930 the Republicans had only one half of the Senate.[22]

The Senate majority may also be tested by comparing it with the popular vote cast in three successive senatorial elections. Such a comparison reveals that in 1933 and 1947 the party majority in the Senate reflected a popular plurality, not a popular majority.[23] It is impossible, of course, to show what the result would have been if those who voted for minor-party or independent candidates had been able to indicate their second choices.

Madison pointed out in the Constitutional Convention that the equality of states in the Senate would enable a minority to block the majority.[24] The provision that the Senate advises and consents to treaties by a two-thirds vote is patently inconsistent with the principle of majority rule. Under this extraordinary provision, a minority of 33 Senators can impose an absolute veto on action desired by the president and by the other 65 senators.

Unlimited debate in the Senate has, on a number of occasions, permitted a single Senator or a small group of senators to block action desired by a majority. If senators want to stop a colleague from talking on and on, they can "gag" him only by invoking the cloture rule; but such procedure is felt to be inconsistent with "senatorial courtesy," and cloture can be adopted only by a two-thirds vote. It is rarely employed.[25] The filibuster is directly related to the equal representation of the states, and to the minority rule that is embodied in equal representation.

Through the House of Representatives. If a party obtains small majorities in a large number of districts, it may elect more representatives than another party which has larger majorities in fewer districts and a greater total vote. Thus in 1942 Republican candidates polled more popular votes than the Democratic; but Democrats obtained 222 seats in the House and Republicans 209.[26] In 1930 the Republicans, with more popular votes than the Democrats, elected 220 Representatives and the Democrats 214; but, because of the deaths of Republicans after the 1930 election, the Democrats gained control of the House. Nevertheless, as a rule, representation of the two parties in the House corresponds rather closely to the distribution of the total vote for congressional candidates. This correspondence results from a canceling out of disproportions in the vote of the five great political sections. If, therefore, the House as a whole is considered to be equitably representative of the party vote in the nation as a whole, we must recognize at the same time that the House does not do with anything like the same accuracy what it is theoretically supposed to do. Representing localities, it is supposed also to fairly represent regions or sections, for these are aggregates of localities having similar interests.[27]

Apart from mathematical considerations, the size of the House, like the setup of the Senate, introduces various factors that make minority control a frequent, if not the usual, thing.[28]

Through checks and balances. We have just been considering the presidency, the Senate, and the House individually; but all three of these institutions share in the legislative process. The Senate and the House possess an absolute veto on each other, and the president a qualified veto on both. The president, with the support of one third plus one of the members of either house, can block legislative action.[29] When the president exercises his veto, exactly where does the majority actually rule, in the presidency or in the two houses of Congress? When the two houses, failing to agree, adopt the report of a conference committee, what popular majority does the conference committee represent?

If majority rule were an assured thing, all three institutions should represent the same party majority. But frequently government is divided against itself, one institution controlled by one party and the other two institutions by another.[30]

One rationalization for divided government is to the effect that no majority exists, that the people are in process of changing their minds, and that their minds are finally made up in the succeeding presidential election. Another apology has it that divided control, when brought about in a mid-term election, indicates that the people have had enough of one political philosophy and are prepared to change to a different one, but they want the ship of state to stand idle for a time before sailing on a new tack. In the author's opinion, neither explanation has much merit.[31] The fact seems to be that a popular majority does express itself in every election to the extent that it is possible for it to do so; and it seems equally certain that a majority of voters do not at any time consciously seek a deadlocked government. Such a situation is due to the fact that we have three governments instead of one. Moreover, we do not invariably elect them at the same time, and we choose them on different bases.

RESPONSIVENESS TO PUBLIC OPINION

It is expected that the elected officials of a democratic government will show a degree of responsiveness to public opinion, not only the opinion that has decided the latest election, but also any new or changed opinion that subsequently develops. In foreign affairs, public opinion is of vital interest from two points of view. First, the people determine, or should determine, in broad outline foreign as well as domestic policies. Second, public opinion in a democracy is a means of implementing and executing foreign policy. When it shows unity, understanding and determination, public opinion can give, as nothing else can, a guarantee to foreign governments of the permanence of our policies and of our intention to carry them out.

An opinion or opinions? Certain underlying feelings and ideas dominate the minds of most voters and determine their general attitude. In the long run, the most important of these appear to be: (1) the economic interest of the individual and of the particular interest-group to which he belongs, and (2) allegiance to a party or to a local machine. In certain regions or at certain times, other basic feelings and ideas may control; such as those attributable to age and sex, those that come from moral standards, and those derived from racial origins or religious affiliations.

Opinion also includes reactions to the behavior of the government as a whole, of the president, of Congress, of Cabinet officers, or of administrative agencies. Voters are inclined to react unfavorably to inept leadership, factionalism, inaction in emergencies, signs of incapacity or corruption, and accumulating irritations of any description. Their response tends to be favorable when an attractive personality is linked with persuasive leadership, when foreign policy is courageous, and when the conduct of government gives an impression of unity and vigor.

Thus, we have opinions, instead of one opinion; and the opinions are variously compounded; but usually it is economic interest that exerts most influence.

National and local opinions. The various factors that account for a voter's attitude vary from section to section, from region to region, from state to state, and from county to county. States and congressional districts behave differently and contradictorily in elections, because the final and decisive combination of attitudes represented by the voting majority is produced in different localities by different influences.

Under ordinary circumstances, the reason for divergent and contradictory opinions is to be found in the geographical distribution of economic interests. In some states and particularly in some congressional districts, a majority or most of the voters are farmers; while other electoral subdivisions show a predominance of industrial wage earners. The agricultural interest, the industrial interest, or the labor interest includes a large number of subinterests. These are, generally speaking, the real "special interests" of which we hear so much. In a particular congressional district, most of the voters may have the same special interest; or a special interest may hold the balance of power. In such cases, the representative of the district in Congress will necessarily be controlled or at least strongly influenced by that interest.

Consequently, members of Congress tend to become, and in practice they usually are, representatives of special interests and generally respond to the demands of those interests, even when such demands have no relation whatever to any national public opinion. On the other hand, when a special interest is absent from a district, its representative is inclined to feel unconcerned, except from the standpoint of party regularity or logrolling.[32]

Much the same can be said of other influences—racial, religious, moral, or what-not—which may be important in a state or a district, but relatively unimportant in the nation. The geographical basis of representation gives certain special groups and special feelings an advocate or a number of advocates in Congress.

The district, however, is never a true sample of the nation, and it is incapable of integrating opinion on national questions. Consequently, it is localism rather than nationalism which is imposed on the representative and which controls him.[33] It is highly improbable that an assembly composed of such representatives will automatically reflect the opinion of the nation; and an important but unfortunate by-product of the system is that it tends to make the representative primarily interested in getting tangible favors for his district and for his constituents.

Opinion in foreign affairs. In the formation of opinion on international questions, conceptions of the national interest have played a larger and more vital role than in the field of domestic policy. This fact appears most clearly when the national security is directly and clearly threatened or when the country is actually at war. Then the people willingly accept a single leadership; they work together for a common cause; they think alike, so far as the immediate end is concerned; and, to an exceptionally high degree, they are willing to subordinate their individual, group, and local interests to the general good.

So far as "normal" or peacetime attitudes are concerned, it now seems extremely improbable that American public opinion will return to the prewar type of isolationism or pacifism; but the modern overlapping of foreign and domestic policy makes it likely that all those particular opinions which characterize domestic politics will also dominate politics in the field of foreign relations.

American opinion on international problems has never been free from local and special influences. When an international objective has been remote or obscure, the peculiar feelings and the material interests of individuals, localities, and groups have become major determining factors. Isolationism had its well-known sectional expression. It gained encouragement from party politics and probably also from racial groups; but the basic influences in the maintenance of this attitude were strongest in the mid-continent, where the rural districts and small towns retained to a relatively high degree the characteristics of an older America—the insularity, self-centeredness, and self-sufficiency of individuals and communities, along with a general conservative outlook.

Sensitiveness and responsiveness. Those who are satisfied with the setup of our national government can get a good deal of comfort from its sensitiveness to public opinion. But sensitiveness does not necessarily produce intelligent responsiveness.

Sensitiveness is greatest when a public opinion seems likely to affect the next election. As an election approaches the sensitiveness increases. This ear-to-the-ground attitude is most evident in the House of Representatives and least evident in the Senate. A fixed and long term of office tends to reduce sensitiveness and responsiveness on those matters that are likely to be forgotten by the voters as time passes or as other more exciting matters claim their attention. Accordingly, at a time such as the present, when problems pile up and new situations appear in rapid succession, an election set by the calendar for some distant date may have slight relation, prospectively or actually, to any meaningful interaction between people and government.

Localized representation and cumbrous legislative machinery also stand in the way of intelligent responsiveness. In the House and to a lesser extent in the Senate, we have come to depend very largely on group pressures to bring about governmental responsiveness.[34] But responsiveness, when thus brought about, may reflect a special or minority opinion, rather than a prevailing majority or national opinion. Appointment of committee chairmen in accordance with seniority fails to give fair and prompt reflection to shifts in public opinion. It tends to give the most influence to those districts which are the slowest to move with changing currents of opinion. These are the rock-ribbed districts and they tend to be predominantly rural. Thus in 1933, when the Democrats came into power, 22 of the 31 principal positions of leadership went to representatives from Southern states.[35]

Public-opinion polls have indicated a close correspondence between foreign policies and public opinion. They have also indicated the inadequacy and instability of opinion and much confusion in the public mind. Public opinion has grown partly out of events, but in many cases the policies themselves have preceded and crystallized opinion. This fact might be construed either as popular response to governmental leadership or a response by government to popular feelings.

Sometimes the sensitiveness of government is too acute and its responsiveness too quick; and government may respond too slowly, too quickly, or wrongly, not because it is indifferent to public opinion, but because its leadership is unrepresentative or inadequate.

LEADERSHIP

No clear political opinion of national significance can come into being without leadership. Since Edmund Burke's famous *Letter to the Electors of Bristol,* every member of a popular assembly has had to face these questions: Should I vote my own convictions or obey instructions? Should I follow or lead my constituents? The answer seems to be clear: a representative should both lead and follow. Of course, leadership should come in part from sources outside the government; but political and governmental leadership is indispensable. Such leadership should come from both or all parties and from both majority and minority members of the government. We require leadership not only *by* the government but also *of* and *within* the government.

Opinion and leadership. Modern public questions and government itself are remote from the average person's experience and observation, and are too complex for general understanding.[36] These questions, moreover, do not arrive leisurely one at a time. Some come in the form of crises; most of them are urgent; and all form a massive and disorderly accumulation. Under the best of circumstances, the most that can be expected of public opinion is that it should express a philosophy, lay down the principles that should control the making of policy, fix the goals that government should have in view, and indicate the direction in which it should move. For the wise exercise of this function, we need a leadership capable of impressing on the masses the elementary facts of economics, of organized society, and of international relations. Only by doing so can leadership become statesmanship, and efficiency be reconciled with democracy.

In foreign affairs, circumstances are likely to conceal the inadequacies of governmental leadership and postpone their ill effects. In some respects, it is difficult to explain foreign affairs and foreign policy to the people. Every public pronouncement at home is a pronouncement to the world. So the demands of secrecy and the rules of diplomacy impose certain inhibitions. These demands and rules, however, seldom seriously restrict the essential possibilities of leadership, and they hardly affect at all the problem of integrating policies and explaining the relations between foreign and domestic situations.

Governmental leadership, whether operating internally on the government itself or externally on the people, depends not only on the personal qualities of the would-be leader, but also on his position, power, and prestige.

Congressional leadership. By making the Senate and the House of Representatives co-ordinate with the president, our governmental organization implies that one or both of these bodies can exercise leadership; but an institution can rarely become a leader, for it is anonymous, abstract, and unable to speak with a single voice. If institutional leadership were possible, our check-and-balance system would merely confuse the situation. When one party controls the presidency and the other Congress, which institution speaks for the government and which for the opposition?

In the House of Representatives, few members possess qualifications for national leadership; many can be local leaders, within the restrictions of localism; but at Washington, being parts of a multitude, they lack position, prestige, and power. Those who rise above the crowd—the Speaker and the chairmen of committees—seldom meet the demands of national leadership. In the Senate, the chances are better. It is, for one thing, a smaller body. Its members are on the average bigger men; they are responsible to larger constituencies; and they can make themselves known and heard as independent personalities. Then, too, the Senate possesses constitutional powers which make this institution, in some important respects, a rival of the presidency.

In Congress, particularly in the lower house, internal leadership and control become major problems, because of the numerous membership and localized representation. Within the House, leadership belongs to the Speaker, the majority and minority leaders, the Steering Committee, the Rules Committee, and the chairmen of the various standing and special committees. The appointment of chairmen of the standing committees in accordance with seniority has the merit of recognizing a kind of experience; but it prevents a free development of leadership by new and younger members, who are often best fitted for it by personal qualifications and political logic. In not a few cases, the senior majority member of a committee has been practically incapacitated by age.[37] In the Senate, the seniority principle is followed with somewhat the same results; but qualified leadership obtains more recognition and the new member has a better opportunity to make his influence felt.

Presidential leadership. Andrew Jackson showed the potentialities of leadership in the presidency; and since 1900 the trend has been for leadership by the government and within the government to become pre-eminently presidential. When presidential electors practically became figure-heads and the people voted to all intents and purposes directly for presidential candidates, popular interest shifted from the congressional contests and tended to concentrate on presidential elections. In recent years this concentration has become more pronounced, reflecting the diminishing prestige of members of Congress, the increased importance of the presidential office, and the desire and need of the people as a whole for a responsible spokesman.

Our governmental organization gives to the presidency alone the basis and the instruments of leadership. He alone can claim to be chosen by the whole nation. He speaks for it in foreign affairs; and in time of war he becomes in effect the government. His office, one of vast and accumulating power, is universally respected; it provides him with a sounding board and ensures him a nation-wide, if not a world-wide, audience. The presidency is in a measure what the man makes it, and presidential leadership is highly personalized. At the same time, the office magnifies the man, tends to hide his defects, and creates what is called the "presidential myth."

Presidential leadership at its full strength subordinates and controls Congress, determines national policy, solidifies the party, and, at its worst, may so manipulate public opinion as to perpetuate the incumbent president in what amounts to an elective dictatorship. Manipulation of public opinion may be accomplished by skillful use of patronage, distribution of material benefits, personal showmanship, emotional or misleading propaganda, and the creation and exploitation of emergencies.

Nevertheless, presidential leadership, as Corwin says, is "sporadic and discontinuous. Its tactic has, to be sure, become fairly well stereotyped; but its availability cannot be counted on."[38] It should be noted also that the opposition has no place in the presidency. The peculiar advantages of the office are monopolized by the majority party. No one in the minority can debate on equal terms with the president.

Administrative leadership. With respect to leadership, the bureaucracy makes a highly impressive showing. The range, the complexity, and the technical nature of administrative activities in the modern age call for expertness and experience and give peculiar authority to those who, from day to day and in infinite detail, carry out the government's responsibilities. The administrator, however, is much more than an executive; he publicly advocates objectives not yet embodied in the law, he proposes and drafts legislation, advises the president and members of Congress, and testifies before congressional committees. On many questions he has knowledge that no elected legislator can possibly possess. Upon the knowledge and judgment of the bureaucracy, the president, the Senate, and the House are to a large extent dependent. In addition, the bureaucracy has its own considerable sphere of legislative and policy-making power.

Administrative leadership, however, is highly specialized and compartmentalized, scattered among segments of policy and among special private groups. Though impressive both in quantity and quality, administration provides not a single leadership, but an agglomeration of leaderships, revealing almost as much diversity as can be found in the country itself.

Shortage and wastage. John Jay wrote in *The Federalist* that an efficient national government would attract "the best men in the country . . . especially as it will have the widest field of choice, and never experience that want of proper persons which is not uncommon in some of the states."[39] The founding fathers were aware, however, that the distribution of legislators among states and districts was not calculated to ensure the choice of the country's best men. Persons qualified to govern the country are unevenly distributed over the nation. They tend to appear and to congregate in the urban centers where great enterprises are directed, competition is keenest, and rewards are greatest. Localized representation precludes a free choice among all the best men in the country and, along with other factors, means the predominance of the mediocre.[40]

The truth seems to be that during much of our constitutional history our political leadership has neither been great nor adequate. It might be comforting to believe, as some say, that every crisis in American history brings forth an appropriate leader in the person of a great president. Whether any such coincidence has ruled in the past is questionable; but in any event, we need leadership to prevent the growth of the conditions that create emergencies. In a later chapter, we shall refer again to this idea that "the hour always brings forth the man."

RESPONSIBILITY

In a sense, anyone who has power in the government has responsibility also and probably feels his responsibility. But such responsibility is vague, loose, and subjective. More is required for truly responsible government. Such a government means that those who are entrusted with governmental power shall be accountable to the people. It means further that the people shall be able to enforce accountability by rewarding the good officials and punishing the bad. The feeling and the exercise of responsibility should belong both to the servant and to the master. A truly responsible government must fix responsibility and enforce it. Unless or until responsibility is located, there can be no enforcement. It is equally axiomatic that power and responsibility should be commensurate with each other. Power without responsibility and responsibility without power are almost equally objectionable.

What and who are responsible? It is not possible for our national government, as a single authority or operating unit, to be held responsible to the nation; for we have not one government but three governments. Normally, a good deal of "passing the buck" goes on among the three authorities; and, when control is divided between two parties, the situation is aggravated by partisan maneuvering and by deliberate efforts to shift blame. From the institutional standpoint, our system of separated departments, when they operate without some effective unifying control, scatters, confuses, and conceals responsibility.

From the viewpoint of personal responsibility, the situation is much worse, for a maximum of 532 individuals participate with constitutional authority in the task of legislation. If "the more power is divided the more irresponsible it becomes,"[41] then responsibility in our government is pretty thoroughly atomized.

In the Senate and House of Representatives, one may locate responsibility, to an extent and after a fashion, by considering the record of each member on critical roll-calls. In the House, however, only a fraction of the representatives play any significant part in the shaping of legislation. If we assume that power is concentrated in the leaders, responsibility is still widely diffused, and its distribution varies according to the subject matter of the bills.[42]

The situation in the Senate is in some respects better than in the House, and in other respects worse. What goes on in the Senate gets more publicity; but, because leadership is less binding and the individual more independent, it is seldom possible to focus responsibility on a senator of a group of senators except when party control is in effective operation.

In the presidency, the responsibility of the institution is the responsibility of a single individual; and the conditions that contribute to presidential leadership contribute also to presidential responsibility. Yet, "it is not an easy task to distinguish between those acts for which the president should be held answerable and those over which he has no control."[43] He owns only a share of the legislative authority; the Senate may at times dictate or veto his foreign policy and reject the men whom he selects for executive positions; and the two houses may use the appropriating power to control his executive actions.

Administrative responsibility. "It is an arresting fact," says Leonard D. White, "that the great improvements in government since 1910 have been designed to make the public service more effective in the management and direction of public affairs, not to keep it responsible or make it more amenable to control."[44] As the scope of governmental power broadens and as public activities become more detailed and more technical, administration gathers to itself an increasing command of specialized knowledge, as well as the support of powerful electoral groups. In consequence, the bureaucracy tends to take on, within the governmental structure, an independent existence and a self-aggrandizing character. Bureaucratic power, armed with expertness, presents a major aspect of the problem of reconciling authority and liberty. That problem cannot be solved unless administration can be made responsible; and it can be made clearly and fully responsible only as the supervision of administration within the government finds definite location in a responsible authority.

Whatever may have been the intent of the founding fathers, and whatever may be the theory of the Constitution, each administrative agency is subject to the control of three elected authorities—the president, the Senate, and the House. It is difficult enough to serve two masters, but it is evidently more difficult to serve three. In practice, however, the administrator serves more than three. Actually, his responsibility is to committees of the House and Senate and to individual members. If a scandal develops or a congressional investigation reveals gross corruption or other malpractices, the guilty officials may have their responsibility definitely fixed. But suppose administrative shortcomings are general but not scandalous, suppose the bureaucracy merely tends to be wasteful, unjust, arbitrary or arrogant, Where does the responsibility lie? With the president? The Senate? Some committee? Or some committee chairmen?

Is responsibility enforced? Governmental responsibility to the people means little unless the people themselves feel and execute their responsibility. The responsibility of which we are speaking should be to the nation—to the people as a whole; but only the president is chosen in a national election. Positions of power in the House come to members by seniority, as rewards for long service on a committee, but not necessarily for good service. If a leader of the House blocks legislation desired by a majority of the nation, only the people of his district can punish him. It is local rather than national opinion that controls him. The responsibility of a senator is to his state. Too often in our senatorial and congressional elections and frequently for local reasons, the good are punished along with the bad, and the bad are rewarded along with the good.

In order to feel responsibility the voter must feel power, but under existing arrangements he is more likely to sense frustration. So far as Congress is concerned, he votes at each two-year election for only one of the 96 senators and for only one of the 435 representatives. In no election can a voter belong to anything more than a state or a local majority. In the nation as a whole his vote may be wasted, and the general result may be largely accidental. Because of its six-year staggered term, the Senate may, in any event, be relatively unaffected. Even when the voter has had a hand in changing control of Congress he can have no confidence that the new Congress will behave much differently from the old.

The people cannot be expected to enforce responsibility with any consistency unless they are interested in government; and they are more likely to be interested when government is comprehensible and operates in the public view. Our national governmental organization is so complex, its operations so cumbrous, and its internal maneuverings so intricate as to baffle completely the ordinary understanding. Congress, as Woodrow Wilson wrote when that body was simpler than it is now, "is too complex to be understood without an effort, without a careful and systematic process of analysis. Consequently, very few people do understand it, and its doors are practically shut against the comprehension of the public at large."[45]

In foreign affairs, especially, popular control calls for a wide and informed interest. For it is often difficult, until years have passed, to demonstrate that a foreign policy is sound or unsound. In the meantime, a president guilty of fatal error or neglect may be elected or re-elected because of domestic prosperity, because he has shown peaceful intentions, because he has spoken in tones of morality, because it is felt that his knowledge and experience make him indispensable, or because he has allied himself with some great interest groups. In the control of foreign policy, the citizen's intellectual burden has probably more than doubled since 1941. His interest and his information have recently improved, but there is no reason to believe that the improvement is yet sufficient.[46]

Not only government but the electoral system as well puts too heavy a burden on the voter. He is expected to vote in the presidential and congressional elections and in the preceding primaries; but he also has a multiplicity of choices to make in state, county, and municipal primaries and elections, to say nothing of township and school district elections, and a variety of questions to decide such as constitutional amendments, charters, bond issues, etc. The states are primarily to blame for the "long ballot"; but its influence is felt in the congressional elections. These are a part of the total electoral burden, the effect of which is to encourage, if not to compel, electoral irresponsibility.

The House of Representatives suffers most from popular ignorance or indifference. Public opinion polls have shown that more than half of the persons interviewed did not know the name of their congressman or the length of his term; and 27 per cent, in January 1946, did not know that a congressional election would be held that year.[47] Evidently, the people normally are not interested in localized elections for national legislators. The enthusiasm aroused by a presidential contest and the comparatively large vote cast in a presidential election demonstrate the drawing power of a truly national office and the appeal made by a relatively simple and apparently decisive electoral choice. The "mid-term" or "off-year" vote is usually much less than in the preceding presidential election. It was 73 per cent in 1930; 87 per cent in 1934; 84 per cent in 1938; 60 per cent in 1942; and about 40 per cent in 1946.[46] Even in presidential elections, the congressional vote has never in the last fifty years equaled the vote for presidential electors,[49] unless it did so in 1948.

Responsibility and leadership. By subjecting governmental power to a process of fragmentation and deadlock, the founding fathers made it impossible to utilize effectively the principle of responsibility; and their failure in this particular, unavoidable as it may have been at that time, places obstacles in the path of leadership and thus further promotes public irresponsibility. Power, responsibly held and responsibly exercised, attracts men of high calibre, brings out the best in them, encourages the assertion of leadership, and facilitates popular control. Such has been the general effect of the presidency, despite the shortcomings of that office.

The national governmental organization, when it fails to produce leadership, generates a vicious circle of irresponsibilities. An uninformed electorate is a gullible one. When intellect is weak, emotion is strong. Hence the prevalence in this country of claptrap, deception, and trickery, the common indulgence in half-truths, the tendency to conceal the full meaning and long-run implications of policies, the absence of moral courage, the sloughing-off of principles and philosophies, the resort to crassly materialistic appeals, and the failure to rely on the higher and better instincts of the people.

CHAPTER IX

THE PARTY SYSTEM

The typical or average American is probably more familiar with the general pattern of political parties than he is with any other feature of government. He probably takes a certain comfort in the fact that the United States has a *two*-party system instead of a *multiple*-party system. The chances are that he is either a Republican or a Democrat. In any event, he looks upon the system as a rather evenly balanced affair, which it usually has been. While he may describe himself generally as a Democrat or a Republican, he probably thinks of himself, or others think of him, as a progressive, a liberal, a conservative, a pro-this, or an anti-that. In other words, he belongs to a wing or a faction of his party. Factionalism is a feature of the system. He may be an independent, with or without leanings in one direction or another. As such, he is part of the independent vote, which is one of the features of our system. He may belong to a third party or to a minor party. In spite of the dominant role of the two major parties, third parties and minor parties are also features of our system. He may, finally, be one of many millions who either do not vote or are disinclined to. The stay-at-homes likewise belong to the system. In whatever classification he may put himself, he probably complains a good deal about politicians and parties.

The party system is an instrument, and a very complex one, fashioned by political needs, that the electorate uses to control government. While parties are outside the Constitution, they are inside as well as outside of government. They figure in both political and governmental processes. They affect both the democracy and the efficiency of government. To what extent, we ask, does the system form and focus public opinion? Is the electorate able to give clear directions to the elected authorities? In general, does the system tend to correct or to offset

180

the questionable features of our government? Or does it tend to fit itself rather closely to the constitutional structure and mechanism? It is organized and it operates in close connection with the governmental organization. If that is changed, would not the party system also change or at least work differently?

The system has its strong points. No one can maintain that it is a total failure or that it always works badly. The purpose here is to note its shortcomings, its weaknesses, and its hazards, and in what respects improvement would be desirable.

OPINIONS AND POLICIES

The party system and popular elections should be means of enforcing the government's responsibility to the people. Following a debate within the government, between the majority and minority, the process of nominating, campaigning, and electing should permit the party in power to account for its stewardship and the party in opposition to present its claims. When the popular debate is over, the electorate should make its decision and lay down a new mandate, which the winning party should carry out. Such is the the ideal; but in practice, while the party system succeeds as a mechanism for filling offices, it does not do so well in other respects.

Party philosophies. Democracy in operation requires that the major parties should agree on certain fundamental matters; for example, on the essential principles of free government, on the rule of law, and on the need of protecting and preserving the nation. Only once in our history have they failed to agree on these matters; and civil war resulted. From that time to recent years, our party system has shown no indication of any similar strong tendency toward an opposition on fundamentals; but, should the communists become strong, such an opposition would again confront the nation.

Within their common frame of reference, healthy political parties should reveal disagreement, or, at the least, a divergence. They should present a choice to voters who have different ideas about public policy. Without such a choice, it is not possible to have a public debate, a crystallization of opinion, or a meaningful electoral decision. The electorate cannot decide details and technicalities, nor pass on too many questions. What it should do is to determine the general attitude of government toward public problems and the philosophy—political, economic, or social—which is to be controlling. The electorate is powerless to make such a decision unless the parties offer alternative points of view.

It has been said that legislation represents an "advancing consensus," that a political party rarely proposes the repeal of a law, and that the only real difference between the parties concerns the tempo, not the direction, of legislation.[1] This view, however, is not inconsistent with the idea that parties should or do disagree or diverge with regard to philosophies and policies, for the question of tempo does not arise in isolation; it arises in connection with specific proposals for action.

The two major parties are often contrasted in terms of Hamilton versus Jefferson, conservatism versus liberalism, centralization versus states' rights, big government versus limited government, special privilege versus the common man, social service versus administrative efficiency, or right versus left. Such contrasts are as often misleading as enlightening. Usually, the chief difference between the parties relates to the manner in which government should act in the immediate future to meet the economic expectations of the people. Generally speaking, Republicans look at this problem from the standpoint of the industrialist and the big businessman, emphasizing the value of free private enterprise. They are disposed to interfere with the economic system chiefly for purposes of stimulation and promotion, removal of its abuses, and maintenance of its internal balances. Democrats, on the other hand, look at government in its relation to the economic system mainly from the standpoint of the wage earner, emphasizing the value of regulation, while aiming by direct measures to bring about a wider distribution of national income.

This divergence has been illustrated rather consistently by the respective attitudes of the parties toward tariff policy; but, when we look at the whole range of domestic policy and particularly at regulative and social legislation, we see that neither party has remained consistent or has shown any conspicuous philosophical integrity. While making the most of its traditions, each has adapted itself to circumstances and to party strategy. The southern Democrat, more partisan than his northern colleague, is as much Republican in his way of thinking as he is Democratic. But his party cannot win a national election without victories in northern states. In the North, the Democratic party has drawn the bulk of its strength from the cities and lower-income groups, while the Republican party normally draws its strength from rural areas and higher-income groups. To the considerable extent that party affiliation rests on an income basis, the division accords roughly with the philosophical divergence just noted.

In the sphere of foreign policy, it is even more difficult to point out any durable difference between the parties on fundamental matters, for in the past foreign policy has usually been a secondary consideration. About all that can be said is that in foreign as in domestic affairs the spirit of conservatism has been somewhat stronger ordinarily in the Republican party than in the Democratic.

Localized basis. One of the striking characteristics of national party organization is its adaptation to the historic geographical decentralization of government. The basic and in many cases the dominant influences operate in the counties, the districts, the cities, and the states. It is in the local units—at the "grass-roots"—that opinion takes concrete form, and leadership acts in direct contact with the voters. The sources of political power are best exploited locally, in the cities and counties, even in the wards and precincts. For that reason, the strongest organizations are locally created and locally entrenched. The national organization is largely derived from the local, by processes of delegation and interplay; and it is only during a presidential campaign that national leadership asserts itself with vigor and can succeed more or less in mobilizing and unifying local leaderships.

From the beginning, sectionalism and regionalism have inevitably entered into the sources and distribution of party strength. From this point of view, the "Solid South" has presented an outstanding peculiarity of the American party system, for the southern states have been not only Democratic: they have been almost exclusively committed in their internal politics to a one-party system.

Pressure groups, direct action, and minor parties. Pressure groups cut across parties and press upon parties. During the eighties and nineties, industrial interest and the industrial corporation exercised a continuous and, in general, a dominant influence in the party system and in government. From the turn of the century, however, the political influence of capital declined, while the power of organized labor rose to an extraordinary peak. Agricultural discontent when deep-seated, widespread, and persistent, has lost none of its political potency. Pressure groups also operate locally and exploit localism. Direct political action is a localized procedure. It aims to pick or pick off candidates locally and one-by-one, in accordance with "box-scores," black-lists or white-lists. The Anti-Saloon League demonstrated the remarkable power that could be developed by an organized group devoted to a single purpose and pressing directly on the party and electoral systems. Local electoral pressure, or the threat of using it, has been one of the American Legion's weapons. Recently, organized labor, with its "liberal" allies, has been the most conspicuous practitioner of direct political action.

Groups or factions may organize as third parties or minor parties. These have figured in all national elections, serving as vehicles of dissent and protest, influencing strategically the policies of the major parties, and sometimes holding the balance of power in pivotal states.[2] On rare occasions, a third party may bring about a realignment of the major parties or, still more rarely, may take the place of a major party. But, as they normally function, most "splinter" parties have two noteworthy characteristics: (1) they are largely confined to and identified with a state or a section, and (2) they are pressure groups in a special form, designed to strengthen or weaken a major party and in this way to decide the election.

Strategy. In the practical effort to win elections, neither party finds it possible to maintain its philosophical integrity, for an absolute integrity would mean an undue inflexibility. Thus, while appealing to its distinctive traditions, pretending consistency, and asserting individuality, each party becomes a conglomeration of elements and opinions, ranging from one extreme to another.

Under the electoral college system, the aim of the party managers in a presidential campaign is to carry enough states to produce a majority in the electoral college. As previously pointed out, the system enhances the political importance of states with large electoral votes.

The "doubtful" states, on which elections swing, are mainly in the industrial Northeast, extending westward from Massachusetts to the Mississippi and including states with large electoral votes, such as New York, Pennsylvania, Ohio, Michigan, and Illinois. In addition to the Northeast, the far west is usually debatable. These two sections are likely to decide elections; and in the Northeast the labor vote holds a highly important strategic position.[3] Neither party can risk any outright antagonizing of this block of voters; and the Democrats have practically no chance of winning a national election without substantial labor support.

Thus the electoral college system appears to give a disproportionate power to the labor group,[4] indeed to any special group whose votes may be needed in a doubtful state. Under that system, the group is not compelled to measure its strength in the whole nation, where it may be relatively weak. It need only act locally where it is relatively strong.

Some effects of party strategy. The general process that makes the two parties represent similar conglomerations of opinion and that produces a fairly even balance between the parties was explained 50 years ago by Henry Jones Ford:

Party . . . contains a principle of conservatism, inasmuch as it must always seek to keep faction within such bounds as will prevent it from jeopardizing party interests. An important consequence of this party instinct of comprehension is the tendency of opposing party organizations to equalize each other in strength. The practical purpose of their formation causes each to compete for popular favor in ways that tend toward an approximately equal division of popular support. . . . If a party becomes so hopelessly discredited that it has no chance of success, it disappears like the Federalists or the old National Republican Party, and a new party takes its place based on contemporaneous divisions of public sentiment.[5]

Thus party strategy keeps each party available as a substitute for the other, but prevents it from becoming much of an alternative, so far as opinions and policies are concerned.

Another result of the jigsaw nature of party strategy operating on a localized electoral basis is to concentrate party action and political discussion in some areas while neglecting others. These neglected areas are in effect partially or wholly outside the party system. In most cases they are on the outside because of traditional party allegiance. They may be there for a precisely opposite reason—nonpartisanship.[6] In a presidential election, any state plurality of more than one is wasted. Accordingly, if a state is "safe" and a plurality assured, why bother to get out the vote? Or why bother to instruct the voter and awaken his interest?[7]

In the 1944 election 54 Democrats and 6 Republicans were elected to the House of Representatives without opposition, while 106 Democrats and 80 Republicans obtained 60 per cent or more of the major party vote. Only 42 Democrats and 52 Republicans received less than 55 per cent of the major party vote. Not all of the 94 "close" districts were "doubtful"; and in 1946 the party tacticians practically narrowed the main contest for the House down to less than 100 districts. Probably at least 300 districts received little or no attention from the party management.[8]

It is true that in the states and districts that are practically outside the party system and where nomination is equivalent to election, there are frequently active contests in the primaries, along with greater public interest and participation.[9] But a primary contest is by no means a substitute for a party contest. A primary campaign tends to be pre-eminently a personal campaign. Of course, to the extent that party debate takes place over the radio, the South has the same access to information and discussion as any other section; but, where party allegiance is unalterable and minds are unchangeable, one is likely to find no great incentive or strong inclination to listen to both sides, or even to one side. In general, one may believe that the unequal distribution of two-party functioning, particularly as it affects the South, contributes to provincialism and stagnation.

Policies. We have formed the habit of looking on the presidential campaign as a real, if not as the only, contest for control of the national government. In such a campaign, we come nearest to a national debate, to a national crystallization of opinion, to a national definition of party policies, and to an electoral decision by the whole nation.

According to the early theory, the national convention made the authoritative statement of party policy, a pronouncement that bound the presidential candidate, the party candidates for the Senate and House, and the party as a whole. The resolutions or platforms adopted by the convention treated issues with boldness and clarity; and the convention's statement of policy had considerable binding effect. As a result of party composition and party strategy, the platform degenerated, and, some time between 1880 and 1900, became more or less a collection of platitudes and an exercise in "straddling," largely disregarded in the campaign and almost forgotten after the election.

The national convention, in any event, was never fitted for an intelligent review and forecast of public policy; and attempts made to prepare a program in advance of the convention, through formal special committees, have had little success. When the presidential candidate is a real popular leader and when his nomination is assured in advance, he usually dictates the platform. In any case, he may expressly repudiate it in part, ignore it, or give his own interpretation to it; and he develops policies as the campaign progresses. These policies, like the platforms, are determined largely or wholly by considerations of strategy, by the need of holding or winning doubtful groups in doubtful states.[10]

In a presidential campaign, the views of the presidential candidate exercise a degree of influence over the candidates for the Senate and the House. They are free, however, if they wish, to follow the policy declared by a state or district convention or to make their own platforms. When the presidential candidate is unpopular, or when any of his policies seem strategically inappropriate locally, the congressional candidate usually goes his own way. In a mid-term congressional campaign, the president in office has less unifying and nationalizing influence than he had as a candidate. The congressional candidates of the opposition party are decidedly on their own. In general, localism prevails, and issues are obscured far more than when public interest is nationally aroused. The reduced vote in the "off-year" election may itself decide the outcome in "close" districts.

The direct primary has tended both to exaggerate local issues and to substitute personalities for philosophies and policies. This system of nomination made it easier for reform or dissident elements to contest the power of the local boss; but the direct primary also encourages factionalism based on local conditions and, locally, it tends to submerge national issues and broad philosophies.

It must be remembered, too, that most of our electoral jurisdictions do not permit the voter to concentrate on national issues. Ordinarily, he is compelled at the same time to referee other contests—state, county, municipal, or what not—each with its special controversies and confusions.[11]

Electoral decisions. Thus we have in our political campaigns a multiplicity of promises and boasts, of charges and counter-charges, related for the most part, not to each other or to the general welfare, but to sectional and group interests. Because the party strategists must attract and hold various groups of voters having divergent or conflicting conceptions of interest, one party or both may resort to "glittering" generalities, may "straddle" positions, dodge issues, stress personalities, and exploit emotion. Nationally no real clarification takes place, and the election becomes a blurred reflection of ill-defined likes and dislikes, along with a dozen or more disputable "mandates" on specific questions. The election may not even show conclusively any general popular attitude of approval, disapproval, or preference, or any indication of the speed at which government should move in a given direction.

With respect to foreign policies, the results have been even more inconclusive, partly because one set of issues has cut across the other, and it has been impossible for voters to express themselves at one time in two separate spheres. In practically all cases, domestic issues and influences have decided the outcome. Such was the case in 1900, when Bryan vainly declared "imperialism" to be the paramount issue; in 1916, when Wilson won on his party's domestic record and on the claim that "he had kept us out of war"; and in 1920, when Wilson called for a "solemn referendum" on the League of Nations and when Harding, urging a "return to normalcy," straddled the international issue so that no decision actually took place. In 1940 and 1944 war overshadowed domestic issues, as well as postwar international questions, and "Don't swap horses in the middle of the stream" became the winning slogan.[12] In 1948, foreign policy was not an issue except for minor details.

Political shifts. Under the American party system, as it now is, one may be fairly certain that, sooner or later, the presidency, and probably the two Houses also, will pass from one party to the other. It is somewhat misleading to call this shift a "political tide," a "political cycle," or the "swing of the pendulum." The shift has no proved rhythm. It might be regular if economic and international factors remained constant. In that case, the cycle would result from the sameness and balance of the two parties and the tendency in the electorate to get tired of personalities and to desire change for the sake of change. The party in power finds itself unable to keep its various elements satisfied; it accumulates critics and enemies; it develops factionalism; its leaders grow old and lose their initiative. Conversely, the opposition party may have its advantages; the one object of coming back to power may give it a special cohesion and unity; criticism is easier than action; and, as time passes, the people tend to become more conscious of the deficiencies of the Ins, while forgetting the past record of the Outs.

Party shifts occur for many reasons unrelated to the soundness or unsoundness of party professions, or to the faithfulness with which the party in power has practiced its professions. It may be said that the most we can expect of the people is that they should choose capable leaders and then throw them out if they fail to keep the country prosperous and safe. But a party and electoral system in which the people, when they shift from one party to the other, vote usually *against* and seldom *for* indicates a negative and *ex post facto* control, a sort of stable-locking after the horse is stolen. It is not the kind of popular control which a fully realized and fully implemented democracy implies. The fact that our electoral campaigns do produce some discussion of issues and policies, inadequate though the discussions may be, shows that the people desire to decide policies, as well as to choose men. The 1948 election supplied evidence of that desire.

PARTY SOLIDARITY

At the turn of the century, political scientists generally agreed that the United States had strong party organization, and was compelled to have it in order to unify our separated governments.[13] The observations of that time sound strange today; for now, though we need strong party organization more than ever, we do not have it. Organization and leadership on a national scale call for a considerable degree of solidarity throughout the nation and among the party's constituent elements. Solidarity in turn calls for means of control and discipline.

Harmony and discipline. "Harmony" is always greatly desired and much discussed. Unless an actual split occurs, the appearance of harmony or an approach to it is usually achieved in a presidential campaign, for in such a contest everything seems to be at stake. But this tactical harmony is seldom lasting. Disciplinary authority is largely dependent on the power to control the subordinate and local leaders of the party and to influence, if not to dictate, the nominations for key political offices. Such nominations include those for the Senate and the House and probably, under our governmental organization, for the governorships as well. Nevertheless, national party leadership has little power to name or control local leaders, to influence or dictate nominations for the Senate or the House, or to decide party candidates for gubernatorial positions.

Party harmony, as well as popular allegiance to one party or the other, is difficult to achieve and retain at the national level when each party is a similar conglomeration of factions representing wide extremes of opinion, and when party pronouncements on policy have no continuing authority. Naturally, partisanship, party "politics," and "politician" have become terms of ill repute, while independence, insurgency, nonpartisanship, and bipartisanship are deemed worthy of high praise. This intellectual and moral weakening of the party undermines the foundation and sanctions of its leadership and discipline. Localized representation and elections are among the main factors in the undermining process; and that process almost reached its conclusion when the wave of democratization and anti-bossism at the turn of the century attached the direct primary system of nomination to the localized basis of representation.

The direct primary. The direct primary works against national control of nominations to the Senate and the House. Because the system arranges for a contest within the party, it puts a premium on personalities, while it invites and creates internal conflict. Under the direct primary a minority may decide the nomination, first, because the turnout of voters is as a rule comparatively small, and second, because the vote may be distributed among three or more candidates.[14] When the primary is "open," the members of one party may decide nominations in the other; and when a man may run in both party primaries, as in California, the result is an almost complete destruction of the party system within the state. Finally, the political-action organization, as it operates in the primaries, substitutes a narrow special interest for the larger integrating purpose of the party.

Independence. Independence of a kind strengthens the party system and, in fact, is essential to its effective operation. This salutary sort of independence comes from an intelligent willingness to shift from one party to the other on the basis of a broad consideration of policies and from the standpoint of the general interest. Other kinds of independence weaken, not only the party organization, but the party system itself.[15] One of these kinds unduly exalts nonpartisanship. The pressure group and the political action committee illustrate another kind of independence, which in effect coerces candidates and does so in order to promote a special interest.

The growth of governmental responsibilities and of the bureaucracy has weakened party solidarity, because at its foundation and throughout most of its superstructure administration deals with adopted policies, which are no longer in the area of party conflict.

REALIGNMENT

To perform its function, the party system should be more than nominal. As Schlesinger says, "parties must not become so meaningless that they drag down the whole level of political understanding."[16]

In general, our party system has yielded to a moving radicalism. Some would call it an advance; some, a retreat; but it cannot go on indefinitely without drawing near to the ultimate issue of authority vs. liberty. As we approach this issue, we may feel increasingly the threat in one form or another of communism. Thus the party struggle may become, not a normal contest between moderate conservatives and "liberals" within the framework of democracy, but a struggle with communism based on a disagreement over fundamentals and involving the very existence of the nation and its way of life.

The communistic movement is a Soviet instrument, but it gains much of its power to infiltrate and create confusion from the fact that it represents itself with some plausibility as a medium of domestic protest, social reform, and pacifism. This new development "has injected into the democratic system of parties new factors of an international type," and they present "not only an external but also an internal challenge, which is active in the very vitals of the State."[17] So far as formal membership is concerned, the Communist party in this country is inconsequential. With respect to its infiltrations, its ability to create confusion, and its eventual possibilities, the movement has already become a menace. Our party system, combined with and resting upon local representation, is sensitive to relatively small groups and balance-of-power tactics. It offers inadequate protection against communism, if communism should succeed in skillfully camouflaging its subversive aims. The Wallace third party in 1948 did not decide the election, but it illustrated how communism can use our political processes while partially hiding its sinister purpose. Localized representation and elections, moreover, would seem to facilitate infiltration into Congress.

PARTY LEADERSHIP

We have already pointed out how the governmental organization without reference to political parties, tends to multiply and scatter leadership and how, along with other influences, the organization affects unfavorably the quality of leadership. If we are to have party responsibility and party government, the leadership of the majority party should be the leadership of the government and should provide the governmental leadership of the nation. At the same time, the leader or leaders of the minority party should head the political opposition within and outside the government.

If there are world-wide trends at work in our own country toward popular impotence and personal government, it becomes crucially important to understand whether they are encouraged or discouraged by the political process. As we have already noted, governmental organization and operation account in a measure for a lack of political interest and an insufficient sense of civic responsibility. Party strategy not only obeys the conditions imposed upon it by governmental peculiarities, but it naturally exploits popular shortcomings. We have also noted that the localized organization and strategy of the party, along with the direct primary system of nomination, work against a nationwide integration of opinion. Consequently, the political process tends toward a degeneration of political debate and toward emphasis on personalities. But emphasis on personalities does not necessarily give us enough leadership or the right kind.

Selection. In a presidential campaign, the presidential candidate becomes to a high degree the leader of his party and, if he wins the election, he retains that position, unless, as rarely happens, he is definitely repudiated.

It has been a general rule in American politics that, to be eligible for top national leadership and to win national notice as a presidential possibility, a man must be widely known and long in the public eye. It is held, as a general rule, that he should have served, and preferably should be serving, as a recognized member of his party in a high political position, such as governor of a state, senator, Cabinet officer, or Speaker of the House.[18] It is also usually and properly maintained that his philosophy and his **policies**, his stand on national questions, should be publicly **known.**

These general rules and logical assumptions are subject in American politics to many and important exceptions. Not infrequently, a party has turned to someone who is comparatively unknown, or without distinguished experience in office, or even without previous activity in or affiliation with the party.[19] The movements for General Eisenhower's nomination in 1948 reflected for the most part a demand for a popular personality, regardless of his political philosophy and his views on questions of policy.

The national convention makes the final selection;[20] and, in the naming of candidates, the principal aim is the winning of the election. The party must draw its factions together, at least for the campaign; it must avoid a split, if it is possible to do so; it must generate enthusiasm and "get out the vote"; and it must attract or hold enough independent voters to carry the required number of states, including the pivotal ones. When an especially stubborn contest occurs between two principal aspirants, the convention in the end often drops them both in favor of a "dark horse," who is acceptable to both wings. The Republicans acted in that way in 1920 and the Democrats in 1924. Thus the party avoids a split; but, in doing so, it largely abandons the principles which should control the process of selection.

The various qualities that make a good candidate can be classified under three main heads: personality, policies, and geography. With regard to policies, "availability" usually means that the candidate has not identified himself with any faction in the party and that he has skillfully escaped the political embarrassments that accrue from positive and bold leadership in controversial matters. From the standpoint of geography, the most "available" candidate as a rule is one who resides in a large and pivotal state.[21]

Party strategy and the wishes of the presidential candidate largely determine the nomination for the vice-presidency. Because of the emptiness of the office and the manner in which men are selected to fill it, the vice-presidential candidates are usually, though not always, inferior to the presidential.[22] A "running mate" is ordinarily named to "balance the ticket" from the geographical and factional viewpoints. Not infrequently, the two nominees hold divergent philosophies and disagree on policies. Yet when by the accident of death the vice-president becomes president, party leadership automatically changes, without opportunity to reconsider the man, the feelings of the party, and the national situation.

Regardless of the quality of the president's leadership in office, it has become a rule, with almost no possibility of an exception, that if he seeks renomination he can have it. If he refuses renomination, he may be able to name his successor, as Theodore Roosevelt did in 1908.

The party-electoral process may select able and positive leaders, but the chances are against them. On the whole, the tendency is to emphasize the personal conception of politics and leadership: "It is the man, not the party, that counts." The factional make-up of the party encourages this tendency. In general and usually, the party-electoral process tends to screen out the type of man that it should select. The party performs satisfactorily and consistently only one function, that of filling offices; but it often fails to fill the offices with the best men.

Minority leadership. The defeated presidential candidate is a casualty in more ways than one. During the campaign, the minority party has selected and rallied round its leader and attempted to make him head of the government. Yet, after his defeat, though still recognized vaguely as titular leader, he has no position in the government from which to act as leader. During the campaign, he has been the authoritative defender or critic of the government, the party's chief interpreter of the country's needs, and the final framer of the party's policies. His party had hoped to make him, not only the chief executive, but also the legislative leader of the nation. Yet, when the voters decide that his party shall be the opposition, he finds himself temporarily, often permanently, shelved. He has no seat in Congress where the opposition is supposed to function. Not one defeated presidential candidate or ex-president during the modern period has become a member of Congress and thus a direct participant in the making of policy.

In Congress, where as a rule the minority party must assert its opposition, the situation, as we have seen, is unfavorable to the development of national leadership. The "safe" states rarely produce a presidential leader of the nation; but, curiously enough, we get from the politically more stagnant areas—the Solid South and the "rock-ribbed" districts—a disproportionate number of our congressional leaders. Leadership develops best in the minority party when the political tide seems to be running in its favor. At such a time, a strong compulsion exists to cover up factionalism and present a united front, yet it is the very time when competition among leaders is the strongest. When the opposition party is in control of Congress, the senatorial leaders, perhaps also the Speaker of the House, have an opportunity to engage in a running debate with the president.

On the other hand, these congressional leaders have assumed a share of responsibility for the conduct of government. They are also usually lacking in administrative experience. So the circumstances of their congressional leadership may make them less "available" for the presidential nomination.

PARTY RESPONSIBILITY

Party responsibility and party government are inseparable. Unless the majority party possesses and exercises actual control, *as a party*, it cannot be held responsible *as a party*. The function of the minority is criticism of the party in power and the presentation of an alternative program. Party responsibility and party government require that the minority be held responsible, not for government, but for the character of its opposition.

Do we accept the principle? The American people have made no clear choice between government by men and government by parties. The feelings and forces that weakened the party outside the government also weakened it within the government. Admitting that the president should be a "party man" and that the members of his Cabinet should be loyal to him, we nevertheless see something reprehensible in a similar party allegiance and a similar loyalty on the part of members of Congress. Though we are well aware that no public purpose can be achieved without organized action involving solidarity, discipline, and loyalty, the application of such action to the control of our complex governmental processes has fallen into intellectual and moral disrepute. When parties come to the serious business of government, we ask them to lay aside "politics."[23]

The pressures and opportunities for party unity in the work of government are greatest under certain combinations of circumstances, such as those that appeared in 1897, 1913, and 1933. At each of these times prior to the party overturn, there had been popular discontent and a widespread demand for remedial legislation. At each time the party previously in power had in one way or another repudiated its leadership. It had also shown its factional disunity and its legislative inefficiency. But beneath the surface, conditions unfavorable to party responsibility and party government operate steadily and with cumulative effect. These unfavorable conditions include the loss of legislative prestige, the theory and plan of representation and election, our scheme of separated departments, the nature of modern public responsibilities and public questions, the disintegration of opinion, the role played by localism and special interests, the intricacies of the electoral and lawmaking processes, and the general decline of popular interest in government.

An immediate obstacle arises from the fact that the party, prior to its entrance into government, has not resolved its internal factionalism and become a suitably organized instrumentality for governmental control or minority opposition. It is still in the process of clarifying its philosophy, formulating its program, testing or developing its leadership, and finding in policy and leadership a common solvent for its intractable elements.

Within the government, scattering and concealment of individual responsibility hamper the development and enforcement of party responsibility. The substantial separation of party organization from party representation in government further diffuses responsibility. A party-controlled government cannot be a completely personalized government; but possession of power in party and government must be sufficiently concentrated in persons or in a person and sufficiently visible to permit the party membership to fix responsibility for party leadership and party action. Furthermore, the pressure groups operate directly upon government, and in their operation create a system of essentially nonpartisan and irresponsible leaderships. Thus, it comes about

... that the real representatives are not the responsible legislators, that the most decisive part of the session is likely to take place in the lobby, and that the duly elected "representative" constantly tends to become a puppet whose strings are pulled by someone in the background. And the public generally expects that results will be got by pressure or persuasion, by methods which it vaguely hopes will be legitimate but which it knows often are not so.[24]

In Congress. Party responsibility and party government require that the president and his party followers in Senate and House act together on politically controversial questions. In order to achieve party unity throughout the government, it is necessary to achieve unity in the Senate and the House. At the end of the nineteenth century, the speakership, the senatorial bosses, the caucus, and the convention system of nominating candidates provided considerable concentration of leadership and fairly adequate means of discipline. At present, the caucus, or, as the Republicans call it, the party conference, is chiefly an arrangement for discussing party policies and legislative tactics; and the individual party members are not bound to follow the decision of the caucus or conference.

As features of this party meeting or as supplements to it, both parties have developed machinery for their governance— a committee on committees, a committee on patronage, a steering or policy committee, a floor leader, and a party whip. In addition, there are the various legislative committees, each with its powerful chairman selected according to seniority. Under the somewhat accidental operations of seniority, committee chairmanships sometimes fall to men of sharply divergent views. Some chairmen may be at the party's right; others, at its left. Seniority may mean that the party goes in one direction in one field of policy and in a different direction in another field. The committee system tends, not only to accentuate disunity within the party, but also to reduce the scope of debate and competition between the two parties.

Through presidential leadership. Party government can hardly materialize unless the president decisively leads his party. Except in time of war and to an extent in the conduct of foreign affairs, presidential leadership within the government has been closely associated with party leadership. Moreover, as Woodrow Wilson pointed out, if the president is also leader of the nation, "his party can hardly resist him."[25]

When a president, favored by circumstances and aided by

accidents, comes into office with the personal qualities and the
political genius required to achieve party government, he is
compelled as a practical matter to dominate his congressional
following. Franklin D. Roosevelt stated the principle of party
responsibility through presidential leadership when he was attempting in 1938 to "purge" Senator George of Georgia:

> To carry out my responsibility as President, it is clear that if there
> is to be success in our Government there ought to be co-operation
> between members of my own party and myself—co-operation, in
> other words, within the majority party, between one branch of gov-
> ernment, the legislative branch, and the head of the other branch,
> the executive. That is one of the essentials of a party form of gov-
> ernment. It has been going on in this country for nearly a century
> and a half. The test is not measured, in the case of an individual,
> by his every vote on every bill—of course not. The test lies rather
> in the answer to two questions: first, has the record of the candidate
> shown, while differing perhaps in details, a constant active fighting
> attitude in favor of the broad objectives of the party and of the
> Government as they are constituted today; and secondly, does the
> candidate really, in his heart, deep down in his heart, believe in
> these objectives?[26]

Actually, party responsibility, as Franklin D. Roosevelt conceived it, meant that the president should impose on members
of Congress his own views of party policy, views that he
had reached presumably after considering the state of public
opinion and after consultation with other party leaders. Our
governmental organization, however, does not lend itself to the
continuous practice of such an interpretation; and even Franklin D. Roosevelt could not consistently maintain his leadership
or the unity of his party. It has long been an almost invariable
rule, in the states as well as at Washington, that executive
leadership of the legislature is most effective when the executive is new in office and least effective as his tenure draws to
an end. Patronage is a most important factor common to all
executive-legislative relationships; and, as time passes, there is
less patronage to dispense.

Aside from his personal qualities, Franklin D. Roosevelt's
strength as a party and a national leader may be attributed

chiefly to the measure in which he exploited emergencies or otherwise circumvented the processes that normally weaken executive leadership. His program distributed, on a scale hitherto undreamed of, substantial material benefits to strategically indicated electoral groups. The same program resulted in rapid administrative expansion and a constantly replenished supply of patronage. By discarding the two-term tradition, Roosevelt made it difficult for any of his followers to contest his leadership or to think of transferring their loyalty.

When Mr. Truman became President in 1945, a condition developed similar to that which had appeared in 1901 when Theodore Roosevelt succeeded to the office. Truman, like Theodore Roosevelt, pledged himself to carry out the policies of his predecessor; but, in each case, the policies to be followed were either nonexistent or soon outdated. Both the elder Roosevelt and Truman had, as vice-presidential candidates, "balanced the ticket"; and, because of this fact, their assumption of party leadership led to dissatisfaction in that wing of the party which had lost its identification with the president. The presidential succession, as constitutionally arranged, is not well adapted to party responsibility and party government.

Repeatedly in recent years, we have seen a Democratic president veto bills which had been voted for by a substantial number of Democratic members; and, on occasion, a combination of Democratic with Republican votes have overridden such vetoes. To the extent, that the president's disapproval works as it was intended to work—as a qualified and not as an absolute veto— it usually forces nonpartisanship or bipartisanship on members of Congress, for the reason that normally no one party can muster out of its membership a two-thirds majority in each house.

Presidential leadership tends to be personal leadership, since only personal leadership can appeal to all the discordant elements of the party and the separated fragments of government. The impersonal factors favorable to unity are simply not strong enough under ordinary conditions to overcome the adverse factors. Moreover, our method of naming candidates for president and vice-president normally discourages the selection of highly capable leaders.

When government is divided. When control of the government is divided, as it often is, between the two parties, party responsibility and party government in any genuine form are obviously impossible. The best that can be hoped for is government by co-operation; and the most that the public can do is to hold each party responsible for the manner in which it co-operates with the other. Divided government tends in a way to accentuate party lines and to solidify the majority in Congress. Such a situation has usually resulted in a slightly increased use of the presidential veto and in more frequent attempts in Congress to override vetoes.[27] On both sides, the temptation is strong to substitute maneuver for constructive legislation. When government divides, the next presidential campaign has already started.

Party votes. A perfect party vote, which is essential to perfect party responsibility, is one in which all Democratic members, present and voting, are on one side and all Republican on the other. Party votes should occur only on party questions; but the American political process, failing to draw clear-cut distinctions between the parties, has developed no definite understanding under which questions can be classified as party or nonparty. Evidently, a very strong tendency exists to reduce the area of party conflict. Nevertheless, among the predominantly or traditionally domestic matters, there are always a number of questions that have figured prominently in the preceding election campaign or concern the organization of Senate or House or enter into the strategy of the next campaign or in some way offer an advantage to one party or an embarrassment to the other. These are usually regarded as party questions. A perfect party vote on any question is so extremely rare as to be practically negligible. More common but still infrequent are the votes in which the bulk of the Republican membership is ranged against the bulk of the Democratic. In many cases, the members of one party are solidly or almost solidly for or against a measure, while the other party either divides its vote or joins in to make the result unanimous or approximately so. During the last two Congresses, that is, from 1945 to 1948, such voting has been fairly typical of congressional action. On many party questions, however, neither party is able to demonstrate much unity. Splitting on both sides is likely to take place when the proposal involves cross-currents of interest or philosophy or ranges sectional against partisan alignments.

The Special Session in 1948. In view of what has been said about presidential campaign strategy, party leadership, and party responsibility, a word should be added about the special session called by President Truman in 1948. He issued his call after the national conventions had met and agreed on their platforms, and when the presidential and congressional campaigns were getting started. He evidently aimed to put responsibility on the Republican party, which controlled the two houses of Congress. In effect, he asked the Republicans in Congress to accept and follow the leadership of a Democratic president and candidate for president, though the Republicans had repeatedly declared their lack of confidence in him as president and had just selected Governor Dewey as their own candidate and national leader.

The special session, therefore, could have little meaning so far as party responsibility was concerned, whatever part it may have played in the election. As a matter of fact, the legislative branch of our government usually does not operate at all during a presidential campaign. It waits for the people's verdict; and we are accustomed to view the period between the party conventions and the next presidential inauguration as an interregnum in which policy-making is at a practical standstill. This is an unfortunate fact with dangerous possibilities; but it appears inevitable under our form of government, especially so when control of government is divided between the parties.

BIPARTISANSHIP

In foreign affairs, presidential leadership or executive-legislative co-operation can rarely function merely as a means of formulating and carrying out a majority-party program. In the first place, neither the president nor the congressional leaders can always control their party colleagues, even when these constitute a majority in each house. Secondly, a party rarely wins two thirds of the seats in the Senate; and, to get a treaty approved, the president must obtain more or less support from the minority party. Finally, control of the government may be divided between the two parties, as it was in the fateful years, 1919-20, and in the equally fateful years of 1947 and 1948.

On the outbreak of war in 1939, President Roosevelt called for the adjournment of "partisanship and selfishness." Interparty co-operation began with conferences between the President and congressional leaders, both of the majority and the minority. It took a more definite form after we entered the war with the establishment of the Advisory Committee on Post-War Problems. Subsequently, majority and minority leaders of Congress became members of the American delegation at San Francisco and at later international conferences. Thus co-operation covered both executive initiation of policies and congressional approval. For a time the results appeared remarkably satisfactory.

After Mr. Truman became President, the joint conferences became less a settled procedure; the executive failed to keep the congressional leaders currently informed; and interparty co-operation tended to lose any vital connection with the initiation of policy. The limited bipartisanship which is possible in our form of government functioned to an extent in the passage of the Greek-Turkish aid bill and the so-called "Marshall plan"; but a more important influence came from the reluctance of congressmen to repudiate the nation's spokesman and to create the spectacle of a disunited country.[28]

True bipartisanship, unlike nonpartisanship in its ordinary aspects, implies a working agreement between the two parties for the purpose of placing foreign policies outside the range of the party system and of party conflict. A complete application of bipartisanship would require a coalition government; but a real coalition is impracticable, if not impossible, in our governmental organization. Bipartisanship in practice has never involved a definite agreement between the parties or any arrangement for carrying out the somewhat tenuous understanding that developed. Neither party can be united within the government or possesses the means to make itself united and to bind its members. Interparty agreement depended for the most part on such leadership as the President could exercise over the Democratic members of Congress, and Senator Vandenberg could assert over the Republican members. Much of Senator Vandenberg's influence depended in turn on a dual leadership in the Senate based on a separation of international political questions from domestic questions.

Many ascribed to bipartisanship, not merely a degree of political convenience, but also a high patriotic and moral quality. Commentators and public men expressed anxiety over the fact that the commitment to bipartisanship did not clearly include economic foreign policies or the domestic policies that concern or affect international relations.[29] It was felt that if bipartisanship were not thus extended, the political process might eventually alter or destroy the entire structure of policy. Obviously, if bipartisanship were thus extended, it would comprehend practically all public policies, not only tariffs, foreign lending, and universal military training, but also measures relating to domestic production, prices, wages, tax-reduction, and public expenditure for social purposes.

Such an enlargement of the scope of bipartisanship would seem extremely difficult, if not impossible; but if the idea were to be carried to its logical conclusion, the result for all practical purposes would be a voluntary and agreed abolition of the democratic political process, which would become completely, as it is now largely, a meaningless exercise in shadow-boxing, a useless flexing of atrophied political muscles. The recent trend has been in that direction.[30]

We have evidently wished through this expedient to escape the evils inherent in a divided and potentially deadlocked government, along with the possibly disastrous consequences of minority obstruction in the Senate. From this point of view, the demand for bipartisanship amounts to a confession that our government, as organized and operated, does not work intelligently, safely, and in the national interest. The assumption is that for the present and for an indefinite future democracy is incompatible with efficiency. For the effect of bipartisanship is to estop discussion. It refrains from putting important questions to the people. So far as popular decisions on specified policies are concerned, elections become preordained plebiscites. Popular control vanishes, along with the responsibility of government to the people. Politics become more personalized, but public leadership less necessary and less likely. If party differences are resolved by conference at Washington, why inform the public and awaken its interest?[31]

Bipartisanship is, or should be, an emergency expedient temporarily necessary in time of war or at other times when national security and the unity essential to security take precedence over democracy.[32] The author does not question the desirability of interparty co-operation as it has operated in recent years in the field of foreign affairs. But he does question bipartisanship as a permanent principle of governmental operation or as a way to remove the defects of government.

CHAPTER X

EFFICIENCY IN GOVERNMENT

We had something to say in Chapter III about how a modern American government ought to act. First among the requirements are *deliberation* and *wise decision*. Two outstanding marks of wise decision are *continuity* and *integration*. Continuity involves *consistency*, and integration implies *comprehension, co-ordination*, and *planning*. Along with deliberation and wise decision, we want *vigor* and *promptitude*, legislative as well as executive. Government does not always need to act quickly; but it should be so designed as to be capable of deciding urgently when urgency is called for. What we want in this age is capacity for *both* deliberation and speed.

To meet these requirements we need, first and last, the best men in both elective and appointive positions; and organization should make it as easy as possible for the elective authorities to supervise and control the administration.

A GLANCE AT RESULTS

The test of a cook is what she puts on the table and "the test of the pudding is in the eating." But it is extremely difficult, as we pointed out in the first chapter, to judge a government by its output.

As we look back on our legislative history and try to take a wide bird's-eye view of our domestic policies, we shall see much constructive and progressive accomplishment. But we shall also see some disturbing signs. Of these the most disturbing is also the most familiar; namely, the tendency toward piece-meal and special legislation, particularly in the economic and social fields. The special and local influences back of this tendency grow by what they feed upon and appear to become constantly stronger. They are frequently opposed to one another and to the general interest; they work strongly against co-ordination and integration; they make comprehension, review, and revision of public policies more and more difficult.

From the beginning, federal legislation has revealed the presence of such influences. They have been evident in tariff-making, in pork-barrel appropriations, in veterans' benefits, in the regulation of business, in taxation, in federal aid to the states, in agricultural and labor legislation especially, and to an extent in the conservation of natural resources.

During the New Deal era, the substitution of deficit spending for a balanced budget marked the surrender of government to a party strategy based on the special interests and disintegrating demands of classes, groups, and localities. From the onset of the 1929 depression, there was much talk of planning and the government tried to organize planning; but probably never before in the history of the country had national policy shown a closer correspondence with the influences which, on the whole, are opposed to genuine integration. Efforts to co-ordinate proved largely unavailing. The New Deal was said to be proving the capacity of government to respond promptly to national needs; but if this were so, the response occurred without deliberation. For the New Deal brought into clear view another disturbing sign—the tendency toward discontinuity, toward peaks and valleys in the speed and volume of legislation, periods of feverish activity alternating with periods of legislative calm.[1]

In the few years since the Second World War, lack of integration has been apparent, particularly in connection with price and labor policies. During this recent period, the government, judged only by results, has hardly proved its capacity for strong, sound, and consistent policy-making. Nor has it given assurance in domestic affairs of speedy or timed action, when such action is called for.

In the field of foreign affairs, we may take much comfort from our national good fortune during the first hundred years or more of constitutional government. We may also get considerable satisfaction from present-day policies and actions. In the spring of 1948 American opinion and American foreign policy had been, since the turn of the century, in process of reorientation and readjustment. It was a process also of profound disillusionment. We probably had the power, the resources, and the moral qualifications to prevent the two world wars, if our government had sufficiently grasped realities, had developed the necessary leadership, and had acted with the requisite vigor and promptitude. While we have suffered from a long-drawn-out, costly, and perilous lag, no one can say that this lag came from mistakes that might easily have been prevented.

From the turn of the century to the latest phase, we have not only been slow but we have also tended to deal with world affairs "by bits and pieces." Because of the vast spread of international problems and their delicacy and complexity, we find it more difficult now, in the light of our world obligations, to meet the requirements of comprehension and integration, continuity, and consistency. Since international affairs have come to overlap and resemble domestic affairs, the marks of domestic policy tend to become marks of foreign policy.

Many of our recent difficulties may be attributed to the scope and nature of our new international responsibilities. The urgency of foreign situations and rapid changes in them have made it almost humanly impossible to avoid piece-meal and hand-to-mouth measures. Quick understanding, unerring foresight, and perfect co-ordination are difficult enough in domestic affairs; but they are more so in foreign relations. Our policies should be adaptable to changing international situations; but it is not always easy to determine at any given time what the situation is or what it is likely to become. As a practical matter, the failure of a policy may be due to the attitude or actions of another government or to other conditions over which we seemingly have no control. Moreover, governmental policy-makers in a democracy, however efficient it may be, cannot enjoy the freedom of action possessed by dictators.

So we can draw no general conclusions from the failures or from the successes of our foreign policy. In the foreign field, as in the domestic, the best that can be done, as already said, is to decide in a common-sense way (1) how a government ought to act in order to meet its responsibilities, and (2) whether it is designed to act in that manner. If it is designed to act in a different manner, it may conceivably still succeed; but we have no right to expect it to, and if we continue to rely upon it, we may sooner or later find ourselves in trouble. How is our government designed to act? And does it act according to its design?

CONGRESSIONAL CONDUCT

We call Congress the legislative branch, but actually it consists of two institutions of government. Each exercises independently, not only the legislative function, but also other functions. It is with the legislative function that we are here primarily concerned.

Notwithstanding the thousands of bills that annually drop into the congressional hopper, neither house is now a principal initiator of legislation. Most proposals originate in pressure groups or in the executive branch.[2] The present legislative function of Congress is largely to approve, revise, delay, or disapprove proposals that originate elsewhere. Such must inevitably be the function of any modern democratic legislative body.[3]

Neither house of Congress is wholly bad or deserves the ridicule that it receives from some quarters; but in the exercise of its present legislative function, Congress has failed to give reasonable assurance that it can meet modern requirements.[4]

The two-chamber system. Two-chamber systems are not all alike. In some governments, the upper house has only a suspending or delaying power, and in others provision is made for a joint session to resolve disagreements. Unlike most foreign governments that have two chambers, our system leaves the two legislatures co-ordinate, gives each in most respects an absolute veto on the other, and makes their agreement depend on voluntary accommodation.

There can be little doubt that this system has in some instances made for better legislation. As the fathers desired and foresaw, the Senate compared with its neighbor has been as a rule the more deliberative body, and it has acted on occasion as a check on the impulsiveness, as well as on the discipline, of the lower house. Though the difference between the two houses is not now the same in kind or as extensive as the fathers intended it should be, it still exists. Each house is, in some respects, more efficient than the other and, in some respects, more inefficient. In certain cases, the virtues of one assembly check and counterbalance the vices of the other. At times, also, when one house follows the other in the consideration of a bill, the prolongation of the policy-making process gives time for public discussion and for the crystallization of public opinion.

On the other hand, the practical purposes served originally by the establishment of two assemblies either have lost their primary importance or are no longer appreciably furthered by the two-house system. Both authorities perform the initiating along with the reviewing and checking function. Not infrequently a piece of legislation shows the worst of both houses rather than the best of both or of one. Bicameralism does not necessarily or usually prolong legislative deliberation. On many questions the legislative process goes on in the two houses at the same time, and the only formal checking or delaying action is in the conference committee which usually decides fairly quickly if it decides at all. Generally, however, the two-house system does produce more or less delay but in an indiscriminate manner. By dividing responsibility, it probably sacrifices, as often as it furthers, deliberation. When disagreements occur, the conference committee becomes, on the points in dispute, a kind of third legislature, the members of which are neither representative of the nation nor responsible to it. The bill as reported out of conference is often passed with only perfunctory discussion and sometimes with little if any explanation.[5] Bicameralism certainly causes duplication of work and waste of energy.[6]

The two-house system is a part of the general setup which produces divided government and impairs or destroys party responsibility. Incidentally, the system complicates government and confuses the public. It provides a double chance for special interests to exercise pressure and enlarges opportunities for obstruction.

Attempts have been made from the beginning to bring the two houses into a smooth, co-operative working relationship, usually by means of joint committees; but these formal agencies of co-operation, while often helpful, have never affected more than a small part of the work of Congress.[7] The repeated proposals for the organization of co-operation amount to an admission of the difficulties inherent in bicameralism; but experience has shown that it is impossible to accomplish much by attaching co-operative devices to a structure built for nonco-operation. Faithful to its original intent, the system inevitably generates reciprocal jealousy.[8]

Deliberation in the "numerous" assembly. Because of the schemes of representation from which they are derived, both houses have become large bodies. The House of Representatives, particularly, is not a working group but an unwieldy "multitude." It has long since ceased as a body to be deliberative. Debates on the floor are rarely of any consequence. Even the smaller, more dignified and abler Senate produces few speeches that command public attention, clarify problems, and define issues. Freedom of debate is frequently abused for purposes of obstruction. Full meetings of either house are usually perfunctory and laxly attended. The longest debates are not always on important questions of policy.[9] Most fruitful discussion takes place in the lobbies, in committee rooms, or altogether outside of Congress. Public debate has largely passed to the radio and press, to public meetings, and to relatively small public or private groups.

Even if the House were to enroll the 435 ablest and best-informed men in the country, such a blue-ribbon assembly would still be an anachronism. No fact is better attested by common experience than the inappropriateness of a large assembly for the handling of complex problems. In the House of Representatives, to say nothing of the smaller Senate, face-to-face businesslike conference is impossible. Such a body, particularly when its members represent localities, hides individual responsibility, lends itself to exploitation by professional manipulators, and encourages log-rolling.

But neither house enrolls the ablest and best-informed men in the country nor the country's outstanding leaders.[10] We have previously pointed out that conditions in the United States have produced a wastage and shortage of public leadership and that the governmental organization itself contributes to this result. In this connection the Senate seems to demonstrate that the size, set-up, and responsibilities of a legislative body bear a close relation to the quality of its members. For the Senate is endowed, more than the House, with dramatic duties, its members represent comparatively large units, and to a greater degree than in the House, they work in the public view.

The general factors that condition the lower chamber tend to exclude and to a high degree have excluded the "talents and experience of the ablest men."[11] In addition, the House, because of its size and its representative basis, prodigally wastes the energies of its membership. This waste of energy results from complicated procedure and emphasis on maneuver, the loss of time involved in getting adjusted to the machinery of the House, the lack of opportunity for new members, the supplying of irrelevant services to constituents, the political demands peculiar to localism, the seniority system, the tendency to specialize, and the sheer dead-weight of numbers. Most members of the House can never understand more than a few of the bills on which they vote.[12]

Integration in the "numerous" assembly. In national assemblies, said Joel Barlow, "passion is lost in deliberation; and interest balances interest; till the good of the whole community combines the general will."[10]

We have seen that the political party performs very imperfectly its intermediate integrating function. It largely fails to translate the various local and group opinions, unco-ordinated and often conflicting, into terms of policy or into a comprehensible program. Thus, the task of formulating and co-ordinating policies falls almost entirely on the formal machinery of government. It becomes its task to create a cosmos of law and action out of a chaos of opinions and pressures.

No doubt many feel that the general interest is attained in Congress, as Joel Barlow thought it would be, by a balancing or adjusting of particular interests or by a kind of mediation among them. These particular interests are usually spearheaded and supported by pressures. In practice, a mass-mingling of local delegates at Washington fails to mediate rationally among pressures.[14] Some important interests and ideas are underrepresented or unrepresented by pressures,[15] while others are overrepresented and in some cases misrepresented. The result is not a blending of opinions, but a mosaic or patch-work produced by an effort to satisfy one by one each articulate and politically important group demand.[16] Policies remain unco-ordinated.

In foreign affairs review and planning should be continuous processes; and some single authority should do the integrating. This authority should have a national point of view; it should be highly qualified; it should be informed; it should have understanding and good judgment; it should function all the time; its facilities for research and study should be adequate; it should exhibit statesmanship in decision and in action; and it should be able to lead the people. The two houses of Congress do not remotely approach these requirements. Such a job cannot be done by two numerous and independent assemblies, based on provincial representation, overburdened, lacking adequate information and understanding, distracted by irrelevancies, torn by individual and factional pretensions, and without power to initiate or finally to decide.

Promptitude in the "numerous" assembly. The numerous assembly is equally unfitted for tasks that demand foresight, timing, and speed. Such a body permits little concentration of thought and discussion on the prior essentials. When it contains men capable of quick and sure judgment, it denies them opportunity for quick and unhampered decision. A numerous assembly, confronted with heavy tasks, complicated demands, and conflicting pressures, tends to move cumbrously and slowly.[17] A body as large as the House of Representatives must operate normally within a rigid framework and through an intricate set of rules, offering many and special opportunities for postponement and obstruction. The Senate, being smaller, can be freer and more flexible; but in the upper house, made up as it is, individualism flourishes and comes to full flower in that paralyzing device, the filibuster.[18]

It seems to be a universal and firmly fixed idea that legislative assemblies should be part-time undertakings. Whatever the reasons may be, it is usually difficult to keep Congress in session for more than a matter of months. It is natural that senators and representatives should want long recesses; but public problems do not wait conveniently until Congress convenes. The continuous and the unexpected are especially characteristic of foreign affairs. The congressional recess and the special session are now outdated survivals of a more leisurely age.

Despite its design, Congress does not always work slowly. Under the presidential spur, it moved fast during the early months of the New Deal. Considering the magnitude of the European Recovery Program, Congress approved it as speedily as one could reasonably expect. It is possible, however, to cite an equal number of cases where Congress has failed to act urgently on clearly urgent matters.[19]

Deliberation in committees. The committee system is supposed to make the numerous assembly workable. So far as internal deliberation is concerned, the two houses do their work largely in committees. These "little legislatures" serve several purposes. They screen the various bills introduced into Congress. They gather information on public problems with a view to the possibility of legislation. They discuss and largely decide the detailed provision of bills. They exercise control over administration. They provide informed leadership for Congress on specific bills. By investigating conditions in the country and through public hearings, they not only gather information but also contribute to the clarification of public opinion. By uncovering facts, they aid in the enforcement of the law.

To serve such purposes, any type of legislative body dealing with a variety of complex and technical questions would require subordinate committees or commissions. The committees of Congress are marked by the fact that their members are drawn from the membership of Congress. Thus, so far as public problems are concerned, the committee members are, for the most part, men of average ability and of ordinary information and experience. Yet, to function in Congress, they have to become specialists, and many do so within the limits of their committee work.

The congressional committee system is maintained, said

James Bryce, "because none better has been, or, as most people think, can be devised."[20] So long as each house retains its present size and composition, the committees are probably indispensable. In their more or less separate compartments, they do much good work, in spite of their manifest shortcomings, their repetitions and duplications, their "meanderings and futilities,"[21] and their waste of time. The occasional select committee introduces a degree of flexibility into the system, provides a special choice of members for a special task, and, perhaps most important of all, permits a disregard of the seniority rule.

Each committee is a power in its field; and the committee chairman wields power over his committee and acts as its representative. As a rule committee chairmanships are awarded by seniority. It is true that seniority means experience, which may have value; but this experience, it must be kept in mind, is only *uninterrupted experience in a committee of the House*, not accumulated experience both in the House and in large affairs outside. The conditions that make possible long tenure for a part of the House membership and that place men in chairmanships are not necessarily those that are appropriate to the recruiting of qualified men.[22] The indications of place[23] and of time are both unfavorable. The lower house, though to a lesser degree than the Senate, is under rural leadership in an urban country. A rural member may be a good legislator for an industrial nation, but the presumption is certainly against him. In an age of rapid change, Congress places and keeps in its positions of power men elected long years in the past.[24] From the standpoint of statesmanship, seniority as a custom for the selection of committee chairmanships seems quite as illogical in foreign as in domestic affairs.

The chief defense that is offered for the principle of seniority is that there is no practicable substitute for it. In an assembly as large as the House and constituted like it, this contention is probably correct.

Committees and integration. Does the committee system produce comprehension and co-ordination of policies? By specializing the work of House or Senate and by compartmentalizing its membership, the committee system, as Bryce observed "destroys the unity of the House as a legislative body" and "lessens the cohesion and harmony of legislation."[25] The system is likewise unfavorable to a general review and revision of laws and regulations.

The committees have shown a tendency to multiply. The Congressional Reorganization Act of 1946,[26] aiming at "increased efficiency in the legislative branch of the Government," reduced the number of committees from 48 to 18 in the House and from 33 to 16 in the Senate. The act defined jurisdictions and required these committees to keep records, record their votes, and report the bills on which they have acted. It was prescribed, with certain exceptions, that a member of the House shall serve on not more than one of the major committees and a member of the Senate on not more than two. Four professional staff members were provided for each standing committee.

Some of the provisions of the law represented long overdue improvements. It may be questioned, however, whether these improvements equaled in significance those made in 1921, when Congress not only reduced the number of its committees but also passed the Budget and Accounting Act. The reduction in the number of committees in 1946 as in 1921 was to a considerable extent a paper reduction, brought about by the elimination of committees that had little or nothing to do.[27] The act left the seniority rule untouched, gave it proportionately a more extensive application, and in practice aggravated its effects.[28] The act strengthened the tendency toward specialization, but did not do away with overlapping and duplication.[29] After the passage of the act, subcommittees increased in number.[30] Considerable doubt could be entertained regarding the professional qualifications and the net usefulness of the augmented committee staffs. It has been estimated that the act carried reorganization only halfway toward the goal, which had been decidedly limited in the first place, and that backsliding from the act up to May 1947 amounted to about 20 per cent.[31]

In the modern conduct of foreign relations, unity, certainty, and continuity are prime essentials. In the past, this field, so far as Congress was concerned, belonged in large measure to the Senate; and in the Senate there was a kind of centralization of leadership and power in the Foreign Relations Committee and particularly in its chairman. As foreign affairs and foreign policies now are, it is unlikely that the chairman of that committee can exercise anything like the same influence in the future. The Foreign Affairs Committee and the Appropriations Committee of the House have grown in power.

A recent use of its power by the Appropriations Committee of the House illustrates the danger that lurks in our complicated and divided system of government. On the recommendation of that committee, the House in June 1948 voted to cut down the sums available to the European Cooperation Administration by amounts variously estimated from a half billion to two billion dollars. This was done some two months after Congress by overwhelming votes in both houses had adopted the European recovery policy (the so-called Marshall plan). Senator Vandenberg declared that the practical effect of the House bill was to "repeal, by indirection, the intent and purpose of this legislation and to reverse this established American foreign policy both at home and abroad."[32] Congress soon put matters to rights, but could not completely remove the impression of instability created by the action of the House committee and of the House. Nor did Congress do anything to prevent a future repetition of the occurrence.

Besides the committees just mentioned, there are others that share in authority over foreign policy. There are the two committees on the armed forces and the Senate Committee on Appropriations. Eight other committees are also heavily involved—those dealing in the two chambers with banking and currency and with interstate and foreign commerce, the joint "watch-dog" committee for the European recovery plan, the House Committee on Ways and Means, the House Committee on Un-American Activities, and the House Rules Committee. This total of fourteen committees does not measure the actual diffusion of leadership or the possibilities of conflict, because other committees are also involved in varying degrees.

Co-ordination and acceleration. Bryce noted that the committee system prevented "the capacity of the best members from being brought to bear upon any one piece of legislation." Neither does the system provide, in itself, for the guidance by congressional leaders of the whole process and program. The party has largely failed to introduce coherence;[33] and the party caucus or conference, the floor leaders, the whips, and the steering or policy committees,[34] fail to meet adequately the need for integrated policy. Much the same can be said of the House Rules Committee[35] and the Speaker.

On a number of occasions, Congress has provided for comprehensive studies and advice, for example, when it set up the Industrial Relations Commission early in the century and the Temporary National Economic Committee during the New Deal era. In the latter case, as in some others, Congress took the over-all view, or was advised to take it, after it had legislated, instead of before.[36]

The Employment Act of 1946[37] launched an interesting experiment. After declaring that it is the "continuing policy and responsibility" of the government "to co-ordinate and utilize all its plans, functions, and resources," for the purpose of creating and maintaining desirable economic conditions, the act requires the president to transmit to Congress, early in each legislative session, an economic report. To assist the president in the preparation of this report and otherwise to keep him informed on economic matters, the act created a Council of Economic Advisers of three members. Furthermore, this legislation established a Joint Committee on the Economic Report, composed of fourteen members, seven from each house. The functions of the Joint Committee are:

(1) to make a continuing study of matters relating to the Economic Reports;

(2) to study means of co-ordinating programs in order to further the policy of this Act; and

(3) as a guide to the several committees of the Congress dealing

with legislation relating to the Economic Report, not later than May 1 of each year ... to file a report with the Senate and the House of Representatives containing its findings and recommendations with respect to each of the main recommendations made by the President in the Economic Report, and from time to time to make such other reports and recommendations to the Senate and House of Representatives as it deems advisable.

Unfortunately, the high expectations that attended the enactment of the Employment Act have not yet been fulfilled.

A co-ordinated program would fall short of full effectiveness unless followed by timed action. The various instruments of majority-party control concern themselves chiefly with priorities and tactics. In this connection, they are useful; but they succeed only partially in accelerating action on the legislative task as a whole. Much the same can be said of the speaker; and the Rules Committee frequently uses its power to obstruct rather than to expedite. The Joint Committee on the Organization of Congress, which drew up the Reorganization Act of 1946, attempted and failed to establish formal machinery for both co-ordination and acceleration, in the form of majority and minority policy committees in each house.[38]

The pressure groups supply a part of the propelling force behind congressional procedure. Pressure is now generated with high speed; and lobbyists are, on the average, abler, more experienced, and in their fields better informed than members of Congress. In most cases, however, they represent special interests or aim at single specialized objectives; they disintegrate rather than integrate; and they obstruct as well as accelerate.[39]

In 1947 the Marshall plan for aid to Europe aroused extraordinary interest in both houses of Congress, not only because of the tense international situation, but also and perhaps chiefly because of the huge expenditure involved and the bearing of the plan on conditions in the United States. Members of both houses proceeded to Europe to investigate conditions and requirements. These steps suggested a comprehensive congressional review and replanning of American economic policy toward Europe, along with a sensible effort to co-ordinate leadership and action in the House. As the House later indicated, the effort was not wholly successful.

In the making of foreign policy, Congress cannot and should not act on its own. It must rely on executive information, initiative and leadership. In recent years these have been supplemented and implemented by bipartisanship.

In domestic affairs, to correct the slowness and incoherence of congressional action, we have also come to depend largely on presidential leadership, supplemented by nonpartisanship. For the heavy and increasing burden of work that presses on Congress, relief has been sought and in a measure obtained through delegation of legislative initiation and legislative power to the executive and to administrative agencies.

PRESIDENTIAL PERFORMANCE

When we come to the presidency, what design shall we refer to, the ancient or the modern? According to the ancient or letter-of-the-constitution design, the president was co-ordinate with Congress only as an *executive* authority and as such he headed a small and simple administrative organization. He commanded an army and navy, both small and ordinarily of little importance. As a *legislative* authority, his duties were, for the most part, accessory or secondary to those of Congress. He helped the two houses with his reports and recommendations, his approval was necessary to make laws out of bills, and he could check Congress with his disapproval. Such, in brief, was the ancient design.

The modern design is different. The president, as an executive, heads the world's largest and most complex administrative organization. At a time when military power may decide the fate of this nation and of the world, he is commander-in-chief of an army, a navy, and air forces which find few precedents in our past peacetime history. The president also is expected to be the leader of his party, of the nation, and of Congress. As a legislative authority, he, more than Congress, is held responsible for results. He is expected to get the work of government done. He is expected to make up for the deficiencies of what is called traditionally the legislative branch. He is looked to for the initiative, the integration, and the drive that Congress measurably lacks.

Thus, the president is a multi-functional officer. He is at once: (1) the chief of state or ceremonial head of the nation; (2) the authority charged with the conduct of foreign relations and the making of foreign policy (subject to the advice and consent of two thirds of the Senate or the approval of both houses of Congress); (3) an initiator of domestic as well as foreign policy, a legislative leader of Congress, and possessor of the qualified veto; (4) the leader of his party; (5) the chief political leader of the nation; (6) the chief executive; (7) the directing and supervising head of the administration (sharing this position with Congress); and (8) commander-in-chief of the armed forces. In any one of these capacities, the president may exercise great power; and any one of them places on him heavy responsibilities and exacting demands.

Power and opportunity. The enormous potentialities of the presidential office were clearly seen prior to the appearance on the national stage of even the first of the modern "strong executives"; and a penetrating student declared in 1898 that, in the presidency American democracy has "revived the oldest political institution of the race, the elective kingship."[40]

The president possesses three sets of powers: (1) his constitutional powers as liberally interpreted and expanded; (2) powers delegated by legislation to him or to administrative agencies more or less under his control; and (3) extra-constitutional and extra-legal powers inherent in his position, personality, leadership, and control of patronage.[41]

Delegations of power come from three main sources: first, conditions in the modern world, second, the responsibilities of government, and, third, the limitations of legislative bodies and the particular incapacities of Congress.[42] The various and extensive delegations to the administration also indirectly increase the president's power. As a result, the implied constitutional prohibition of delegation has now lost most of its vitality and effect.[43]

The president's opportunity for leadership is also an opportunity for the acquisition and exercise of power.[44] Circumstances give opportunity to the president. Emergencies call for action, impose unity on the people and on parties, and subordinate those parts of the government which are inherently unable by themselves to achieve singleness of purpose or direction. At a time of insecurity, accumulated discontent, or pent-up pressures, when public opinion clearly demands action, a single individual, representing the maximum concentration of power and responsibility seems to offer the best hope of quick but deliberate decision with vigorous action.

The founding fathers expected that, for the most part, a single concentrated authority with equally concentrated responsibility would conduct our foreign relations. In time of peace, the Constitution, as well as usage, gives to the president, practically unchecked by Congress, an enormous power to determine our relations with other countries; and the expanded war powers of the president transfer to him in time of war an almost dictatorial authority.[45] In the day-by-day conduct of foreign relations, we have to a large extent not merely presidential leadership but actually one-man government, restrained only by the president's conscience, by public and congressional opinion, and by considerations of personal or party politics. In the making of treaties the president possesses the initiative, and he is constitutionally unchecked by the House of Representatives; but he is subject to an absolute veto by one third plus one of the Senate. The president has in some measure avoided this check and the delays incidental to it by concluding executive agreements and informal understandings.

Power and opportunity in the international field come also from the fact that the president in this field is and must be the nation's authoritative spokesman. Changes in the international situation and in America's responsibilities since the Second World War tend in certain important respects to increase the president's power and enlarge his opportunity. The postwar peace is both peace and war.[46] The national security remains in jeopardy. Foreign affairs become more complex and mysterious. The situation emphasizes the need of a single leadership and of concentrated authority. In the existing state of public opinion and of governmental organization, only the president can fill that need.

The "strong executive." We generally use the term "strong executive" with a special meaning and with particular reference to domestic affairs. When we use the term, we usually think of the relations between the executive and the legislature, and we have applied the term as commonly to governors as to presidents. In the national government, we look upon Theodore Roosevelt, Woodrow Wilson, and Franklin D. Roosevelt as the modern "strong executives." When concentration of power and of responsibility becomes the deliberate aim of a president and when he acts aggressively and successfully on that basis, we have the "strong executive."[47] Such a president marks the meeting of man, of office, and of opportunity.

The essential characteristic of this recurring phenomenon is effective leadership of people, of the party, and of Congress in the field of policy-making. The president formulates the program, if one is formulated, presents proposals and drafts of legislation to the congressional leaders, and takes responsibility for their enactment. To a large extent under modern conditions, the so-called presidential leadership, when it becomes the central force in governmental policy-making, is as much domination or manipulation as it is leadership. Up to this time, the "strong executive" has always been associated with a surge of domestic policy, with an extension of economic and social legislation. He acts as the spokesman and agent of the current "progressivism." Such an identification is natural, because the groups that press for "forward-looking" legislation lend themselves to the kind of strategy that strengthens executive leadership of the party and, through the party, of Congress.

In the conduct of foreign relations, the whole governmental organization is now involved normally and constantly in a manner and to a degree that were unknown and unanticipated in the past. Foreign and domestic problems are intermixed; and policies in one field are dependent on those in the other.

It appears improbable that in the foreseeable future the president can be strong enough in the conduct of foreign relations unless he is already strong in domestic affairs.

Capabilities of the president. The power of the presidency, as well as its position and role in government vary with its occupant. As Woodrow Wilson said of the president, "His capacity will set the limit." In no other part of the government is it so vitally necessary that the holder of the office should by his personal qualifications be fitted for it and that his energies should be brought fully to bear on his duties.

Our political processes, as adjusted to the governmental organization, make it a good deal of a gamble whether the president, and more so whether the vice-president, will be an outstandingly able man, or equipped by experience for the responsibilities that rest on the chief executive. If he becomes disabled or disqualified while in office,[48] we have no recognized and prompt way to remove him; and the constitutional and statutory provisions for the succession do not permit a free choice of the new president when a succession becomes necessary.[49]

In the getting of a qualified president, the multifunctional nature of the office is a prime obstacle. It demands at least four major and different sets of qualifications. He must be fitted, first, for the leadership of people, party, and Congress; second, for the supervision of administration; third, for the conduct of foreign relations; and, fourth, for the supreme command of the armed forces. It would be extremely difficult, under the most favorable circumstances, to find a man possessing all four sets of qualifications.

Since the Civil War, presidents have come mainly from four sources: the state governorships, Congress, the Cabinet, and the vice-presidency.[50] The state governorship has served most frequently as a training ground or stepping stone. It offers a test of leadership and of administrative ability but gives no experience in foreign affairs. Service in Congress may indicate aptitudes for leadership and may bring contact with foreign affairs, but it seems to disqualify, rather than qualify, for administration. The Cabinet and the executive branch as a whole provide administrative experience, indications of leadership, and some contact with international problems; but only twice since the Civil War has a federal administrative job led to the presidency.

Thus, we have had presidents who are not adequately qualified in any respect, such as Harding; others who are good administrators but poor leaders, such as William Howard Taft and Herbert Hoover; and another, Franklin D. Roosevelt, who was a brilliant politician and possibly a good military strategist, but a poor administrator. Theodore Roosevelt, the one chief executive since the Civil War who combined at least three sets of presidential qualifications,[51] came to the office through the vice-presidency and the accident of McKinley's death.

Nor is it possible promptly to adjust presidential qualifications to changes in conditions. During a presidential term, the country may pass from peace to war; but, unless the transition happens to coincide with a presidential election, an unlikely event, we have no opportunity to change the executive, no matter how incompetent he may be. Though his shortcomings may be known, he can usually win a renomination; and his re-election follows unless the voters reject his party along with him. Thus our system makes inadequate provision, not only for the selection of superior men, but also for the removal of those who demonstrate their inferiority.

Under present-day demands no president can bring his energies fully to bear on his duties. With all the necessary delegation and advice, he would have enough to do in any one capacity—as a legislative leader, as popular and party leader, as chief of administration, as conductor of foreign relations, or, in time of war, as commander of the armed forces. Under existing conditions, when he gives proper attention to one function, he is almost certain to neglect some of the others. All place upon him an unbearable burden.

Presidential policy-making. Can the president efficiently make policies and prepare a sound, comprehensive legislative program?

The president's skill must consist chiefly in the picking of advisers and in the weighing of the advice that they give him. His advisers may be formal or informal, publicly known or publicly unknown, responsible or irresponsible, inside or outside of government. A large role is played by pressure groups. Consequently, the president in recent years has often appeared, not so much to control or use his assistants, as to act as chairman of a heterogeneous body, not unlike Congress itself. The result of unco-ordinated presidential policy making, along with presidential political strategy, is that executive proposals do not usually form a coherent scheduled program or proceed from a sound review of legislation already enacted. They constitute, rather, a series or catalogue of piecemeal recommendations. At the worst—and the worst is likely to appear in a presidential election year— the president's proposals may be simply devices to embarrass the opposition and catch votes.[52]

Presidents usually take more or less direct charge of foreign relations; more rather than less in critical matters and in troubled times. The decisions then are too critical to be delegated; but in the present-day world practically all decisions are critical. So also, unluckily, are decisions in other fields; and it is unsafe for a president to give attention to one function by neglecting other functions.[53] It is indispensable that the president have an able Secretary of State; but because foreign policy depends on military strategy, the armed services have become a coequal, if not a primary, force in the shaping of foreign policy. Moreover, because of the need of economic implementation, the various economic agencies of the government also have important parts to play. Thus, the president's co-ordinating function has taken on a new and decisive importance and on substantial matters he cannot delegate that function, as government is now organized. Certainly he cannot long or safely neglect domestic questions; and their reconciliation with foreign problems presents the supreme test of the president's ability to unify government, integrate policy, and act in time. In the foreign field, as in the domestic, the chief executive has seemed to act not as a unifying leader, but as chairman of a heterogeneous assembly representing special interests and contradictory views.

As party leader, moreover, the president, along with the opposition leaders in Congress, is subject to the demands of party strategy. In general, the presidency has tended to become a center of manipulation, engaged in concretely pleasing the dominant groups and in managing, rather than instructing, public opinion. The practice of pampering the people rather than appealing to their fortitude leads the government to take its more distasteful decisions only when situations become critical enough to be automatically convincing. Bipartisanship is neither in principle nor in practice adequate for overcoming the demands of party strategy. How those demands operate on an overburdened and inept executive is illustrated by President Truman's handling of the Palestine problem.[54]

Presidential policy-making has from time to time made use of specially appointed temporary commissions; and these illustrate the kind of instrumentalities for fact-finding and investigation which, if our legislative department were differently constituted, might well take the place in most instances of the congressional committees.[55]

Furthermore, in recent years two significant attempts have been made to provide for permanent qualified counsel in broad fields. The first was the National Resources Planning Board, set up under another name in 1934 and abolished in 1943. The second is the Council of Economic Advisers, established in 1946. The first experiment, restricted for the most part to physical matters, proved disappointing.

The latest effort, though limited in scope to economic conditions, appears more soundly conceived. Placing the Council in the Executive Office of the president, the Employment Act of 1946 recognized the part that the chief executive should play in the formulation and co-ordination of policy. Some evidence appeared in 1947 and 1948 that the Council might improve at times the quality of executive leadership and might, through the president, exercise beneficial influence over congressional action. One may question, however, whether the Council is likely to maintain in the long run any considerable usefulness. Its connection with the chief executive is a weakness and a danger as well as an opportunity. There are also economists of established reputation outside the government, in industry, in labor organizations, and in the universities and research institutions. If and when the Council faces disagreements and criticisms, will it become anything more than just another group of advisers, to be heard or ignored, as political expediency may suggest or as the pressure of administrative agencies and interest groups may dictate?

Shortcomings of the "strong executive." What the "strong executive" has done thus far is to capitalize on the characteristics of his office, good and bad, and to exploit its possibilities to the full, especially its personal possibilities. He extraordinarily personalizes an already highly personal position.

As an accelerator of the legislative machine, he gets quantitative results; and it may be true that in our governmental organization only such a president can bring about any close approach to operating unity. But a result of the temporary acceleration is to produce a mass of laws which may be hastily enacted and ill-digested, followed by a period in which corrections and administration require special emphasis. Thus, we have in legislation an alternation of action and inaction, or, as one writer puts it, of "coma and convulsion."[56]

If the president is to act effectively as an accelerator, he must possess exceptional personal aptitudes for the management of men and of public opinion. Because of the force of the personal factor, a change of presidents may bring about a radical change in the nature of government.[57] To the large extent that the occupant of the office determines its character, the presidency is erratic and unpredictable; and the "strong executive" is even more so.

Theodore Roosevelt, Woodrow Wilson, and Franklin D. Roosevelt were by no means the same sort of "strong executive." The first Roosevelt, to the extent that he succeeded as a legislative leader, worked mainly through the Speaker and the senatorial bosses, while the congressional leaders, through whom Wilson worked, used the caucus to enforce unity. Franklin D. Roosevelt, on the other hand, figured as a "strong executive" mainly because of his personality, his exploitation of "emergencies," of public confusion and of class feeling, the increasing patronage at his disposal, and the spending and other policies which distributed material benefits to special groups.

In whatever manner he may operate, the "strong executive" cannot be a continuous force in government.[58] He cannot function when government is divided between the two parties. Since 1900, we have had 39 years of peace; and during those years we have had a "strong executive," at the most, only 18 years.[59]

But even during his term or terms this kind of president does not function continuously. No president has yet appeared capable of the versatility and the sustained extraordinary effort required to eliminate the antagonisms and inertia that our governmental organization is designed to foster. Experience seems to demonstrate that any executive who desires to put through a legislative program must act with all his resources at the very beginning of his first term.[60] Thereafter, his hold on the legislature becomes precarious.[61]

The "strong executive" is no more a solution of our problem in foreign affairs than he is in the domestic sphere. Presidential leadership stands a chance of working effectively only when the president is an exceptional personality and a strong popular and party leader, when he holds the confidence of the country and the control of his party, when his party has a majority in both houses of Congress, when he maintains close contact with the congressional leaders, and when he keeps them constantly and fully informed. It is possible to meet all of these requirements occasionally, but not continuously.[62]

Woodrow Wilson conjectured in 1900 that the "new leadership of the Executive" might bring about "an integration which [would] substitute statesmanship for government by mass meeting."[63] Theodore Roosevelt's preachments, which in his time sounded platitudinous, were for the most part simply reassertions of the national and general interest along with denunciations of demagoguery, paternalism, and class appeals. In many respects, Wilson's leadership followed a similar pattern. Franklin D. Roosevelt's did not; and it would have taken in 1933 an extraordinary mental grasp, a deeply ingrained intellectual honesty, and an exceptionally strong will to resist the demands of special groups, the disposition to deal with subdivisions of policy, and the temptations offered by demagogic political strategy.

The "strong executive" does not necessarily mean strong government. In domestic affairs this means of expediting policy actually weakens government, because the strategy on which presidential leadership rests tends to augment the political power of special groups and to encourage direct political action, as well as private defiance of public authority. In foreign affairs, the personalizing tendency operated in different ways on Woodrow Wilson and Franklin D. Roosevelt. Woodrow Wilson solved his problem, up to a point, in his own mind and in the Versailles Conference, but failed to impose his plan on the Senate and the American people. He thought personally too much and institutionally too little. Roosevelt's mistake had the same basic source but took a different form. He relied greatly on his personal relations with Marshal Stalin; and the result was a diplomatic procedure which weakened and delayed action, produced confusion and vacillation, and led to later embarrassments and dangers.

We have previously referred to the conception, derived from an interpretation of American history, that the hour always brings forth the man, that in every great crisis we have a great president.[64] If we have been thus favored in the past, a common-sense view of the matter gives no assurance for the future that we shall not have at any given time a weak president when we need a strong one or a mediocre one when we need the best. As a matter of fact, the dates 1789, 1861, 1914, 1933, and 1939 or 1941, when we are supposed to have been blessed with great presidents, do not mark the inception of crises. Rather each of these dates stands for a particular and late phase of a critical situation. If it were true that in some inscrutable way the great man would always appear at the decisive stage, would it not be equally or even more necessary that we should have presidents (to say nothing of senators and representatives) great enough, at the origin of a crisis, to recognize it and, if humanly possible, to check it? At this moment, we are living in a crisis, the course of which will apparently be measured in decades rather than years; and, during such an ordeal, we can scarcely afford to rely on an ultimate miracle.

The veto power. The president's power to approve or disapprove bills seems quite as likely to exemplify and accentuate our legislative shortcomings as to overcome them. Undoubtedly, the veto power has at times prevented bad legislation, not merely through the actual disapproval of bills, but also because the possibility of a veto puts Congress under a measure of restraint, which is sometimes desirable. On the other hand, the purpose of a veto is not always constructive. It may reflect group pressure on the president or merely political maneuvering. As a means of inducing co-operation between president and Congress, it is as likely to work one way as another, and, in any case, it is unimportant compared with the other instruments that presidential leadership has at its disposal. The veto is predicated on an absence of party responsibility and party government and in practice the overriding of a veto by Congress depends on a lack of solidarity in one or both parties in Congress. The veto is a crude blocking or delaying weapon, ill-suited to the needs of strong government and inconsistent with the idea of a clarifying governmental leadership of the people.

Moreover, the veto power serves in one connection to render executive accretions of delegated power practically exempt from congressional revision or repeal. In those cases where Congress does not set a time limit on the life of a law or does not reserve to itself the right to recall its own delegations, the president can veto an amending or repealing act. In that event, Congress can withdraw the delegated power only by a two-thirds vote in both houses. To avoid this situation, the tendency appears to be to increase the number of laws with time limits.

Such a practice makes the legislative task more difficult, and in some instances, puts the president in a position where he cannot exercise his veto power.[65]

The logic of the veto rests on the general peculiarities of our governmental organization and particularly on the basis and composition of Congress. Were we to substitute a single and truly responsible government for our present collection of governments, the executive veto would become as unnecessary as it would be unthinkable.

USE AND CONTROL OF THE ADMINISTRATION

The executive branch is not the concentrated decisive authority that the fathers intended it to be. It consists of the president himself—multi-functioned, overburdened, politically diverted and sometimes inept—his office and his staffs, and a vast, loose complex of departments and agencies. This complex and the personnel that belongs to it we call the *administration*.

President and Congress look to the administration for the preparation of legislation and policies and for judgments on the results of laws and adopted policies. Moreover, president and Congress delegate sublegislative and policy-deciding powers to the administration. For these and other reasons, it has become, in large part and in general effect, a fifth branch of government. It has taken on a separateness similar to that which belongs constitutionally to the president, the Senate, the House of Representatives, and the Supreme Court.

We are here concerned with administration, not as an attachment to government or a mere tool of government, but as a part of government—a part of the general mechanism—which does the same sort of over-all job that president and Congress are engaged in doing and which shares in the task of president and Congress. From this point of view, does the administration make a good enough showing when we apply to it the criteria of efficiency that we have just applied to Congress and the president?

We have seen, besides, that responsibility as a principle of democracy requires that the elected authorities of government should supervise and control the administration. Are supervision and control properly designed?

Power, independence, and disunity. Administrative power is not a single power. Usually it is scattered and more or less unobserved; but it is genuine governmental power; it is already immense; it is constantly growing; and it tends to become independent because it is not properly joined with responsibility.

Administration has grown to such size that it practically defies outside understanding. It can largely act as its own interpreter and, in many instances, must be taken on its own terms. The administrators, with information and experience at their command, have gathered intellectual authority and with it influence. To a considerable extent, the initiative in legislation has passed to the administration, so that in many cases it practically determines the laws that it is called upon to enforce. It draws support and strength from regions, groups, and private organizations whose interests the agencies serve or whose objectives they share. Inherent in bureaucracy is a state of mind that resists curtailments of function and favors aggrandizement.[66]

Bureaucracy appears on the one hand to carry a threat of encroachment and usurpation and on the other to offer the essentials of effective government in the modern world. Bureaucracy, however, has its own internal divisions and subdivisions, along with checks and balances, more various and intricate than any conceived by the framers of the Constitution. Separate agencies have tended not only to multiply, but also to develop and operate within closed compartments.

The setup of Congress, as we have seen, strongly favors a specialized and compartmentalized handling of policy and puts a premium, especially, on local interests and group objectives. It is natural, therefore, that the administration, since laws create it, should to a large extent follow the group pattern; and the affiliation of various agencies with groups is a familiar fact.[67] Congress, moreover, often acts without an understanding of the relationship of specific enactments to one another or to broad and long-run principles. Because the relationship is not apparent, it is natural and in some cases probably desirable to establish a separate agency for a seemingly new purpose; but, after the agency has been thus set up, its powers of resistance and the inability of Congress to review its actions combine to perpetuate the situation. Besides, administrators usually desire to be independent; and congressional jealousy of the president sometimes takes advantage of the idea that unified administration strengthens the executive.[68] Finally, a class of agencies, first illustrated by the Interstate Commerce Commission, are viewed as "arms" of the legislature and, in theory and partially in fact, have been made specially exempt from presidential control.

As Congress relies more and more on the administrative agencies for the appraisal and initiation of policies, it becomes more and more subject to particularistic influences;[69] and the president in his use of the administration for policy-making becomes subject to the same influences. On occasion, interagency conflict comes into the open; and not infrequently different administrators have made contradictory statements of policy, thus weakening governmental leadership and adding to the confusion of an already confused public. The introduction and extension of the merit system and of professionalization made epochal contributions to operational efficiency, but did not solve the problem of co-ordination. It is true that administration has developed numerous co-ordinating procedures; but these operate most successfully on the lower levels, where no system of superior direction can, under ordinary circumstances, make itself felt.[70]

When we look at foreign-affairs administration, we see that the situation tends to become similar. Until the First World War the small size and single-mindedness of the State Department made its internal co-ordination comparatively easy. At the same time, it enjoyed, in its relations with other government departments, an unquestioned precedence, along with great prestige and authority. Between the two wars, the Department did not and could not keep to itself the immediate handling of foreign economic relations; but it retained most of its traditional prestige and authority, as well as its power to integrate, co-ordinate and supervise. During the Second World War and at its end, the Department's problem became vastly more difficult, because of the greatly increased importance of economic and other activities that could not be fitted into the geographic-political offices, or capably handled by them. It has been necessary, therefore, to create another set of offices in the Department for the handling of world-wide as distinguished from areal problems.

As a result of departmental expansion and increased specialization, the supervisory and co-ordinating function of the secretary of state within his department has become as important as his own thinking function in connection with external problems. Administration develops a bureaucratic character and gives to its officials the greatest power and security when its policies and activities are compartmentalized according to classes and fields of expertness. In foreign relations, however, we have complex, fluid, and vague situations which must be treated as wholes with comprehensive and balanced judgment, with imagination, and with foresight. In the policy-making phase of foreign relations, what we need, down to the lowest officials, is experienced, disciplined, and exceedingly flexible statesmanship, rather than narrow expertness. For the task of execution, we need technical expertness, capable of prompt, flexible, and timed action. These needs make over-all integration a permanent necessity, if we are to avoid the inconsistencies and vacillation that come from failure to reconcile specialties and viewpoints.

With reference to public leadership and responsibility to the public, the Department of State labors under peculiar handicaps. Its functions have set it apart from the American public; for it has little operating administrative contact with the people; it gives them few direct and tangible services. Moreover, the feeling of caste, of power, and permanence, along with sojourns abroad, have tended to isolate professional diplomats from American public opinion.

Consequently, one of the chief and most difficult problems

in the modern conduct of foreign relations is how to organize and co-ordinate the concerned agencies. While the Department remains the central and major agency for the conduct of foreign relations, it is not so easy now for it alone to decide foreign policy or for the secretary of state to act alone as adviser to the president on foreign relations. Power over the determination, implementation, and execution of foreign policy belongs also and often decisively to the military services.[71] Important parts are also played by the Treasury Department, the Department of Commerce, the Department of the Interior, the Department of Agriculture, the Maritime Commission, the Tariff Commission, the Export-Import Bank, and others. When Congress approved the European recovery program, it established a new and separate Economic Co-operation Administration to carry out the program.

Unity in the government is a foundation for co-ordination and a result of it, as well as an essential means of implementing and executing foreign policy. Yet in recent years we have seen evidence of both disunity and actual conflict.[72] The situation obviously places on the president (or on Congress) increasingly heavy demands for procedural co-ordination, as well as for substantive decisions. The conditions that make co-ordination and unity difficult to attain account in part for lack of foresight, promptitude, courage, and strength. It is unlikely that administration can be much reduced in size or greatly simplified, or that co-ordinating committees, interdepartmental or interbureau, can provide the necessary leadership and direction. So we must examine the pattern of supervision at the top.

Presidential supervision. The president has a supervisory and directing task incomparably greater and more difficult than that of any industrial executive. But, as previously pointed out, we have no means to put and keep the job in the hands of a qualified administrator.

Administration on so vast a scale calls for a few executive authorities below the president. The Cabinet now represents only a part of the administrative field. If we select any major governmental problem we find that no one Cabinet officer nor any combination of Cabinet officers directs or probably should direct all of the agencies concerned with that problem. The Cabinet "has become an administrative anachronism."[73] The establishment of the Executive Office of the President, the improvement of his staff agencies, and the enlargement of his secretariat—all accomplished during recent years—represent important and indispensable reforms. Nevertheless, even the staff agencies suffer from the division of control between president and Congress.[74]

Administrative proposals for legislation should be kept consistent with one another and with the broader objectives of presidential leadership.[75] Nominally, the Bureau of the Budget is the president's central co-ordinating instrument; but with respect to the co-ordination of legislative proposals, its work leaves much to be desired. For one thing, the heads of agencies maintain direct contacts with the committees of Congress; and Congress insists on the maintenance of these contacts. At the same time, the agency head, if his proposal is confidential or out of the ordinary, may clear it directly with the president. In either case, the Bureau of the Budget is by-passed and, in some cases, the president, too.[76] It is evident also that the Bureau cannot effectively co-ordinate unless or until the president has formulated his policy-program. In any event, staff agencies cannot do the work of administrative vice-presidents.

In the conduct of foreign relations, it appears that we cannot depend upon the president for continuous and effective co-ordination of policy or unification of government and of popular leadership. The secretary of state can no longer act in the field of foreign affairs as an assistant president or administrative vice-president. The National Security Act of 1947, rather than merging the military organizations into one department, really set up an assistant president between these organizations and the president to aid the latter in the exercise of his duties as commander-in-chief. The principle of this act might well be applied to the whole field of international, including military affairs. An assistant president or vice-president for foreign relations would take over from the Department of State the function of integrating policy which that Department can no longer appropriately or authoritatively perform. Such a high officer would simplify the tasks and reduce the burdens of both the president and the secretary of state. But it would be difficult if not impossible in the existing governmental organization to bring about such a radical reformation at the top, or, if it were brought about, to make it work successfully.

Congressional supervision. In practice, Congress exercises a considerable degree of control over administrative agencies.[77] The Constitution provides for congressional supervision. In any kind of political organization, the supreme policy-making authority should embody the headship of government; and, in this position, it should impose accountability on its agents. It is not illogical, therefore, under our legislative-executive organization, that both Congress and the president should possess and exercise supervision and control over the administration. But in this respect our legislative-executive organization contradicts administrative science, all experience outside of government, and common sense. Division of authority not only divides and therefore confuses the responsibility of government to the people, but it is also inconsistent with accepted principles of administrative direction. No man can serve two masters. In Congress, moreover, control is again divided between the two houses; and congressional control in each house is subdivided among the committees and still further among the individual members. Because of this division, which has an extra added feature in the field of foreign affairs,[78] it has been said that the State Department carries on two sets of foreign relations: with foreign governments and with the Senate. And in the international field Congress is no more united than in the domestic.[79]

Congress ordinarily exercises its control through legislation, appropriations, senatorial confirmation of presidential appointments, formal investigations, questioning in committee hearings, and conferences with administrative officers.[80] With regard to administrative expenditures, the General Accounting Office serves as a congressional instrument of control. The Foreign Assistance Act of 1948 created a joint "watch-dog" committee, composed of three members of the Senate Foreign Relations Committee, three from the House Foreign Affairs Committee, and two from each of the Appropriations Committees, to receive reports from the administrator of the European Recovery Program, to observe the progress of the work, and to study the subject of additional legislation. Assuming that Congress is to share supervision, this joint committee may be helpful; but it does not introduce unity and responsibility into the government's supervision of foreign-affairs administration. On the contrary, it confirms and would apparently accentuate the division between president and Congress.

The methods and instrumentalities used by Congress may at times be extremely useful, but on the whole and in the long run, they are unsatisfactory because neither house of Congress, as now established, is qualified for efficient, unified, and continuous administrative supervision.[81] Plural bodies, much smaller and better selected, are universally considered unfit for administrative control. Even if the administrative agencies were solely responsible to Congress, control would still be inefficient, probably more so;[82] and no amount of staffing can make the committees effective instruments of supervision.[83]

Incidental effects and perversions of congressional control have appeared; and these are, it would seem, either unnecessarily wasteful or positively damaging. The time of busy administrators is wasted by investigations and hearings. Delays occur in the confirmation of appointments. Senatorial confirmation, as influenced by "senatorial courtesy," as well as the distribution of patronage generally among senators and representatives, places the appointment of administrators, in many cases, in the hands of individual members of Congress.[84] The members, especially when they are chairmen of committees, interfere in too many cases with the details of administrative operations.[85] This power of interference tends on the one hand to increase the errand-boy work of congressmen and on the other forces the administrators in self-defense to buttress their own positions by enlisting the support of the public or of special groups.

Reorganization. We have now a fairly long history of efforts to reorganize federal administration.[86] The latest attempt is represented by the Brown-Lodge Act, passed in 1947, establishing a commission headed by Ex-President Hoover to study and report on the subject. Experience has shown in the first place that reorganization is a continuing task. In the second place, legislative-executive relationships make a full accomplishment of the task extremely difficult, if not absolutely impossible. Congress has admitted its own inability to perform the task independently; but it is reluctant to delegate the work unconditionally to the president. A sound reason for this reluctance is found in the fact that administration cannot be reorganized without reference to policy and without an effect upon it. There are other reasons, less sound, why Congress resists substantial administrative changes.[87] But the president is also hampered because the pattern of administration follows to a large extent either the pattern of legislation or that of political strategy.

EFFICIENCY OF CHECKS AND BALANCES

Our legislative-executive organization consists of four authorities or groups of authorities: the president, the Senate, the House of Representatives, and the administration. The administration of course is not constitutionally or legally an independent entity. Its power is exercised by its miscellaneous parts; but also to an extent the Senate and the House similarly exercise their power. The result is looseness, disunity, and capacity for self-paralysis.

In foreign affairs. In the conduct of foreign relations, the most conspicuous check is found in the power of a minority of the Senate to disapprove a treaty negotiated by the president. The president has sought to evade this check, and one can argue that it did not prevent the ratification of the United Nations Charter. But it probably kept us out of the League of Nations. From the standpoint of democracy, nothing can be said for this check. From the standpoint of efficiency, it works against unity and certainty in the conduct of foreign relations.

In general, the tendency has been for the Senate to assert

its prerogatives;[8c] and a similar tendency has now appeared in
the House. In both branches, the tendency becomes stronger
as domestic policy blends with foreign policy and as Congress,
in the international sphere, feels more and more the pressure
of local and special interests. For either house to abdicate in
this sphere would now mean a fairly complete surrender of its
position in government. So long as the present governmental
system exists, no such general abdication is probable, if it were
desirable.

The fact that either house can act or obstruct in an unpredictable manner produces uncertainty, confusion and delay, not
only in congressional action but also in executive leadership.
When changes in the international situation require modifications of policy or new policies, the possibility of opposition in
Congress acts as a restraint on presidential initiative; and,
though public opinion may seem to be with him, he must
guard against the possibility of a competing public or party
leadership in Congress, such as that which worked the undoing
of Woodrow Wilson. Presidential fear of public opinion and of
Congress, along with party strategy and the limitations of the
presidential office, produces a tendency to deal with "bits and
pieces" rather than with the whole, to improvise action for meeting specific crises as they arise, to make small commitments, and
to edge into policies without publicly discussing, and perhaps
even without seeing, their general implications and consequences.

Undoubtedly, a good deal of value attaches to the procedure
of consultation between the president and secretary of state on
the one hand and congressional leaders on the other. But any
such consultation is one between independent authorities, each
having a different electoral responsibility; and the forces that
the check-and-balance system generates necessarily intrude
into executive-legislative conferences. When the president is not
in a dominant position, and when resort is had to legislative-
executive co-operation or, in the event of divided government,
to bipartisanship, the tendency is for power and leadership to

grow in Congress, with the result that we have in effect more than one foreign office and more than one spokesman for the nation.

The possibilities of delay as well as of publicly advertised disunity in our system are aggravated by the size and setup of the two houses and by the characteristics of the presidency and the administration. The fault lies, not with any one of our governmental authorities, but with each of them and with all of them. For we have a government that is itself structurally disunited. In the field of foreign affairs, we sometimes have one governmental authority, sometimes two, and sometimes three; or, to put it in another way, we have for some activities a three-fold check, for some a double check, and for some no check at all. Institutionally divided, the government is also, for about one fourth of the time, divided with respect to party control and liable to the compromises that such a situation compels, as well as to the possibility of deadlock.

Compromise. Our governmental organization produces an excess of compromise. It makes bargaining a primary procedure and a political habit. The causes, it would seem, lie in the separation of authorities and in their check on one another, in our two numerous assemblies, and in the sectional and localistic basis of representation.[89] In many cases too it is the minority, rather than the majority that actually rules.[90] The organization creates many centers of obstruction, large and small, that need to be placated before action can be taken.[91] When leaderships are scattered, they are forced to bargain among themselves.

Compromise is said to be "the way of democracy." It is, in a sense and to an extent. When it proceeds from a realization that no one person or group can hold a monopoly of the truth, that the ultimate good is seldom fully known, and that, in any case, an irreconcilable conflict within the state is undesirable, compromise stabilizes democracy and contributes to the continuity of policy. On many questions, middle-of-the-road action may be not merely the surest and safest, but the only way to avoid a deadlock. The compromising of means and of details may make possible the accomplishment of a great constructive undertaking. Such were the famous compromises of the Constitution.

On the other hand, compromise may mean the surrender of a vital principle. It may be worse than defeat and less practicable than no action at all. A compromising habit on the part of legislators and negotiators invites resistance and pressures, discourages discussion, and, in the end, makes reasonable adjustments more difficult, if not impossible. Compromise, too, may result from ignorance and incapacity. It may indicate weak, irresponsible, or ineffective leadership. It may or may not be useful in the presence of an irrepressible conflict.[92]

Compromise, as we find it in our government, artificially induced, exaggerated, and often misapplied, is one of the symptoms of governmental disorder. It may overcome obstruction and get action, but at the price of inconsistencies in policy, disregard of relationships, and increased need for supplemental or corrective legislation. Since international negotiations also involve compromise, our organization presents the danger of exhausting all possibilities of compromise within the government, thus creating a situation in which effective negotiation or other flexible action may become difficult, if not impossible.

Unifying efforts. Most of those who still defend checks and balances or accept the system as unchangeable hope nevertheless for the introduction of unifying practices, in order to make the system act more or less contrary to its own character. Our constitutional history reveals six noteworthy efforts to unify government. The first two of these—control by public opinion and the operation of the party system—sprang from the democratizing urge; but both developments were, or should have been, unifying in effect and thus contributory to efficiency. In the end, met by the resistance of an intricately arranged and thoroughly fortified system, neither development accomplished its purpose.

A third development occurred in connection with the war powers of the president. In time of war, public opinion and Congress largely abdicate their normal governing functions and the president becomes, in an extraordinary and more or less undefined measure, a one-man government. This phenomenon is often pointed to as a praise-worthy example of flexibility and adaptability. The truth seems to be that, in time of war and increasingly also in lesser emergencies, we confess the unworkability of checks and balances. In times that we call "normal," we can after a fashion tolerate governmental inefficiency and excuse it in ways that have become habitual; but, when national security is threatened, we demand a kind of government that can lead the nation and act with total comprehension, with vigor, and with speed. In the present state of the world, however, there is no longer any clear distinction between war and peace, between the abnormal and the normal. Consequently, an admission that checks and balances are unworkable at one time amounts to a substantial admission that they are unworkable at all times.

Fourthly, the "strong executive" is held to be the answer in peace as well as in war; but as we have seen, this kind of executive is the exception rather than the rule and is insufficient even as an exceptional development. The cult of the "strong executive" offers another confession of the weaknesses of checks and balances.

The fifth unifying effort is a simple and natural one. When, as in 1947, we find ourselves with divided government, we fall back as a last resort on "co-operation." From Washington's inauguration to the present time, Americans have always recognized that president and Congress should work together so far as possible; and, during the whole of our constitutional history, the governmental organization has shown varying degrees and kinds of co-operation. But the need and desire have not succeeded in eliminating the separateness and the antagonisms that the governmental system provides for. An effort to cut doors in partitions and install speaking-tubes says more eloquently than words that a house divided against itself is not a good thing.

The sixth experiment in unification is sound so far as it goes. It is illustrated by joint legislative-executive commissions to conduct research and investigations and to make recommendations simultaneously to president, Senate, and House. The aim is to unify on the level where policy is initiated. Moreover, through developments other than the joint commission, the tendency has been toward unification on this level. Nevertheless, the congressional committees, as well as the two houses, are jealous of their functions; and recently, Congress has shown a disposition to set up research staffs of its own.[93] In any event, no means of centralizing governmental research could fully compensate for the general diffuseness that would hamper subsequent steps in the making of policy.

NOTES

CHAPTER II

[1] *Records of the Federal Convention of 1787*, Max Farrand, ed., Vol. 3 (1911), pp. 301-02; Henry Jones Ford, *Rise and Growth of American Politics* (1898), p. 72; John A. Hawgood, *Modern Constitutions Since 1787* (1939), p. 18.

[2] "Pierce Butler to Weedon Butler, May 5, 1788," in *Records of the Federal Convention of 1787*, Farrand, ed., Vol. 3, pp. 301-02.

[3] Benjamin F. Wright, "The Origins of the Separation of Powers in America," *Economica*, Vol. 13 (May 1933), pp. 168-85.

[4] *The Federalist* (Sesqui. Ed.), pp. 366, 376, 410.

[5] "Everyone knows that a great proportion of the errors committed by the State legislatures proceeds from the disposition of the members to sacrifice the comprehensive and permanent interest of the State, to the particular and separate views of the counties or districts in which they reside." The same, p. 307.

[6] *Records of the Federal Convention of 1787*, Farrand, ed., Vol. 2, p. 52.

[7] "Throughout the eighteenth century, party was regarded as a gangrene, a cancer, which patriotic statesmen should combine to eradicate." Ford, *Rise and Growth of American Politics*, p. 20.

[8] "By a faction, I understand a number of citizens, whether amounting to a majority or minority of the whole, who are united and actuated by some common impulse of passion, or of interest, adverse to the right of other citizens, or to the permanent and aggregate interests of the community." Madison in *The Federalist* (Sesqui. Ed.), pp. 54-55.

[9] Charles A. Beard, *The Republic* (1943), pp. 21-26.

[10] *The Federalist* (Sesqui. Ed.), pp. 5-6.

[11] The same, p. 27.

[12] For discussions of the doctrine of separation of powers, see Malcolm P. Sharp, "The Classical American Doctrine of the Separation of Powers," *University of Chicago Law Review*, Vol. 2 (April 1935), pp. 385-436; Wright, *Economica*, pp. 169-85; Thomas K. Finletter, *Can Representative Government Do the Job?* (1945).

[13] "The accumulation of all powers, legislative, executive, and judiciary, in the same hands, whether of one, a few, or many, and whether hereditary, self-appointed, or elective, may justly be pronounced the very definition of tyranny." *The Federalist* (Sesqui. Ed.), p. 313.

[14] The same, p. 337.

[15] "One great object of the Executive is to controul the Legislature. The Legislature will continually seek to aggrandize. . . ." Governeur Morris in Constitutional Convention, *Records of the Federal Convention of 1787*, Vol. 2, p. 52.

[16] *Records of the Federal Convention of 1787*, Vol. 1, p. 431; Vol. 3, p. 400; *The Federalist* (Sesqui Ed.), p. 478; Thomas Reed Powell, "From Philadelphia to Philadelphia," *American Political Science Review*, Vol. 32 (February 1938), p. 7; Beard, *The Republic*, p. 285; James Bryce, *American Commonwealth*, Vol. 2 (1910), p. 271.

[17] *The Federalist* (Sesqui. Ed.), pp. 403-09.

[18] The same. *Records of the Federal Convention of 1787*, Vol. 1, p. 428; Vol. 3, p. 538; Sharp, *University of Chicago Law Review*, pp. 412-13.

[19] *The Federalist* (Sesqui. Ed.), p. 92; No. 58, pp. 381-82.

[20] *Records of the Federal Convention of 1787*, Vol. 1, p. 144.

[21] *The Federalist* (Sesqui. Ed.), p. 459.

[22] The same, p. 92.

[23] "Safety from external danger is the most powerful director of national conduct. Even the ardent love of liberty will after a time give way to its dictates." Hamilton in *The Federalist* (Sesqui. Ed.), p. 42.

[24] *The Federalist* (Sesqui. Ed.), p. 54.

[25] The same, p. 59.

[26] Art. 1, sec. 8.

[27] Art. 2, sec. 2.

[28] *The Federalist* (Sesqui. Ed.), pp. 312-15; Sharp, *University of Chicago Law Review*, p. 407.

[29] *The Federalist* (Sesqui. Ed.), p. 321.

[30] The Constitution provides for a joint sitting or joint action only for the trial of impeachment cases and for the counting of the electoral votes for president.

[31] Art. 2, sec. 1.

[32] Art. 1, sec. 6.

[33] Art. 1, secs. 2, 3,; Art. 2, sec. 4; Art. 3, sec. 2.

[34] George Washington, Message to House of Representatives, Mar. 30, 1796; *Records of the Federal Convention of 1787*, Vol. 3, p. 371.

[35] Art. 5.

[36] *The Federalist* (Sesqui. Ed.), p. 488.

[37] Art. 2, sec. 2.

[38] Art. 1, sec. 3.

[39] "If these observations be just, our government ought to secure the permanent interests of the country against innovation. Landholders ought to have a share in the government, to support these invaluable interests and to balance and check the other. They ought to be so constituted as to protect the minority of the opulent against the majority. The senate, therefore, ought to be this body; and to answer these purposes, they ought to have permanence and stability." Madison, in *Records of the Federal Convention of 1787*, Vol. 1, p. 431.

[40] To become a law, a bill must be passed by a majority of both houses and signed by the president. If, within ten days after receiving a bill, he returns it with his objections, it can then become a law only when passed by a two-thirds vote of each house. If he does not sign or return a bill within ten days, it becomes a law anyway, unless Congress shall have adjourned, in which event it does not become a law, being killed by what is called the "pocket veto." Art. 1, sec. 7.

[41] "[Those] who can properly estimate the mischief of that inconstancy and mutability in the laws, which form the greatest blemish in the character and genius of our governments . . . will consider every institution calculated to restrain the excess of law-making, and to keep things in the same state in which they happen to be at any given period, as much more likely to do good than harm. . . ." *The Federalist* (Sesqui. Ed.), p. 478.

[42] "We should either take the British Constitution altogether or make one for ourselves. The Executive there has dissolved two Houses as the only cure for such disputes. Will our Executive be able to apply such a remedy?" Gov-

erneur Morris in Constitutional Convention, *Records of the Federal Convention of 1787*, Vol. 1, p. 545.

[43] Art. 2, sec. 3.

[44] Edward S. Corwin, *The President: Office and Powers* (1940), p. 310. "[The] President is to act for the people, not for the *States*." Madison, in Constitutional Convention, *Records of the Federal Convention of 1787*, Vol. 2, p. 403.

[45] "The Legislature will continually seek to aggrandize. . . . It is necessary then that the Executive Magistrate should be the guardian of the people, even of the lower classes, against Legislative tyranny. . . . The Executive therefore ought to be so constituted as to be the great protector of the mass of the people. . . ." Governeur Morris in *Constitutional Convention*, the same, p. 52.

[46] *The Federalist* (Sesqui. Ed.), pp. 441-45. Hamilton argued that this method of election united "in an eminent degree all the advantages the union of which was to be wished for"; and he maintained that the process of election afforded a "moral certainty, that the office of President will never fall to the lot of any man who is not in an eminent degree endowed with the requisite qualifications." The same, pp. 441, 444.

[47] The electors were to vote by ballot for *two* persons. The one receiving the highest number of votes was to be declared the president.

[48] Art. 2, sec. 1.

[49] The same.

[50] *The Federalist* (Sesqui. Ed.), p. 458.

CHAPTER III

[1] Alaska, Hawaii, Puerto Rico, Guam, American Samoa, Panama Canal Zone, and the Virgin Islands.

[2] Estimated.

[3] Vermont and Texas.

[4] Ernest Barker, *Reflections on Government* (1942), pp. 123-41.

[5] Leverett S. Lyon and Victor Abramson, *Government and Economic Life*, Vol. 2, pp. 764-65.

[6] For example, the Panama Canal, the Inland Waterways Corporation, the Tennessee Valley Authority, and the various irrigation and power projects in the West.

[7] Lyon and Abramson, *Government and Economic Life*, p. 915.

[8] Reference is to the interest-bearing debt. Brookings Institution, *The Recovery Problem in the United States* (1936), p. 665.

[9] "The bearing of these particularistic tendencies on the necessity for the integration of policy is obvious. The broadening and intensification of public control make integration more essential. Yet the same process enlarges administrative hierarchies with their peculiar form of particularism and at the same time generates around each agency clusters of private and parochial pressures. The conditions that demand an integrated consistency of policy in government as a whole seem also to create forces driving persistently toward disruption and disintegration. The atomizing influences of economic specialization are likely to press most strongly on government under those conditions that make the function of major policy formation most nearly indivisible." V. O. Key, Jr., "Politics and Administration," in *The Future of Government in the United States*, Leonard D. White, ed. (1942), pp. 151-52.

[10] "The problem of timing is partially a matter of policy integration, that is, the timing of the action of one agency in relationship to that of another. It is even more, however, a question of the timing of the actions of all agencies in accordance with the demands of external conditions." The same, p. 148.

"And there seems to be no place in the modern world for a government that merely marks time. Recent experience the globe over has proved this beyond question. There must be deliberation, to whatever extent is needed for making decisions in the light rather than by guess, and then, without loss of precious time, action must ensue. Opportunity there must be for the voter, without compulsion or pressure, to replace the ins with the outs. But once the general will is freely and emphatically expressed, action should ensue or cease according to that will." Clarence A. Dykstra, "The Quest for Responsibility," *American Political Science Review,* Vol. 33 (February 1939), pp. 13-14.

[11] The power of the Supreme Court to interpret the Constitution is implied in the instrument itself and was probably understood and accepted by its framers. Nevertheless, it is unlikely that the founding fathers had any idea or intention that the Court's legislative and political character would ever be as conspicuous as it is now.

[12] These powers are sometimes called quasi-legislative or sub-legislative. Actually, they are legislative powers, though generally having a narrower application than those exercised by Congress and the president.

[13] Woodrow Wilson, *Congressional Government* (1913), p. 11.

[14] "Thus Congress, though it is no more respected or loved by the people than it was seventy years ago, though it has developed no higher capacity for promoting the best interests of the State, has succeeded in occupying nearly all the ground which the Constitution left debatable between the President and itself; and would, did it possess a better internal organization, be even more plainly than it now is the supreme power in the government." James Bryce, *American Commonwealth,* Vol. 1, pp. 223-24.

[15] Henry Jones Ford, *Rise and Growth of American Politics* (1898), pp. 279-93.

[16] Wilson, *Congressional Government,* Chaps. 12-13.

[17] Edward S. Corwin, *The President: Office and Powers* (1940), p. 315. See also, the same, pp. 17-30 and 313-14; and Merlo J. Pusey, *Big Government— Can We Control It?* (1945), pp. 49-73; Woodrow Wilson, *Constitutional Government in the United States* (1911), pp. 56-69.

[18] Each state has as many electoral votes as it has senators and representatives, and the votes for president and vice-president are counted by states.

Difficulties that early appeared in the election of president and vice-president were dealt with in the Twelfth Amendment, and further corrections were included in the Twentieth Amendment.

[19] Up to the ratification of this amendment, each newly elected Congress had met for its first regular session *thirteen months* after its election; while the old or "lame duck" Congress met in regular session about a month after the election, though it no longer represented the popular will and may have been repudiated at the polls. Moreover, a new president did not take office until four months after his election. Under the Twentieth Amendment, the "lame duck" session is eliminated and a new Congress meets on the third of January following its election and the president's inauguration takes place on the twentieth of January.

[20] Felix Frankfurter, *The Commerce Clause and the Constitution* (1937), p. 2.

CHAPTER IV

[1] William MacDonald, *A New Constitution for a New America* (1921), p. 5.

[2] ". . . It is not speculation to hazard the forecast that representation will never again be made effective upon a merely local or geographical basis. The modern community has outgrown the limits of locality, which, from the be-

ginning of man's experience down to the end of the eighteenth century, were natural to all communities. When essential human interests and the associations built upon them have ceased to be local, it is idle to suppose that locality can continue to serve as a sufficient basis for political representation." George H. Sabine, "What is the Matter with Representative Government?" in *The People, Politics and the Politician,* A. N. Christensen and E. M. Kirkpatrick, eds. (1941), p. 411.

[3] *Proposing an Amendment to the Constitution . . . for the Election of President and Vice President,* S. Rept. No. 1230, 80 Cong. 2 sess., p. 1.

[4] Edward T. Folliard in *Washington Post,* Nov. 3, 1946.

[5] Mark Sullivan in *Washington Post,* May 4, 1947.

[6] James Bryce, *American Commonwealth,* Vol. 1 (1910), p. 310.

[7] "What are some of the weaknesses that have been revealed in legislative-executive relationships? The following situations are frequently cited: (1) There is haphazard correlation of legislative policies. The President and the Congress frequently reach a deadlock on important legislation. (2) Budgetary and fiscal policies are handled piecemeal. Over-all planning and control are lacking. Authority and responsibility are too widely diffused. (3) Congress exercises no systematic review of its laws. It relies on sporadic investigations, on secondary sources, on inadequate staff, and on an over-lapping committee structure that cannot be readily geared to administrative activities. (4) Party programs and legislative leadership have no formal means of exerting influence. National concerns suffer at the expense of sectional and special interests. (5) The internal machinery of Congress is inadequate to permit more expeditious treatment of important legislative business. A log-jam of bills—such as has frequently happened in recent sessions—is the surest sign of obstructions in the flow. Members of Congress carry heavy secondary and nonessential loads of work. (6) Legislative research and staff facilities are inadequate. Congressional policies and salaries fail to attract the expert assistance required to formulate legislation. (7) Insufficient protection exists against pressure groups and lobbyists.

"These are but a few of the commonly acknowledged shortcomings. Critical opinions have been voiced also concerning the seniority practice in Congress, the complexity of legislative rules, the inordinate powers of certain committees, the obstructions of orderly debate in the Senate, and the absence of methods of affording a congressional forum for cabinet members." Floyd M. Riddick, "American Government and Politics," *American Political Science Review,* Vol. 41 (February 1947), pp. 61-62.

[8] *New York Times,* Oct. 1, 1947.

[9] *The Federalist* (Sesqui. Ed.), p. 337.

[10] Bryce *American Commonwealth,* Vol. 1, p. 68.

[11] Of the 235 direct vetos, between 1889 and 1934, only eight were for executive protection. Katherine A. Towle, "The Presidential Veto since 1889," *American Political Science Review,* Vol. 31 (February 1937), pp. 51-53.

[12] A. C. Millspaugh, *Democracy, Efficiency, Stability* (1942), pp. 195, 286.

[13] Pendleton Herring, *Presidential Leadership* (1940), pp. 8-9.

[14] Speaker Sam Rayburn, in an address at Dallas, Texas, Dec. 10, 1941, quoted in Paul H. Appleby, *Big Democracy* (1945), p. 160.

[15] The same.

[16] Alexis de Tocqueville, *Democracy in America* (rev. ed., 1900), Vol. 2, pp. 330-35.

[17] "The Public Service of the Future," in *The Future of Government in the United States,* Leonard D. White, ed. (1942), p. 212.

[18] At least two districts in 1946 nominated men alleged to be communists.

One obtained the Democratic nomination in the Fourth Wisconsin district, *Washington Post*, Oct. 4, 1946; and the other the Republican nomination in the Twenty-fourth New York district, *New York Times*, July 29, 1946.

[19] Bryce, *American Commonwealth*, Vol. 2, p. 124.

[20] Ernest Barker, *Reflections on Government* (1942), p. 192.

[21] *The Federalist* (Sesqui. Ed.), p. 188.

[22] "Woodrow Wilson also erred in believing that administration has no close connection with the constitutional system and the general framework of government. Inadequate machinery is the principal cause of administrative inefficiency and ineffectiveness. . . . Political science would do well to level heavy guns on the amassed lethargy which stands in the way of structural reforms.

"In a realistic analysis, the intimate interdependence of the constitutional and administrative structures will be closely observed. . . ." Marshall Dimock, "The Study of Administration," *American Political Science Review*, Vol. 31 (February 1937), pp. 32-34.

[23] James Bryce believed it to be essential to the excellence of a representative system of government that the representatives "individually, and the Cabinet they form, shall have a reflex action on the people, that is that while they derive authority from the people, they shall also give the people the benefit of the experience they acquire in the Chamber, as well as of the superior knowledge and capacity they may be presumed to possess." Bryce, *American Commonwealth*, Vol. 1, pp. 302-03.

"If Congress had a few authoritative leaders whose figures were very distinct and very conspicuous to the eye of the world, and who could represent and stand for the national legislature in the thoughts of that very numerous, and withal very respectable, class of persons who must think specifically and in concrete forms when they think at all, those persons who can make something out of men but very little out of intangible generalizations, it would be quite within the region of possibilities for the majority of the nation to follow the course of legislation without any very serious confusion of thought. . . ." Woodrow Wilson, *Congressional Government* (1913), pp. 58-59.

"Public opinion in a democracy responds to leadership, and needs the stimulus of leadership in order to crystallize one way or the other on specific proposals. Legislators are perfectly correct in sounding opinion so that they may determine whether or not they are moving in a direction calculated to meet popular needs. It is completely fallacious for legislators to wait on public opinion to tell them what to do, because public opinion waits on leadership to supply the grist of fact and suggestion so that it can fulfill its function, which is the acceptance or rejection of proposals. In a sentence, when faced with a specific problem, public opinion will respond to proposals, but cannot generate them; generation of proposals is the function of the legislators." Frank V. Cantwell, "American Government and Politics," *The American Political Science Review*, Vol. 40 (October 1946), p. 935.

"But, however the methods change, the vital principles in evoking the best of the forces latent in democratic opinion remain the same. Three in number, they have not altered since public opinion was effectively born in Britain, America and France in the eighteenth century.

"The first principle is the importance of the leader, the dominating individuality. The best kind of leader, the people always feel instinctively, is the man who thinks not of party or section but of the welfare of the whole nation. The masses have never failed to rise to a Pitt, Peel or Gladstone who tried to speak for the interests of *all* Britain, or to a Jackson, Lincoln or Wilson equally intent on the good of the whole of America. The people have almost never failed to stick by such men." Allan Nevins, "Arousing the Giant that is Public Opinion," *New York Times Magazine,* July 28, 1946.

[24] Wilson, *Congressional Government,* p. 93.

[25] "The danger to American democracy lies not in the least in the concentration of administrative power in responsible and accountable hands. It lies in having the power insufficiently concentrated, so that no one can be held responsible to the people for its use. Concentrated power is palpable, visible, responsible, easily reached, quickly held to account. Power scattered through many administrators, many legislators, many men who work behind and through legislators and administrators, is impalpable, is unseen, is irresponsible, cannot be reached, cannot be held to account. Democracy is in peril wherever the administration of political power is scattered among a variety of men who work in secret, whose very names are unknown to the common people. It is not in peril from any man who derives authority from the people, who exercises it in sight of the people, and who is from time to time compelled to give an account of its exercise to the people." Theodore Roosevelt, Special Message to Congress, Dec. 8, 1908.

"Acton's saying that 'power corrupts, and absolute power corrupts absolutely' has in recent years again been put into vehement circulation, strangely enough by those who more than others seem thirsty for power and who propose policies which inherently necessitate its more massive use. But the cases where men have been ennobled by the possession of power are just as numerous as those where they have been corrupted. Power corrupts only those already corrupted. Government is power; democratic government is democratic power; whether it shall be corrupt or noble depends, not on a more or less sincerely wry-faced disavowal of power, but on a universal and responsible intervention in the daily process of its exertion." Herman Finer, "Towards a Democratic Theory," *The American Political Science Review,* Vol. 39 (April 1945), p. 268.

[26] "If a democratic people really desires the government to seek assiduously the ends of the state, it will construct the constitutional system so that the administration will be responsible and unified. The checks and balances system makes it necessary and inevitable to violate public administration's central principles. In a realistic analysis, the intimate interdependence of the constitutional and administrative structures will be closely observed. The fixity of our written constitution, the multiplicity of our governing units, and the failure to provide for responsible leadership and administration make our constitutional system a difficult one within which to build principles of public administration." Dimock, *American Political Science Review,* pp. 32-34.

[27] Appleby, *Big Democracy,* p. 38.

[28] Ernest Barker observes that we must have division of labor or of function between the electorate, party, parliament, and cabinet; but there is another principle, he says, that of co-operation and interconnection. "Each has to act as part of a system; and each has therefore to act with reference to, and in harmony with, the other parts." Barker, *Reflections on Government,* pp. 56-60.

[29] "In fine, Burke's remedy for factious strife and abounding corruption was frankly to adopt party rule by conferring upon party full power to act, coupled with complete responsibility for what was done. It was from partisanship, thus strengthened and steadied, that the nation might hope 'to see public and private virtues, not dissonant and jarring and mutually destructive, but harmoniously combined, growing out of one another in a noble and orderly gradation, reciprocally supporting and supported.'

"The event has shown that just by such partisanship the regeneration of English politics was accomplished." Ford, *The Rise and Growth of American Politics,* pp. 348-50.

[30] ". . . Among all the modern fallacies that have obscured the true teachings of constitutional history, few are worse than the extreme doctrine of the separation of powers and the indiscriminate use of the phrase 'checks and balances.' The doctrine of the separation of powers has no true application to judicial matters. Consideration of this important question should not be clouded and confused by including the independence of the judges, with which it has nothing to do. But the present confusion does not end with that. There is an equal lack of discrimination between the legal checks for which our history gives such strong support, and the political balances for which, so far as I can see, there is little historical background whatever, except the fancies of eighteenth-century doctrinaires and their followers. Political balances have no institutional background whatever except in the imaginations of closet philosophers like Montesquieu. When in modern times representative assemblies took over the rights and duties of earlier kings, they assumed a power and a responsibility that had always been concentrated and undivided. There is no medieval doctrine of the separation of powers, though there is a very definite doctrine of limitation of powers.

"Some modern conservatives can see no practical difference between limitation and separation today, and I must confess that many historians have not seen any difference between them in earlier times. The gist of nearly all that has been said here thus far is to show that such difference has existed from the middle ages to the present. I am now concerned with showing that it ought still to be maintained. The limiting of government is not the weakening of it. The maxim that the king can do no wrong is a legal, not a political maxim. The true safeguards of liberty against arbitrary government are the ancient legal limitation and the modern political responsibility. But this responsibility which in modern times has become fully as important for our welfare as the ancient legal limits, is, I think, utterly incompatible with any extended system of checks and balances." Charles Howard McIlwain, *Constitutionalism, Ancient and Modern* (1947), pp. 141-42.

The excerpts below illustrate the confusion between the ideas of separation of powers and checks and balances on the one hand and those of limited government and judicial independence on the other:

"Separation of powers is basic in Anglo-Saxon jurisprudence: It is contrary to the experience of mankind that justice can be done by a process which combines all the powers of government in the same hands. For more than a century and a half we have been taught that such a system is the very definition of tyranny. One of the irrefutable verdicts of history is that authority must be limited in the interest of essential liberty." C. Perry Patterson, *Presidential Government in the United States* (1947), p. 172. "American constitutionalism is an adjustment between liberty and authority. This is the meaning of the line of federalism, the principles of separation of powers, checks, and balances, the Bill of Rights, the Supreme Law of the Land, granted powers, reserved powers, prohibited powers, and judicial review." The same, p. 244.

CHAPTER V

[1] It has not seemed practicable or essential to present in this chapter a complete list of proposals. Those here noted are believed to be typical or representative of various lines of thinking; but it is not intended, as it would not be possible, to present completely and literally the ideas of any one person or of any one school of thought, or the arguments advanced in support of the ideas. It should be understood, furthermore, that many of the less ambitious proposals are made by men who favor bolder and more far-reaching reforms but

who feel that "this is not the time" or "the people would not accept." The inhibitions which rest upon and stifle political discussion in this country prevent us in many cases from knowing what our public leaders and political scientists actually think. It is obviously difficult in such cases to determine the weight or even the meaning of their published statements.

[2] "Were the Senate and House thrown into one, the country might suffer more by losing the Senate than it would gain by improving the House, for the united body would have the qualities of the House and not those of the Senate." James Bryce, *American Commonwealth,* Vol. 1 (1910), pp. 187-88.

[3] W. F. Willoughby, *Principles of Legislative Organization and Administration* (1934), pp. 213-35, presents a cogent argument against bicameralism in state legislatures; but, with regard to the national government, he says:

"When one turns to the federal government the problem of the desirability of retaining or abolishing the bicameral system presents itself in somewhat different form. Within the field of their competence, our state governments are what is known as unitary governments. In marked contrast with this, our national government is a federal government; that is, one where the powers of government instead of being concentrated in a single piece of governmental machinery are divided between two sets of governments, the one representing the country as a whole and the other the constituent states. In such a form of government the bicameral system serves an important purpose. Were provisions made for but a single legislative chamber with representation in it apportioned according to population, a situation would be brought about where the influence of the less populous states would be almost completely submerged, and the power to control the conduct of national affairs would rest in but one part of the country, namely, that embracing the more populous states east of the Mississippi River, and, to a considerable extent, in the still more restricted area of the New England and North Atlantic States. Whatever may be the theoretical arguments in favor of such a system, it is one which the American people are not as yet prepared to accept. . . . So long, therefore, as the American people desire to retain their federal form of government, it is probably necessary that, notwithstanding the many manifest disadvantages that the system presents in its practical workings, the bicameral character of the national congress should be retained."

Says George B. Galloway (*Congress at the Crossroads,* 1946, p. 84):

"While this system has many theoretical disadvantages and practical drawbacks, and has recently been abandoned in one state (Nebraska), the American people are not prepared to abolish bicameralism in Washington."

[4] W. Y. Elliott, "Getting a New Constitution," *Annals of the American Academy,* Vol. 185 (May 1936), p. 120.

[5] Arthur N. Holcombe in *Organization of Congress,* Hearings before the Joint Committee on the Organization of Congress, 79 Cong. 1 sess. (1945), pp. 617-18.

[6] Willoughby, *Principles of Legislative Organization and Administration,* p. 536.

[7] Joint steering committees were frequently appointed in the early days.

[8] Marshall Dimock in *The Organization of Congress,* Symposium on Congress by Members of Congress and Others, Joint Committee Print, 79 Cong. 1 sess. (August 1945), pp. 30-38; *Legislative Reorganization Act of 1946,* Report of the Special Committee on the Organization of Congress, S. Rept. 1400, 79 Cong. 2 sess., p. 4. Estes Kefauver and Jack Levin, *Twentieth-century Congress* (1947), pp. 127-32; Roland Young, *This Is Congress* (1943), pp. 243-44.

[9] "Pick out the ten or fifteen most able and most respected leaders of the

majority party in each house, vest them with the title and powers of the new steering committee, and put them to work. What could they do? In a large degree they could determine *what* Congress should consider; they could exercise pretty full control over the order in which various bills should be discussed; they could use their procedural controls as weapons of persuasion to marshal a certain number of votes this way or that—on issues where the congressman concerned is not bound by local considerations in his home district and is therefore relatively free to vote either way. But on the major questions which involve large segments of people in various groupings—economic, social or regional—these leaders could do little to determine *how* Congress would vote unless they were armed with some form of sanction for bringing recalcitrants into line.

"The problem of sanctions is crucial—and obstinate. Such sanctions as are available are usually bound up with the personnel aspects of party—jobs which may be distributed under the direction of the individual member of Congress. But these are not at the disposal of the steering committee and there seems little likelihood that the President will be willing to relinquish control over this most potent instrument of persuasion. The party caucus is not feasible as a tool to promote party solidarity when it is employed on an issue which lies athwart both parties—as so much of our major legislation does. Stated conversely, how can we have party responsibility on an issue when the party as a whole has not agreed upon a policy? American parties being what they are— loose coalitions of individuals and groups with widely ranging interests and aspirations—unanimity on policy matters is out of the question. This fact is well known and has been demonstrated repeatedly in every session of Congress. It goes to the very heart of our two-party tradition and this is not the place to review well-known history, but the question of party responsibility in Congress is inextricably bound up with the very nature of our party system and cannot be revolutionized simply by changing the tumblers in the combination which operates the legislative mechanism.

"Party responsibility in the form of a program of definite policy commitments on the major issues does not lie within the realm of possibility as long as our present two-party system continues." Lawrence H. Chamberlain, "Congress— Diagnosis and Prescription," *Political Science Quarterly* (September 1945), pp. 443-44.

[10] For an excellent discussion of the question of limiting obstruction, see Willoughby, *Principles of Legislative Organization and Administration*, pp. 476-500.

[11] The Committee on Congress of the American Political Science Association recommended that the committee chairman be chosen by the Committee on Committees of the majority party or that the service of a committee chairman be limited to six years. Other suggestions are that he should be elected by a majority vote of the majority-party members of the committee (Kefauver and Levin, *Twentieth-century Congress*, pp. 137-38), that he should be chosen by the party caucus, or that all chairmen should retire at 65 or 70 years of age.

For other suggestions see Jerry Voorhis, "Congress and the Future," *Review of Politics* (April 1945), cited in *The Organization of Congress*, Joint Committee Print, p. 288; Charles P. Trussell, "Congress Checks Its Tool Kit," *Nation's Business* (February 1945), cited in the same, pp. 265-66. For the difficulty of the problem, see above and Pendleton Herring, *Presidential Leadership* (1940), p. 37. For a defense of seniority, see Willoughby, *Principles of Legislative Organization and Administration*, pp. 349-54.

[12] Kefauver and Levin, *Twentieth-century Congress*, pp. 58-64.

[13] *Organization of Congress,* Hearings, p. 716-17.

[14] See Galloway, *Congress at the Crossroads,* pp. 41-45; Prof. Harold D. Lasswell, quoted in *New York Times,* May 13, 1946.

[15] Governor Dewey is said to have proposed in 1941 that the Constitution be amended to permit ex-presidents, ex-vice-presidents, and all unsuccessful major-party candidates for president to become senators-at-large for life. Henry Hazlitt, *A New Constitution Now* (1942), pp. 214-15.

[16] "Thus, if the amendment were adopted, there would be in the national legislature a small group who could be the open defenders of the national interest. They could afford to be outspoken and could frequently furnish a nucleus around which legislators, elected by local and group interests, could rally when they felt deep down in their hearts that group and sectional pressures exerted by some of their more vocal constituents were not to the real advantage either of the country as a whole or of their own less vocal electorate. Under this plan men and women like the late Wendell Willkie, Alfred E. Smith, and Eleanor Roosevelt could be drawn into the national legislative counsels." Galloway, *Congress at the Crossroads,* pp. 287-88.

[17] W. Y. Elliott, *The Need for Constitutional Reform* (1935), p. 35.

[18] The same, pp. 9, 36-37, 193-96.

[19] "Mr. Ramspeck. Therefore I am suggesting, Mr. Chairman, for the consideration of this committee, that we go back to the job that the Constitution gave us, the legislative job. I am suggesting that we adopt a constitutional amendment which would prohibit a Member of Congress, or Senator, from contacting the executive branch of the Government except in regard to legislation.

"That we reduce the House of Representatives by half and provide for the election by the people of a Representative who would represent them before the executive branch of the Government, to assume all this other business that, through lapse of time, has become part of the job which we are undertaking to do and which we cannot do, in my judgment, without sacrificing the time necessary, under present-day conditions, to properly consider the legislative matters facing this Congress." *Organization of Congress,* Hearings, p. 296.

[20] Lewis Meriam and Laurence F. Schmeckebier, *Reorganization of the National Government* (1939), pp. 157-59.

[21] Willoughby, *Principles of Legislative Organization and Administration,* pp. 357-60; George II. Haynes, *The Senate of the United States,* Vol. 1 (1938), p. 316; "Report of Committee on Congress of the American Political Science Association," *The Organization of Congress,* Joint Committee Print, pp. 24-25.

[22] Walton Hamilton, *Organization of Congress,* Hearings, p. 717.

[23] David A. Simmons, "Reorganization of the Federal Government," *American Bar Association Journal* (February 1946), cited in *The Organization of Congress,* Joint Committee Print, pp. 255-56.

[24] Willoughby, *Principles of Legislative Organization and Administration,* pp. 185-95, gives a history of this proposal and, with respect to administrative supervision, sums up his conclusions as follows: "The second claim, that the proposed system will provide means by which a better scrutiny of administrative acts may be had, it can be shown; one, that the system has limitations that would seriously restrict its operation; two, that Congress now has, or can easily provide itself with more effective means for subjecting administrative acts to critical review; and, three, that the proposed system would bring with it undesirable collateral results."

[25] *Organization of Congress,* Hearings, p. 181.

[26] "The American people would benefit if they could make a complete change in the executive and legislative branches of the Government at the same time,

but this can be accomplished by providing that the presidential term should last two years and that re-election should be permitted at least three times so that a President would not serve beyond the customary eight years." David Lawrence, *Washington Star,* Nov. 8, 1946.

[27] "Note must be taken of Wilson's intention [in 1916], if Hughes won, to put him in office quickly. House suggested that Marshall and Lansing be gotten to resign, the President-elect made Secretary of State, and then Wilson himself would resign, so Hughes could succeed. The President said after the election that he would have done so . . . ." George Fort Milton, *The Use of Presidential Power, 1789-1943* (1944), p. 217.

The Twentieth Amendment has shortened the interregnum from about four months to about two and one-half months.

[28] "Not for a moment, we believe, will the President listen to the call for his resignation except as a last resort. It would be a confession of pusillanimity of which Harry Truman has never been accused. A quitter he has never been in his personal or political relations. Resignation might erode the bulwark of the Republic at a time when constitutional government is on trial. To be sure, a Constitution is not fixed and immutable and the need for amendments to it (as we have constantly suggested since the death of President Roosevelt created a vacancy in the Vice Presidency) is emphasized by the new impasse. What at the minimum is required whenever there is no Vice President is that the mid-term election shall be transformed into a general election. Another change is necessary to see that no mid term election shall have the effect of producing divided government." *Washington Post,* Nov. 7, 1946.

[29] "If a party is to be held responsible for the enactment of a legislative program, there must be a sufficient concentration of power in the party leaders to enable them to hold their following in line. One effective means is to permit party leaders to determine who should be nominated as representatives of the party. This is a key power sometimes disregarded in discussions of cabinet responsibility under parliamentary government. If we were ready to abolish direct primaries and grant to the national party organization the initial selection of Congressional candidates the disagreements between executive and legislative branches would become insignificant and few." Herring, *Presidential Leadership,* pp. 23-24.

[30] "There is a definite tendency to break down the isolation of the Executive from Congress and to develop ways of working together instead of at cross purposes. . . . We are, I think, in the course of a most important mutation in the growth of the American constitutional system." Thomas K. Finletter, *Can Representative Government Do the Job?* (1945), pp. 69-70.

"One heritage of the past that today is central in any effort to adapt our governmental machinery to present problems is the idea of checks and balances and the separation of powers. These concepts are so deep that they are part of our folkways. The practical question is how to work through and around such assumptions, for this is no time to overhaul our political structure." Herring, *Presidential Leadership,* p. 9.

"For better or for worse, Congress and the President are bound together in the legislative process because neither can act without the consent of the other. To make our government more effective, it is not necessary that the present gap be widened; rather instruments need to be devised whereby the President and Congress can carry on their work more harmoniously." Young, *This is Congress,* pp. 61-62.

"The nub of the problem is to make Congress more responsive to the President and to make the President more responsive to Congress and to do this without departing radically from existing institutional forms. And at the same time we must increase the over-all efficiency of government management. . . ." Alexander Hehmeyer, *Time for Change: A Proposal for a Second Constitutional Convention* (1943), p. 64.

"As I see it, the correct view of our government would accept the functions of the legislature and the executive as complementary rather than emphasize their role as parts of a structural system of checks and balances. Overemphasis on the idea of checks and balances and minimization of political considerations should be equally obsolete. The realm of the political has expanded greatly and must expand still more if democracy is to keep abreast of the conditions under which it must live in the middle of the twentieth century." Paul H. Appleby, *Big Democracy* (1945), p. 156.

[31] Art. 2, sec. 2 provides for the advice and consent of the Senate in treaty-making and appointments; and Art. 2, sec. 3 requires the president to give to Congress from time to time information of the state of the Union, and recommend "such measures as he shall judge necessary and expedient."

[32] "In other words, the policy committees would be an advisory superstructure on the simplified committee system. The policy committee of the majority party in each house would perform still another correlating job—that of combining with the President and his Cabinet to form a Joint Legislative-Executive Council." Robert M. LaFollette, Jr. "Systematizing Executive Control," *American Political Science Review,* Vol. 41 (February 1947), pp. 63-64.

"In order to facilitate the formulation and carrying out of national policy and to promote better teamwork between the executive and legislative branches of the Government, the bill further provides for the creation of a Joint Legislative-Executive Council. This Council would be composed of the majority policy committees in Congress and of the President and his Cabinet. It would seek to bridge the gap between the two branches created by our inherited system of separated powers and to avoid those periodic deadlocks between Congress and the President which have hitherto caused dangerous crises in the conduct of the Federal Government." *Legislative Reorganization Act of 1946,* Report of the Special Committee on the Organization of Congress, S. Rept. 1400, 79 Cong. 2 sess., p. 4.

"Our task is to form a Government that can govern. We shall not get such a Government by informal consultation between the President and the congressional leaders. Yet that appears to be all that he and they have thus far in mind for carrying out their pledges of cooperation. Informal consultation will not be enough. It will not work because the inducements to agree are too weak. Consultation is indispensable but to be effective it should be formal. It should depend not on Mr. Truman's inviting the congressional leaders in for a chat, or on their asking him to receive them.

"The consultation should be based on law and not merely on the good intentions, the moods and personal idiosyncrasies, of a few individuals. Perhaps as good a way as any to achieve this would be to adopt the proposal of Dr. Galloway, the staff director of the La Follette-Monroney Committee, and to create by joint resolution of Congress and an executive order of the President, an executive-legislative council with a secretariat. The great advantage of establishing formal machinery is that it would make solemn the duty of collaboration, that it would focus the attention of the country upon the task of finding agreement, and that it would fix clearly and conspicuously the responsibilities of the individuals who promote or obstruct agreement." Walter Lippmann, *Washington Post,* Nov. 14, 1946.

Finletter (*Can Representative Government Do the Job?* pp. 88-106) would reduce the number of committees in each house, combine the committees of the two houses dealing with the same subjects, form a joint legislative cabinet consisting of the chairmen of the combined committees, and join the legislative cabinet with the executive cabinet to form an executive-legislative cabinet. This joint cabinet, he says, "would necessarily be partisan—that is, chosen from the majority party." For other endorsements of the idea of a formal legislative-executive liaison, cabinet or council, see Charles A. Beard, *The Republic* (1943), p. 258; Elliott, *The Need for Constitutional Reform*, p. 37; Hehmeyer, *Time for Change: A Proposal for a Second Constitutional Convention*, pp. 95-99; Kefauver and Levin, *Twentieth-century Congress*; Merlo Pusey, "Broken Liaison" in *Washington Post*, Aug. 27, 1946.

[33] "Senator Burton believes that the relationship between the President and the Congress may well approximate, with certain qualifications, the relationship between the presidents of some well-managed corporations and their boards of directors. If a corporation president dictates to his board, the senator says, he gets no benefit from the board members' experience. If he leaves everything to the board, he gets no policy. The best results are usually obtained when the president analyzes each important situation as it arises, discusses it with members of the board, makes definite suggestions as to various ways in which the problem can be met, states his preference for one plan of action, gives his reasons for the preference and leaves the final determination of broad policy to the board.

"Application of this procedure to the government would constitute a variation of the council or legislative cabinet plans, for Congress would have to set up some kind of representative group to consult with the President. Logic and common sense lead us back to this suggestion from many different starting points. That is not surprising, because it embodies the advantages of unified leadership along with those of democratic control. As a practical matter, any comprehensive legislative program in this age of big government must be channeled through the White House or worked out in collaboration with the executive branch. In ever-increasing degree, lawmaking is concerned with administrative problems. Guidance in that field must necessarily come from men who are most experienced in carrying out the government's multifarious activities. In many instances also these officials will be first to suggest new lines of policy. Likewise the President, as our chief administrator and as the representative of all the people, is in the best position to organize these ideas, along with plans originating in his own mind and in the party that has elected him, into a mosaic of suggested policy to be discussed, amended and accepted or rejected by Congress. For this very reason, however, it becomes the more important to bring the impact of congressional influence to bear upon national policy making from its inception and to give Congress more effective tools than the rubber stamp and the wastebasket." Merlo J. Pusey, *Big Government: Can We Control It?* (1945), pp. 128-29.

[34] For discussions of this proposal from various points of view, see Willoughby, *Principles of Legislative Organization and Administration*, pp. 185-95; Finletter, *Can Representative Government Do the Job?*, pp. 87-88, 170-79; Harold J. Laski, *The American Presidency, an Interpretation* (1940), pp. 96-110; Kefauver and Levin, *Twentieth-century Congress*, pp. 69-79; C. Perry Patterson, *Presidential Government in the United States* (1947), pp. 257-58; Herring, *Presidential Leadership*, pp. 92-96; Henry S. McKee, *Degenerate Democracy* (1933), pp. 29-30; William MacDonald, *A New Constitution for a New America* (1921), pp. 47-52.

[35] Kenneth Colegrove, *The American Senate and World Peace* (1944), p. 161.

[36] Compare Willoughby, *Principles of Legislative Organization and Administration,* pp. 12-16.

[37] Hehmeyer (*Time for Change: A Proposal for a Second Constitutional Convention,* pp. 73-88) proposes cabinet government, though elsewhere in his book he rejects it. He recommends making constitutional provision for a cabinet, the eight members of which would exercise all the functions of the president except the ceremonial. If the mid-term election showed a reaction against the president, he would make changes in his cabinet to reflect the will of the people. But another proposal by Heymeyer is that only one half of the representatives shall be chosen at the mid-term election. It is evident that if all members were to be elected at the same time, as they are now, it would still be as difficult as it is now to determine the will of the people. Patterson (*Presidential Government in the United States,* pp. 258-80) comes to the conclusion that there is "no halfway and piece-meal readjustment this side of cabinet government which will solve the problem of the proper relation between the President and the Congress in the matter of both legislation and administration"; but he opposes "an unlimited cabinet system." He thinks that a "Congressional cabinet" could be established by a simple Congressional resolution, without amendment of the Constitution. The ministers would be chosen from the membership of both houses by the majority members of both houses. When the two houses are controlled by different parties, the cabinet would be a coalition cabinet. The ministers, according to the author, would give advice only, but the result would be to force the president to act through these ministers. In the author's view, they would become the party leaders; but just why and how he does not explain. He says of the proposed cabinet: "It would be merely a responsible steering committee working in the open and serving as a co-ordinating agency between the president and the Congress in a legislative and an administrative capacity. However, in contrast with the present cabinet, it would be responsible to the Congress for its advice in that it would fall if its policies were not approved. Its advice in legislative matters would take the form of proposed legislation.

"In regard to its relation to national administration, it would be advisory to the heads of the administrative departments who are appointed by the President and Senate. Its members would be the political heads of these departments while the President's secretaries would be their legal heads."

The author goes on to say: "If the President should refuse to cooperate, the Congress has the power to abolish any administrative office or to refuse to appropriate funds for its maintenance." But the fact is that this congressional power cannot now be exercised in the face of a more intelligent, realistic and enforceable executive power; and the author gives away his case when he says: "The President's veto power or any of his powers would still be as active as he saw fit to make them. His active participation in politics by means of popular election would, according to all precedents, be a much stronger guarantee of the preservation of his powers than any paper document could be. There is not the slightest possibility as long as the President is popularly elected that he would become the figurehead that the English King is or the French President was."

Hazlitt (*A New Constitution Now*) recommended that the president be elected by the legislative body but that his legislative and executive powers should be exercised by a premier, directly responsible to the House of Representatives. William MacDonald (*A New Constitution for a New America*) proposed to establish in somewhat similar fashion an outright cabinet system of government.

Elliott (*The Need for Constitutional Reform*, pp. 31-35) proposed, in effect, that the members of House and Senate should nominate the party candidates for the presidency. Such a procedure, in conjunction with other changes that he suggested, might conceivably make the president responsible to Congress.

[38] Edward S. Corwin, *The President: Office and Powers* (1940), p. 1.

[39] "The situation is such that the extension of executive authority is still the only practical method of advancing popular rule." Henry Jones Ford, *Rise and Growth of American Politics* (1898), p. 356.

"It may be that the new leadership of the Executive, inasmuch as it is likely to last, will have a very farreaching effect upon our whole method of government. It may give the heads of the executive departments a new influence upon the action of Congress. It may bring about, as a consequence, an integration which will substitute statesmanship for government by mass meeting." Woodrow Wilson, *Congressional Government* (1913), pp. 12-13.

". . . In any event, the responsibilities of the national Executive for the co-ordination of the important affairs of our national life may be expected to expand year after year." Carl Brent Swisher, *American Constitutional Development* (1943), pp. 1023-24.

"In all the talk of separation of powers there is a great deal of artificiality. In actual practice there must be a combination of the functions of legislating, executing, or adjudicating which in formal theory are supposed to be kept distinct. In practice we have achieved this in sufficient degree to weather an economic storm of awful magnitude and to face a world at war. . . .

". . . In actual practice our system can respond quickly to emergency conditions once the public is convinced of the need. *Presidential leadership sustained by a united people has power for any crisis.*

"In a time of divided purposes Congress can so obstruct action that no president can have his will; but when the goal is clear the branches of government can move as one." Herring, *Presidential Leadership*, pp. 140-41.

"If our democracy fails to meet the demands of the hour, the fault will be not with the system but with ourselves. In the ultimate reckoning the governance of a free people is an affair not of forms but of men.

"Presidential leadership is the answer. . . ." The same, p. 146.

[40] Appleby, *Big Democracy*, p. 163.

[41] Elliott, *The Need for Constitutional Reform*, p. 202.

[42] For the pros and cons of this proposal, see Herring, *Presidential Leadership*, pp. 76-86; Kefauver and Levin, *Twentieth-century Congress*, p. 51; Willoughby, *Principles of Legislative Organization and Administration*, pp. 80-85.

[43] Willoughby, the same, pp. 85-87. An American Institute of Public Opinion poll showed that two thirds of those who knew what the term "veto" means thought that the president should have power to veto some items in a bill without vetoing the entire bill. *Washington Post*, June 8, 1947.

[44] To enable the president to "give unified direction to a clear, coherent national policy," the editors of *Time, Life* and *Fortune* have proposed that the secretary of state and the secretary of the treasury should "become the President's recognized and responsible chief assistants in the making, respectively, of foreign and domestic policy." "Our Form of Government," *The United States in a New World*, No. 5, Supplement to *Fortune* (November 1943), p. 2.

[45] Dimock in *The Organization of Congress*, Symposium on Congress by Members of Congress and Others, Joint Committee Print, 79 Cong. 1 sess. (August 1945), pp. 30-38.

[46] Representative Monroney, quoted in *Washington Post,* Nov. 2, 26, 1946.

[47] Bryant Putney, "Abolition of the Electoral College," *Editorial Research Reports,* Vol. 2 (July 10, 1940), pp. 3-13.

"Bearing all this in mind, I think it is safe to say that *if* the members of the Federal Convention had happened to prescribe the mode of voting for the Presidency and Vice Presidency which is now the rule they would at the same time have provided for an intermediate election in the event of the President's death or resignation. They would have done this not to avoid a governmental deadlock but because the same considerations would have weighed with them as weighed with the authors of the act of 1792 when they provided for a special election in the event of the succession passing to the President *pro tem* of the Senate or to the Speaker of the House. A man who has not been voted on for the Presidency ought not to hold the office for longer than it takes to choose a new President. Indeed the argument applies even more forcibly to the Vice President than to the President *pro tem* of the Senate or the Speaker, since these have in point of fact been elected for office by the members of some constituency, while the Vice President has in truth been elected by no one—he rides into office on the coat tails of the President." Lucius Wilmerding, Jr. Quoted by Walter Lippmann, *Washington Post,* Dec. 7, 1946. On presidential tenure and succession, see *Congressional Digest,* Vol. 26 (January 1947); Lucius Wilmerding, Jr., "The Presidential Succession," *Atlantic Monthly* (May 1947), pp. 91-97.

[48] "By and large, the system of strong presidential leadership has worked well and the people have liked it. . . .

"But there are many things about it, too, that they have emphatically not liked. These are the things that always happen when a nation's leader gets out of control and grows too strong. They have been a direct result of the failure of Congress to fulfill the constitutional intention that it, though sharing the legislative function with the President, should be supreme in it, and through this power should keep the Executive in bounds." Supplement to *Fortune* (November 1943), p. 7.

"The error of our governmental history, so far, has taken the form of too great a fear of executive authority and hence the bestowal of too much upon the legislature. It is in this relationship that the necessary adjustment must be made. The purposes to be accomplished by this necessary readjustment are to procure all that is good in the principle of government by a strong executive; and at the same time to safeguard against its dangers by fastening upon it inescapable personal responsibility, and by reserving the power to thwart its action to the people through the legislature, at any time when its measures and its conduct fail to win public approval." McKee, *Degenerate Democracy,* pp. 25-26.

"Thus the immediate objectives of the future technique of government in constitutional states are twofold. On the one hand, rational methods must be discovered and guarantees must be devised by which the constitutional machinery brings real leaders as experts, and not only expert politicians and demagogues to the top. This is the problem of rationalized control of mass emotionalism, involving, temporarily perhaps, some revisions of traditionally revered standards of equalitarian concepts. In the second place, while the government thus entrusted with power does what governments have to do, namely to govern, a rationalized method has to be found of how governmental leadership should be made amenable to political control of the people or their representatives. This implies evidently a revision of the technical functions of representative assemblies. Relieved of their burden of actual participation in the conduct of the business of the government the parliaments can become true and efficient agencies of political control. It may be hoped that from this new division of functions and powers a new balance of political forces will emerge more in conformity with realities than the present myth of the balance between legislative and executive power. Such an arrangement of weights and counterweights should serve for the tasks of directed economy in the technological age, and, at the same time, it would be better adjusted to the ultimate end of all and every political organization: Political Freedom." Karl Loewenstein, "The Balance Between Legislative and Executive Power: A Study in Comparative Constitutional Law," *The University of Chicago Law Review*, Vol. 5 (June 1938), p. 608.

[49] "Finally, I return to the point that, as matters stand today, presidential power is dangerously *personalized*, and this in two senses: first, that the leadership which it affords is dependent altogether on the accident of personality, against which our haphazard method of selecting Presidents offers no guarantee; and, secondly, that there is no governmental body that can be relied upon to give the President independent advice and whom he is nevertheless bound to consult. As a remedy calculated to meet both phases of the problem I have suggested a new type of Cabinet. At least, if a solution is to be sought in *institutional* terms, it must consist in stabilizing in some way or other the relationship between President and Congress. That, today, with the rapid relegation of judicial review to a secondary role, is the center of gravity of our Constitutional System." Corwin, *The President: Office and Powers*, pp. 315-16.

Corwin would bring the independent agencies into the executive departments, give cabinet members the right to sit in either house and participate in debate, and have the cabinet selected from leading members of Congress. "The proposed Cabinet would contain men whose daily political salt did not come from the presidential table, whose political fortunes were not involved in his, who could bring presidential whim under an independent scrutiny which today is lacking. It would capture and give durable form to the casual and fugitive arrangements by which Presidents have usually achieved their outstanding successes in the field of legislation." The same, pp. 297-308.

". . . We have created a political executive. The President has become a prime minister, not by virtue of the Constitution, but by extra constitutional or political means. In the absence of organized leadership in the Congress, this was both necessary and inevitable. . . . We have made a political executive out of a single individual and have failed to make him responsible to the representatives of the people either as legislators or partisans. . . . Having created a strong government, we must now 'oblige it to control itself.'" Patterson, *Presidential Government in the United States*, pp. 250-51.

[50] "What the people should have, if the government is to be really popular in character, is the power at a given time to force an unpopular party out of the control of the government, and to oblige the party leaders in whom they do not have confidence to lay down their rights of leadership, giving place to others more in accord with the public will. Until such a condition of things is reached, either within the government or the party, no government can be regarded as popular." Frank J. Goodnow, *Politics and Administration* (1900), p. 166.

[51] Hazlitt says that because of fixed elections we fear to criticize the president:
"The limitations imposed by a rigid constitution, in short, may pervert a nation's very thinking, leading it to a sort of national neurosis in which it

refuses to face the truth about the situation that confronts it." *A New Constitution Now,* p. 25. He thinks that our "crude, uncertain and dilatory method of reflecting public sentiment is not to be compared with the parliamentary method," which permits a test of public sentiment on a specific issue at the precise time when that issue is to be decided." The same, p. 89.

[52] Elliott, *The Need for Constitutional Reform,* pp. 9, 31-35; Finletter, *Can Representative Government Do the Job?,* pp. 110 ff.

[53] The same.

[54] Elliott, *The Need for Constitutional Reform,* pp. 9, 31-35.

[55] Finletter, *Can Representative Government Do the Job?,* p. 110; Senator Fulbright, quoted in *Washington Post,* Nov. 8, 1946.

[56] MacDonald, *A New Constitution for a New America.* Hazlitt (*A New Constitution Now*) suggested that the normal term of senators and representatives should be four years or that the Senate should be subordinated to the House.

[57] Elliott, *The Need for Constitutional Reform,* pp. 31-35.

[58] Fulbright, quoted in *Washington Post,* Nov. 8, 1946.

[59] Elliott, *The Need for Constitutional Reform,* pp. 31-35.

[60] Finletter, *Can Representative Government Do the Job?,* pp. 125-28. For an explanation of the proposed Joint Cabinet see above, pp. 259-60, note 32.

[61] Elliott would give the power to the president alone and would have no more than one general election during his term. *The Need for Constitutional Reform,* pp. 31-35.

[62] For an instructive comparison of the British and American systems, see articles by Don K. Price and Harold J. Laski, in *The Organization of Congress,* Joint Committee Print, pp. 322-61.

[63] The only thing left for Parliament to do, says Ramsay Muir, "is to turn the Government out; and it cannot do this when the Government is in command of a disciplined majority of pledged supporters." *How Britain is Governed* (1933), pp. 12-17.

[64] Britain had coalition governments from 1846 to 1852, from 1886 to 1892, from 1910 to 1914, from 1929 to 1931, and from 1940 to 1945. W. Ivor Jennings, *The British Constitution* (1942), p. 70.

[65] In his *A New Constitution Now,* pp. 87-88.

[66] *Principles of Legislative Organization and Administration,* p. 55.

[67] See Arthur N. Holcombe, *The Middle Classes in American Politcs* (1940).

[68] MacDonald, *A New Constitution for a New America,* pp. 44, 127-39, 144-48.

[69] Roscoe Drummond, quoted in *Washington Post,* Apr. 5, 21, 1947.

[70] James Reston, "The Convention System: A Five-Count Indictment," *New York Times Magazine,* July 11, 1948.

[71] "I suggest that these conventions should consist not of delegates chosen for this single purpose but of the nominees for Congress, the nominees for vacant seats in the Senate of the United States, the Senators whose terms have not yet closed, the national committees and the candidates for the presidency themselves in order that platforms may be framed by those responsible to the people for carrying them into effect." Woodrow Wilson, First Annual Address to Congress, *Messages and Papers of the Presidents,* Vol. 18, p. 8290; quoted in Richard M. Boeckel, "National Party Platforms, 1832-1932," *Editorial Research Reports,* Vol. 1 (Jan. 13, 1932), p. 28.

[72] S. J. Res. 200, 80 Cong. 2 sess., Mar. 25, 1948. The same resolution was reported from committees in the Seventy-second and Seventy-third Congresses.

[73] S. Rept. 1230, 80 Cong. 2 sess., H. Rept. 1615, 80 Cong. 2 sess.

[74] Marquis Childs discussed this proposal in the *Washington Post,* July 13, 1946.

[75] *Washington Star,* Jan. 10, 1947.

[76] "One of the knottiest problems in the science of democratic government is that of reducing this basic theory of separated powers to a workable and efficient system. It requires the establishment of a proper balance, and devices of coordination that facilitate action but do not disturb the balance of powers. It also requires formal methods of procedure." LaFollette, *American Political Science Review,* pp. 58-59.

CHAPTER VI

[1] E. M. Sait, *Political Institutions* (1938), p. 444.

[2] "The truth is, that in all cases a certain number at least seems to be necessary to secure the benefits of free consultation and discussion, and to guard against too easy a combination for improper purposes; as, on the other hand, the number ought at most to be kept within a certain limit, in order to avoid the confusion and intemperance of a multiude. In all very numerous assemblies, of whatever character composed, passion never fails to wrest the sceptre from reason. Had every Athenian citizen been a Socrates, every Athenian assembly would still have been a mob." *The Federalist* (Sesqui. Ed.) p. 361.

". . . In the next place, the larger the number, the greater will be the proportion of members of limited information and of weak capacities. . . ." The same, p. 382.

[3] Whether it is possible, constitutionally, to abolish the Senate is a moot question. Article V of the Constitution prescribes that "no State, without its consent, shall be deprived of its equal suffrage in the Senate." It may be argued that this injunction can be ignored, since it was originally intended as reassurance for a few small states along the Atlantic seaboard, that the clause has no application to states admitted since 1789, and that it no longer has any effect whatever, for the reason that the Constitution is not now, if it ever was, a compact among the states. In any case the nation and its unity are now accomplished facts. The Constitution itself replaced the Articles of Confederation, though the latter provided that any alteration therein must be confirmed "by the legislatures of every state." It may be reasonably argued that no constitutional provision can eternally stand in the way of change and that the practically unamendable proviso in Article V is no longer practically or morally binding. Certainly, it is undemocratic.

[4] It may be of interest to note that the British Parliament Act of 1911 enables a money bill to become law if not passed by the House of Lords within one month of its receipt. With respect to other public bills (except bills to extend the duration of Parliament) the House of Lords can interpose a delay of two years. W. Ivor Jennings, *The British Constitution* (1942).

[5] If the chief executive were to be suspected of a high crime or a misdemeanor, he would be suspended or removed by the Council and brought to trial in a federal court. If considered necessary, provision could be made in the Constitution for the suspension and prosecution of a member of the Council or a federal judicial officer who might be similarly charged.

[6] "The verdict of actual practice is that the Electoral College provides a feasible method of choosing a President so long as there is a continuously dominant party in the country, as was the case from 1801 to 1825, and again with two interruptions from 1829 to 1861, and again from 1861 to 1873. Moreover, it remains a more or less feasible method in the presence of two fairly

equal, alternating parties, despite the fact that the majority party in the college may be the minority party at the polls—even overwhelmingly so. But should a strong third party ever spring up the scheme would be confronted with the dangerous possibility of entire collapse. Although just such a danger has impended several times already, the lesson of the situation has been obscured each time by a fortuitously fortunate denouement. But we should not continue to rely solely on the intervention of that Providence which is said to have fools and the American people in its special care." Edward S. Corwin, *The President: Office and Powers* (1940), p. 63.

[7] One would imagine that if the plan had gone into operation on June 21, 1948—the date of the Republican national convention—the Republican delegation would have been likely to include most of the following men: Ambassador Warren Austin, Governor Thomas E. Dewey, John Foster Dulles, General Dwight Eisenhower, Ex-President Herbert Hoover, Ex-Senator Robert M. La-Follette, Jr., Alf Landon, General Douglas MacArthur, Speaker Joseph Martin, Former Justice Owen J. Roberts, Senator Leverett Saltonstall, Harold E. Stassen, Ex-Secretary Henry L. Stimson, Senator Robert Taft, Senator Arthur M. Vandenberg, Governor Earl Warren, and Senator Wallace White. Here are 17 outstanding and representative men. Who the other 4 might be (they probably would be women) may be left to the imagination.

If we look back over the past, we can feel reasonably certain that Grover Cleveland, James G. Blaine, William McKinley, Theodore Roosevelt, Woodrow Wilson, and Franklin D. Roosevelt would have been prominent in the country's political leadership. We can feel sure, too, that Herbert Hoover would have been chief executive, probably earlier and longer than he actually was, that Charles E. Hughes, John W. Davis, and Alfred E. Smith would have been members of the National Council, and that William Jennings Bryan, Warren G. Harding, Calvin Coolidge, and Harry S. Truman would probably have played less conspicuous parts on the national stage.

[8] The following table illustrates how the seats in the Council would be appointed, if the distribution of the popular vote were the same as it has been in certain presidential elections:

Year	Percentage of Popular Vote[a]		Seats in National Council	
	Republicans	Democrats	Republicans	Democrats
1900	52.4	47.6	11	10
1904	60.0	40.0	13	8
1908	54.5	45.5	12	9
1916	48.3	51.7	10	11
1920	63.9	36.1	14	7
1928	58.8	41.2	13	8
1932	40.9	59.1	8	13
1936	37.8	62.2	8	13
1940	45.0	55.0	9	12
1944	46.2	53.8	9	12

[a] All figures are taken from *Gallup Political Almanac for 1946*, p. 257, except figures for 1936, which are calculated from figures given in *World Almanac 1946*, p. 522.

[9] "Some of the methods for reducing choices and expediting decisions in our political system are so familiar that they are not seen in that light at all. Take

the manner of electing our president. No candidate for that office from 1796 to 1944 would have received a popular majority had there been a completely unrestricted field, yet how many citizens realize that it is *only* when the choice is limited by the device of party nominations to a few principal contenders, and very preferably to two, that *any* candidate can win a majority? Incidentally it is germane to observe also that elections in which the voters are offered but two choices are far more likely to produce effective administrations than those in which the choices number three or four. John Quincy Adams was handicapped throughout his Presidency because the range of choice in the campaign of 1824 included, besides Jackson and himself, Clay and Crawford. Lincoln's efforts to avert the Civil War in 1861 were the more certainly destined to fail because of the four-way division in the campaign of 1860 between himself, Douglas, Breckenridge, and Bell. The election of 1912, with its three-way split between Wilson, Taft, and Theodore Roosevelt, generated so much tension and friction that even after thirty years the nation retains its disinclination for another campaign on that model." Paul H. Appleby, *Big Democracy* (1945), pp. 190-91.

[10] Let us take, for example, the results of the 1912 presidential election. The percentages of the total vote were as follows: *The Gallup Political Almanac for 1946*, pp. 230, 259.

Democratic	41.1
Progressive	27.4
Republican	23.9
Other parties	7.6

No party had a majority. If the system of preferential voting had been in operation, the second-choice votes of the "other parties" would first have been counted. If they had all been cast for the Democratic or for the Progressive party, no party would yet have received a majority. It would then have been necessary to count the second-choice votes of the Republicans. What the Republican's second choice would have been is difficult to imagine. It seems probable, however, that, if preferential voting had been permitted in 1912, the Democrats would have come into power, as they actually did; but it is almost certain that the Progressives would have become the other major party.

For another example, let us take the presidential election of 1924. The percentages in that election were as follows:

Republicans	54.1
Democratic	28.8
Progressive	16.6
Others	0.5

Though the LaFollette Progressives cast a substantial vote, it would not have been necessary to count the second-choice votes. The Republicans obtained a majority of all votes cast and the Democrats a majority of the remaining votes. It is possible, however, that, if second-choice voting had been permitted, the Progressive vote in 1924 might have been considerably larger.

[11] Consideration might be given to a somewhat novel scheme which would provide a four-year term when control of the Council passed from one party to another and a two-year term when the party in power won the election. Thus, when an overturn occurred, the new majority would have four years to demonstrate its program; but, thereafter, so long as it remained in power, it would have to go to the people every two years. A good deal might be said for such a plan; and a good deal against it.

[12] *The Federalist* (Sesqui. Ed.), pp. 84-85.

[13] For the differences between government and corporate business enterprises, see Marshall Dimock, "The Study of Administration," *American Political*

Science Review, Vol. 31 (February 1937), pp. 28-40; Appleby, *Big Democracy,* pp. 1-10; Ernest Barker, *Reflections on Government* (1942), p. 223.

[14] Carl Brent Swisher, *The Growth of Constitutional Power in the United States* (1946), p. 73.

[15] The same, p. 249.

[16] The same, p. 75.

[17] Alexander Hehmeyer, *Time for Change: A Proposal for a Second Constitutional Convention* (1943), p. 60.

[18] It is a commonplace that much of the work of Congress is done in the members' offices, in the lobbies, in casual conferences, and even in semi-social gatherings. The committees do not yet in all cases or even in many cases deliberate publicly. Meetings of conference committees are almost entirely out of view, and in those crucial committees important decisions are taken in secret and usually little if any public discussion takes place after a bill is reported out of conference. Not all the final votes in Congress are record votes. "A large part of the strategy of Congress takes place covertly and receives little or no publicity. . . . The nature of political strategy accounts for the fact that much of the open procedure of Congress seems to be of an inconsequential nature." Roland Young, *This is Congress* (1943), p. 135.

[19] "There is a risk that the result of a presidential election may be doubtful or disputed on the ground of error, fraud, or violence. When such a case arises, the difficulty of finding an authority competent to deal with it, and likely to be trusted, is extreme." James Bryce, *American Commonwealth,* Vol. 1 (1910), p. 299.

CHAPTER VII

[1] Madison in *The Federalist* (Sesqui. Ed.), p. 226.

[2] *New York Times,* May 15, 1947.

[3] Madison in *The Federalist* (Sesqui. Ed.), p. 226.

[4] "The whole scheme of the American Constitution tends to put stability above activity, to sacrifice the productive energies of the bodies it creates to their power of resisting changes in the general fabric of the government." James Bryce, *American Commonwealth,* Vol. 2 (1910), p. 116.

[5] Since the Twenty-first amendment repealed the Eighteenth, the existing amendments represent only *nineteen* changes in the Constitution.

[6] Many of these proposals are practically duplications.

[7] Isodor Loeb, "Facts and Fiction in Government," *American Political Science Review,* Vol. 28 (February 1934), pp. 1-10.

[8] Edward S. Corwin, *The President: Office and Powers* (1940), pp. 50-51.

[9] "The members [of the Joint Committee on the Organization of Congress] were expressly forbidden even to consider certain basic matters that go to the heart of any thorough repairing of ancient congressional machinery." Estes Kefauver and Jack Levin, *Twentieth-century Congress* (1947), p. 9.

[10] Robert M. LaFollette, Jr., "A Senator Looks at Congress," *The Atlantic Monthly,* Vol. 172 (July 1943), p. 96.

[11] George B. Galloway, "On Reforming Congress," *Free World* (June 1944), cited in *The Organization of Congress,* Symposium on Congress by Members of Congress and Others, Joint Committee Print, 79 Cong. 1 sess. (August 1945), pp. 64-65.

[12] Address of Mar. 9, 1937.

[13] Henry Hazlitt, *A New Constitution Now* (1942), pp. 251-61.

[14] "The real issue today is not whether the Constitution will be touched or not, but *how* it will be touched. At present it is in danger of being scrapped piece meal and by indirection, leaving only as its monument an excessive

duplication of bureaucracies. . . . If we are to save the Constitution we must amend it to fit the needs of a modern state; but we must amend it in an intelligent, coherent, and lawful manner, rather than by a hodge podge of makeshift evasions." William Y. Elliott, *The Need for Constitutional Reform* 1935), p. 30.

[15] Woodrow Wilson, *Congressional Government* (1913), p. 4. "For a long time the cult of Constitution-worship reigned in circles deemed select and wise. To the high priests of that cult, little or nothing was needed save proper lip-service and genuflections." Charles A. Beard, "Foreword" to Merlo J. Pusey, *Big Government—Can We Control It?* (1945), p. 11.

[16] "Social convulsions from within, warlike assaults from without, seem now as unlikely to try the fabric of the American Constitution, as an earthquake to rend the walls of the Capitol. This is why the Americans submit, not merely patiently but hopefully, to the defects of their government. The vessel may not be any better built, or found, or rigged than are those which carry the fortunes of the great nations of Europe. She is certainly not better navigated. But for the present at least—it may not always be so—she sails upon a summer sea." Bryce, *American Commonwealth*, Vol. 1, p. 310. "Americans . . . are conservative about their institutions because they lack the motive which really impels masses of men to wish to change their institutions. That motive is the denial or the absence of opportunity for the mass of men. In this country today the mass of men do not think they lack, or are being denied, opportunity." Walter Lippmann, in *Washington Post*, Dec. 28, 1946.

[17] "The citizen has little time to think about political affairs. . . . It astonished me in 1870 and 1881 to find how small a part politics played in conversation among the best educated classes and generally in the cities. . . . "The want of serious and sustained thinking is not confined to politics. . . ." Bryce, *American Commonwealth*, Vol. 2, pp. 291-92.

[18] "When the laws of a country are perfect, and equality of rights and privileges reached, there is far more important work at home than in legislative halls. Hence the ablest and best men in the Republic are not found as a class trifling their time away doing the work of mediocrity." Andrew Carnegie, *Triumphant Democracy* (1893), pp. 69-70.

[19] "We are as free politically, perhaps, as it is possible for us to be. . . . ". . . And, therefore, the end to which we must move is a recognition of industrial democracy. . . ." Louis D. Brandeis, Testimony before Industrial Relations Commission, *Final Report and Testimony*, S. Doc. 415, 64 Cong. 1 sess., pp. 63-64.

[20] "The sluggishness of government, the multitude of matters that clamor for attention, and the relative ease with which men are persuaded to postpone troublesome decisions, all make inertia one of the most decisive powers in determining the course of our affairs and frequently gives to the established order of things a longevity and vitality much beyond its merits." Justice Jackson in *Duckworth* v. *Arkansas*, 314 U. S. 400-01 (1941).

[21] "The fight to save the Supreme Court from being packed would be dwarfed by comparison with the furore that would sweep the country if any administration should propose to substitute any other system for the work of the founding fathers." Pusey, *Big Government—Can We Control It?*, p. 109.

[22] Bryce, *American Commonwealth*, Vol. 1, pp. 174-75.

[23] Alexander Hehmeyer, *Time for Change: A Proposal for a Second Constitutional Convention* (1943), p. 9.

[24] Charles A. Beard, *The Republic*, pp. 251-54, quoted in George B. Galloway, *Congress at the Crossroads* (1946), pp. 221, 223-24.

"[It] is a major premise in any discussion of governmental forms and procedures that any national or local pattern for organizing a political society must be related intimately to, and grounded in, the history and habits of that society." Clarence A. Dykstra, "The Quest for Responsibility," *American Political Science Review,* Vol. 33 (February 1939), pp. 10-11.

[25] A member of Congress observed that the check-and-balance system of government is "what our Nation's defenders have been fighting to preserve." *Organization of Congress,* Hearings before the Joint Committee on the Organization of Congress, 79 Cong. 1 sess. (1945), p. 208.

[26] Pusey, *Big Government—Can We Control It?,* p. 109.

[27] "The novelty of the undertaking immediately strikes us. It has been shown in the course of these papers, that the existing Confederation is founded on principles which are fallacious; that we must consequently change this first foundation, and with it the superstructure resting upon it. It has been shown, that the other confederacies which could be consulted as precedents have been vitiated by the same erroneous principles, and can therefore furnish no other light than that of beacons, which give warning of the course to be shunned, without pointing out that which ought to be pursued. The most that the convention could do in such a situation, was to avoid the errors suggested by the past experience of other countries, as well as of our own; and to provide a convenient mode of rectifying their own errors, as future experience may unfold them." *The Federalist* (Sesqui. Ed.), p. 226.

[28] "To these stand opposed another kind of political reasoners, who are so far from assimilating a form of government to a machine, that they regard it as a sort of spontaneous product, and the science of government as a branch (so to speak) of natural history. According to them, forms of government are not a matter of choice. We must take them in the main, as we find them. Governments cannot be constructed by premeditated design. They 'are not made, but grow.' Our business with them, as with the other facts of the universe, is to acquaint ourselves with their natural properties, and adapt ourselves to them. The fundamental political institutions of a people are considered by this school as a sort of organic growth from the nature and life of that people: a product of their habits, instincts, and unconscious wants and desires, scarcely at all of their deliberate purposes. Their will has had no part in the matter but that of meeting the necessities of the moment by the contrivances of the moment, which contrivances, if in sufficient conformity to the national feelings and character, commonly last, and by successive aggregation constitute a policy, suited to the people who possess it, but which it would be vain to attempt to superinduce upon any people whose nature and circumstances had not spontaneously evolved it." John Stuart Mill, *Liberty, Utilitarianism and Representative Government* (Everyman Ed.), pp. 175-76.

[29] "Let us remember, then, in the first place, that political institutions (however the proposition may be at times ignored) are the work of men; owe their origin and their whole existence to human will. Men did not wake on a summer morning and find them sprung up. Neither do they resemble trees, which, once planted, 'are aye growing' while men 'are sleeping.' In every stage of their existence they are made what they are by human voluntary agency."

. . . .

"The result of what has been said is, that, within the limits set by the three conditions so often adverted to, institutions and forms of government are a matter of choice. To inquire into the best form of government in the abstract (as it is called) is not a chimerical, but a highly practical employment of scientific intellect; and to introduce into any country the best institutions which, in the existing state of that country, are capable of, in any tolerable degree, fulfilling the conditions, is one of the most rational objects to which practical effort can address itself." The same, pp. 177, 181-82.

[20] *The Federalist* (Sesqui. Ed), p. 3.

CHAPTER VIII

[1] Representatives-at-large, when provided for, are chosen by the state as a whole, not by districts.

[2] James Bryce, *American Commonwealth*, Vol. 1 (1910), p. 187; Charles A. Beard, *The Republic* (1943), p. 206.

[3] In 1947, 15 states had senators of opposite political affiliation. In 1942 the voters of Colorado elected two senators, one to fill a vacancy; and they chose a Republican and a Democrat.

[4] Vermont, with 359,231 inhabitants, has 2 senators. So also has neighboring Massachusetts with 12 times the population. Nevada with only 110,247 people wields the same voting power in the Senate as New York with 13,479,142. (The figures given are the census figures for 1940.) Fifty senators, coming from 25 states, represent about one-fifth of the nation's population; the minority of 46 senators represents 80 per cent of the American people. The nation in 1940 was 56.5 per cent urban; but the states that were 57 per cent or more *rural* had a majority of the senators. The 25 rural states had a total population of 41,225,703, about 30 per cent of the nation's population.

[5] Henry Jones Ford, *Rise and Growth of American Politics* (1898), p. 240.

[6] A comparatively few representatives are elected at large; that is, by the state as a whole and not by districts. In 25 congressional elections from 1896 to 1944, 2½ per cent of the members were elected at large. Cortez A. M. Ewing, *Congressional Elections, 1896-1944* (1947), p. 51.

[7] On apportionment of representatives, see Laurence F. Schmeckebier, *Congressional Reapportionment* (1941). No reapportionment was made by Congress following the 1920 census. The same, pp. 120-21. In 1941, according to Schmeckebier, the boundaries of districts in three states dated from the census of 1900; in ten states, from the census of 1910; and in one from the census of 1920. Two New York City districts in 1941 had populations respectively of 90,671 and 799,407. In Illinois, the population in 1930 of the 5th District was 140,481 and of the 7th District 889,349. In that state there had been no reapportionment from 1901 to 1941, and in the latter year the down state region contained nearly two thirds of the congressional districts, although one half of the Illinois vote came from Cook County. Harold F. Gosnell, *Grass Roots Politics* (1942), p. 92.

[8] Some states come close to being typical of the nation as a whole; but none of these states possesses the means to integrate their various opinions, except through the political party.

[9] George H. Sabine, "What Is the Matter with Representative Government?" in *The People, Politics and Politicians*, A. M. Christensen and E. M. Kirkpatrick, eds. (1941), pp. 403-11; Roland Young, *This Is Congress* (1943), p. 177.

[10] In the case of representatives, a few exceptions occur. Occasionally in a large city that contains several congressional districts a representative has lived outside his district.

[11] Pendleton Herring, *Presidential Leadership* (1940), pp. 13-15.

[12] Nevada, for example, has 23,442 potential voters for each electoral vote, while New York has 177,182. Thus, a Nevadan has 7-5/10 times the voting power of a New Yorker in presidential elections. A potential voter in Vermont has twice the power of one in Massachusetts. Figures for potential voters are those for citizens 21 years of age or over. *World Almanac* (1946), p. 490. Potential voters are not precisely the same as qualified voters, and of course they are not the same as actual voters.

[13] In the House of Representatives elected in 1944, three of the delegations were tied between the two major parties; and the important New York delegation had the same number of Democrats as Republicans, with the American Labor Representative, Vito Marcantonio, in a position to cast the deciding vote.

[14] When the election of a president is thrown into the House of Representatives, the Senate chooses the vice president.

[15] In the six presidential elections of 1880, 1884, 1888, 1892, 1912, and 1916 no candidate for the presidency received a majority of the popular vote. In 1880, the Republican candidate, James A. Garfield obtained a plurality of only 9,464 over the Democratic candidate, Winfield S. Hancock. James B. Weaver, candidate of the Greenback party polled 308,578 votes. Had the election been truly national and if those who voted for Weaver could have registered a second choice, it is possible that Hancock would have been elected.

A similar situation arose in 1884. Grover Cleveland's plurality over James G. Blaine was only 23,004; but 325,739 votes were polled by minor party candidates. The vote in New York determined the result of this election. Cleveland's plurality there was only 1,149 and, because of the vote given to minor parties, he fell short of a majority in that state.

The election of 1888 was notable for the fact that the successful candidate, Harrison, received not only a minority of the popular vote, but also fewer votes than the defeated candidate, Cleveland. The 36 electoral votes of New York again decided the contest; but Harrison's plurality over Cleveland in that state was only 13,002, while minor parties polled 33,525 votes in New York.

Cleveland won the election of 1892 with a popular plurality of 380,961 over Harrison; but the winning candidate did not obtain a majority of the popular vote, since minor parties polled a total of 1,318,259. Cleveland obtained pluralities in California, Delaware, Illinois, Indiana, Missouri, New York, North Carolina, West Virginia, and Wisconsin. Had it not been for the populist and prohibitionist vote, Harrison might have won enough of these states to give him the election. Cortez A. M. Ewing, *Presidential Elections from Abraham Lincoln to Franklin D. Roosevelt* (1940), p. 134. In 1912 the split in the Republican party and the candidacy of Theodore Roosevelt on the progressive ticket brought about the election of Woodrow Wilson. He received 6,286,214 popular votes; but Roosevelt had 4,216,020 and Taft 3,483,922. In 1916 the Republicans were again united, and Wilson won over Hughes with a plurality of 591,385; but Wilson did not obtain a majority of the popular vote. Minor parties cast a total vote of 860,916. In this election, a change of 1,904 popular votes in California would have given the national election to Hughes.

[16] Georgia uses a "county-unit" system for the election of its governor. In 1946 Eugene Talmage won the election with a minority of the popular vote. Such a frustration of democracy seemed outrageous to many people. Georgia's way of electing a governor, however, is not much different in principle and may not be different in effect from the electoral college method of choosing a president.

[17] A Democratic vote of 3,304,238 in New York gave Roosevelt 47 electoral votes in 1944; but a Democratic vote of 1,097,785, or one third as large in 5 southern states gave him 50 electoral votes.

[18] In Connecticut, for example, 77 per cent of the potential voters voted in 1940; while in South Carolina only 10 per cent voted. Yet, each state cast 8 electoral votes. American Institute of Public Opinion, *The Gallup Political Almanac for 1946* (1946), pp. 226-27.

[19] In the Senate as of January 1928, a Republican majority of 49 represented states having a population of slightly less than those represented by the 45 Democratic senators. In January 1932 the 48 Republican members represented 53,408,531 people, while 47 Democratic members represented 63,844,754. In

both years, there was one independent senator. He is not counted for either party. Where a state has two senators of different parties, one half of its population is counted for one senator and one half for the other. *Congressional Directory*, 70 Cong. 1 sess. (January 1928); 72 Cong. 1 sess. (January 1932). In both cases, the census of 1930 is used.

[20] The table below shows the party in control of the presidency and of the Senate at four-year intervals since 1880.

Year	President	Senate
1881	Republican	Tied
1885	Democratic	Republican
1889	Republican	Republican
1893	Democratic	Democratic
1897	Republican	Republican
1901	Republican	Republican
1905	Republican	Republican
1909	Republican	Republican
1913	Democratic	Democratic
1917	Democratic	Democratic
1921	Republican	Republican
1925	Republican	Republican
1929	Republican	Republican
1933	Democratic	Democratic
1937	Democratic	Democratic
1941	Democratic	Democratic
1945	Democratic	Democratic

The tie in 1881 was between the two major parties. The composition of the Senate was: Republicans, 37; Democrats, 37; minor parties, 2.

[21] The table below shows party control of Senate and House of Representatives in the year following each mid-term election since 1880.

Year	Senate	House
1883	Republican	Democratic
1887	Republican	Republican
1891	Republican	Democratic
1895	Republican	Republican
1899	Republican	Republican
1903	Republican	Republican
1907	Republican	Republican
1911	Republican	Democratic
1915	Democratic	Democratic
1919	Republican	Republican
1923	Republican	Republican
1927	Republican	Republican
1931	Republican	Democratic
1935	Democratic	Democratic
1939	Democratic	Democratic
1943	Democratic	Democratic
1947	Republican	Republican

[22] The distribution of seats was: Republicans, 48; Democrats, 47; independent, 1.

[23] The comparisons appear in the following tables:

	Popular Vote in 1928, 1930, and 1932	Senate Seats in 1933
Democrats	33,121,933	59
Republicans	31,222,365	36
Others	3,208,046	1

Compiled from U. S. Bureau of the Census, *Vote Cast in Presidential and Congressional Elections, 1928-1944, Elections, 1944*, No. 5, pp. 12-15. No available reports of votes in senatorial and congressional elections appear to be completely accurate; and the exactness of the above figures is not guaranteed.

	Popular Vote in 1942, 1944, and 1946	Senate Seats in 1947
Republicans	37,600,752	51
Democrats	36,017,343	45
Others	1,606,464	0

The vote for "others" was not available for 1946. Compiled from United States Bureau of Census, *Vote Cast in Presidential and Congressional Elections 1928-1944, Elections, 1944*, No. 5, pp. 12-15; *World Almanac* (1947), p. 902.

[24] *The Records of the Federal Convention of 1787*, Max Farrand, ed., Vol. 1 (1911), p. 554.

[25] In opposition to limitation on freedom of debate, Senator Russell stated on Feb. 9, 1946: "The suggestion has been made during the debate that the majority of the Senators could even take a Senator off the floor if they thought that an amendment being discussed was frivolous or that his remarks did not appeal to the majority. If we are to start whittling away the rights of the States and the rights of individual Senators by adopting cloture, and then move on to the time when the majority can silence a Senator if his remarks do not appeal to the majority, we should adjourn the Senate sine die ... and go out of that door and place above it a bronze plaque having on it the words, 'Here fell the last citadel of individual rights in an authoritarian world, betrayed by those selected and sworn to defend it.'" *Congressional Record*, daily ed. Feb. 9, 1946, 79 Cong. 2 sess., p. 1246, quoted in Floyd M. Riddick, "American Government and Politics," *American Political Science Review*, Vol. 41 (February 1947), p. 16.

On filibustering and cloture, see George H. Haynes, *The Senate of the United States: Its History and Practice*, Vol. 1 (1938), pp. 402-26. The filibuster was eliminated from the British House of Commons in 1881 and from the United States House of Representatives in 1890. Even the present undemocratic and largely ineffective cloture rule was not adopted in the Senate until 1917.

[26] Other parties obtained 4 seats. American Institute of Public Opinion, *The Gallup Political Almanac for 1946*, p. 263.

[27] See Ewing, *Congressional Elections, 1896-1944*, pp. 79-104.

[28] George B. Galloway, *Congress at the Crossroads* (1946), p. 197.

[29] In 1946, the House failed to override the President's veto of the Case labor bill. The vote was 255 to 135, five votes less than a two thirds majority. The House in 1947 failed to override the President's veto of the income tax reduc-

tion bill. In this case, the vote to override fell short only two votes of the necessary two thirds.

[30] During the 66 years from 1883 to 1948 inclusive, we have had divided government for a total of 18 years, or more than one-quarter of the time. The make-up of the government, when control has been divided, is shown in the following table:

Year	President	Senate	House of Representatives
1883-1885 ....Republican	Republican	Democratic
1885-1887 ....Democratic	Republican	Democratic
1887-1889 ....Democratic	Republican	Republican
1891-1893 ....Republican	Republican	Democratic
1895-1897 ....Democratic	Republican	Republican
1911-1913 ....Republican	Republican	Democratic
1919-1921 ....Democratic	Republican	Republican
1931-1933 ....Republican	Republican	Democratic
1947-1949 ....Democratic	Republican	Republican

[31] In 1885 divided control appeared as the result of a presidential election. Such would have been the case also in 1889, if Cleveland had received a majority of the electoral votes, as he should have. In 1931 the Democrats obtained control of the House in spite of a Republican plurality in the congressional elections. In 1943 Franklin D. Roosevelt would have faced a Republican House if the House had accurately reflected the popular plurality. Most important, however, is the probability that in some, if not all, of the midterm elections which brought about a genuine change in the House majority, the incumbent president would have been defeated had he been running for re-election. It seems probable, for example, that Cleveland would have lost in 1886, Harrison in 1890, Cleveland in 1894, Taft in 1910, and Truman in 1946. It is possible but not probable that Wilson would have met defeat in 1918; but it does not seem at all likely that Hoover would have lost in 1930.

[32] Mrs. Norton of New Jersey commented on a farm bill as follows: "I represent a city district in which there are located no farmers. The nearest I have ever been to a farm is to pass one along the road in an automobile. Therefore, any opinion I may have regarding the farm bill would amount to very little. . . . I intend to vote for the bill as is." Quoted by O. R. Altman, "Second and Third Sessions of the Seventy-fifth Congress, 1937-38," *American Political Science Review*, Vol. 32 (December 1938), pp. 1105-06.

[33] "In February 1946, the National Opinion Research Center polled the leaders of six key groups (agriculture, labor, management, negro, press-radio, and veterans) and a sample of average Americans on what they thought a Congressman should and does rely on most when he votes on a national problem: the opinions of the people who elect him, the opinions of the country as a whole, or his own judgment. Although there were some sharp differences between public and leadership opinion, both polls indicated that the opinions of the country as a whole play little part in determining individual congressional positions." Galloway, *Congress at the Crossroads*, pp. 314-15.

[34] "We solemnly elect our representatives and send them to the State or National capitol to make our laws. But when we want something, or believe that something needs doing, we show little confidence that our representative will

know about it or give his help if he knows. We forthwith begin to devise ways of convincing him that we want it, and of putting pressure upon him to help us get it. What we actually rely on is the extra-legal, voluntary association which we feel can really be trusted to look after our interests." Sabine, *The People, Politics, and the Politicians,* pp. 403-11.

[35] A. C. Millspaugh, *Democracy, Efficiency, Stability* (1942), pp. 305-09. Of 27 Republican House leaders in the Eightieth Congress, all had been elected in 1944, as well as in 1946, and in 1944 (a Democratic presidential year), 23 of the Republican leaders had received 55 per cent or more of the major-party vote and one had been unopposed.

[36] See Walter Lippmann, *Public Opinion* (1922), pp. 16-29. "But there is another and more disturbing explanation for the *political apathy* that seems to exist between the surface noise of discussion and agitation. Political observers sensitive through long years of observation to trends and attitudes detect a kind of *fatalism.* It is a feeling that what is happening is too complex and over-whelming for the plain citizen's comprehension." Marquis W. Childs, "The Political Outlook," *Yale Review,* Vol. 36 (September 1946), p. 5.

[37] Haynes, *The Senate of the United States: Its History and Practice,* Vol. 2, p. 301. On seniority, see also Estes Kefauver and Jack Levin, *Twentieth-century Congress* (1947), pp. 133-42.

[38] Edward S. Corwin, *The President: Office and Powers* (1940), p. 281.

[39] *The Federalist* (Sesqui. Ed.), pp. 14-15.

[40] "The mischief is two-fold. Inferior men are returned, because there are many parts of the country which do not grow statesmen, where nobody, or at any rate nobody desiring to enter Congress, is to be found above a moderate level of political capacity. And men of marked ability and zeal are prevented from forcing their way in. Such men are produced chiefly in the great cities of the older states. . . . Boston, Chicago, New York, Philadelphia, could furnish six or eight times as many good members as there are seats in these cities." Bryce, *American Commonwealth,* Vol. 1, p. 195.

[41] Woodrow Wilson, *Congressional Government* (1913), p. 93.

[42] "The distribution of power in Congress is in many respects similar to the game of button, button, who has the button? One knows that someone has the button, but it is at times difficult to tell precisely where it is. The responsibility for action lies in many hands and in many groups. As soon as you think you know where the responsibility lies, where the button is, it is slipped to some one else. The internal organization of Congress is so involved and so complicated that only very few men, and they specialists in the legislative process, know who are the individuals and the groups concerned with any specific piece of legislation, and there is hardly a man alive who can solve the mystery of Congress for every issue that comes along." Young, *This Is Congress,* pp. 80-82.

[43] Herring, *Presidential Leadership,* p. 115.

[44] Leonard D. White, "The Public Service of the Future," in *The Future of Government in the United States* (1942), p. 212.

[45] Wilson, *Congressional Government,* pp. 58-59.

[46] "About one fourth of the nation's voters want the Government to give out more specific information concerning foreign policy. Another one fourth believe the government is holding back vital information. . . ." American Institute of Public Opinion, *Washington Post,* Aug. 23, 1947.

"More than half say they don't know whether the Turkish government is backed by the people and about four in every ten say they don't know whether the present Greek government has the support of a majority of Greeks." The same, Mar. 28, 1947.

"A recent survey of public opinion revealed that one out of three people in the United States still do not know what the United Nations is and what it does. The same study showed that only one in five knows what is meant by the veto." Secretary of State Marshall, Address before the American Association for the United Nations, *New York Times*, Sept. 15, 1947.

"Recent institute polls have shown a steadily increasing number of voters expressing concern over world affairs. While 47 per cent today say that foreign policy is the most important problem facing the nation, only 16 per cent held that view a year ago." *Washington Post*, Aug. 23, 1947.

"Fewer than half the Nation's voters, the poll indicates, have been paying attention to the discussion over the two men's ideas. That is shown in replies to the following: Have you followed the arguments about Byrnes' ideas and Wallace's ideas for dealing with Russia? Yes . . . 42 per cent; No . . . 58 per cent." *Washington Post*, Oct. 13, 1946.

"Although the whole world has crowded in on him in the last few years, the [American Majority Man] is by no means as passionately interested in peoples abroad as they are in him. At a guess, he is more than twice as interested in purely domestic affairs as he is in world affairs. Some students of American opinion allege that there is a submerged 20 per cent which has no interest in foreign affairs at all, and another 20 per cent which is deeply interested." *Newsweek*, Aug. 4, 1947.

"Some years ago Sir Willmott Lewis, Washington correspondent of the *London Times* and a profound student of American public opinion, made the statement that, leaving out Washington, where the diplomats, Government officials and specialized journalists are concentrated, there are not in the United States 500 men who have an 'intelligent, informed and sustained interest in foreign affairs.'

"That seems a ridiculously small number, but when one analyzes it in reference to his own city or town—particularly bearing in mind that word 'sustained'—most men will agree that 500 is not far from an accurate estimate." Frank R. Kent, in the Washington *Star*, July 11, 1947.

[47] *Washington Post*, Oct. 9, 1946. A poll taken in Philadelphia in 1946 showed that four voters out of five did not know the names of the major-party candidates for senators and governor. Washington *Star*, Oct. 29, 1946.

[48] American Institute of Public Opinion, *The Gallup Political Almanac for 1946*, p. 227. The figure for 1946 is an estimate.

[49] Ewing, *Congressional Elections, 1896-1944*, p. 36.

CHAPTER IX

[1] Arthur W. Macmahon, "Conflict, Consensus, Confirmed Trends, and Open Choices," in *American Political Science Review*, Vol. 42 (February 1948), pp. 1-15.

[2] In the New York elections of 1936 to 1944, the American Labor Party allied itself with the Democrats and in 1940 it was the vote of the American Labor Party totaling 317,009 that gave Roosevelt a majority in the state over Willkie.

[3] On the sectional aspects of party strategy and elections, see Cortez A. M. Ewing, *Presidential Elections from Abraham Lincoln to Franklin D. Roosevelt* (1940); A. N. Holcombe, "Present-Day Characteristics of American Political Parties" in *The American Political Scene*, E. B. Logan, ed. (1936), pp. 1-52; Harold F. Gosnell, "The Future of the American Party System" in *The Future of Government in the United States*, Leonard D. White, ed. (1942), pp. 101-18; Harold F. Gosnell, *Grass Roots Politics* (1942).

[4] It is not implied that industrial wage earners vote solidly one way or the other. As a group, however, laborers tend to vote according to a fairly definite conception of special interest.

[5] Henry Jones Ford, *Rise and Growth of American Politics* (1898), pp. 127-28.

[6] Of the 54 Democratic representatives who were elected without opposition in 1944, no less than 50 were from the South, and, in a majority of the other southern districts, Republican opposition is merely nominal. Three of the unopposed Democrats came from California, while four of the six unopposed Republicans were elected in that state.

[7] In the 1940 election, the percentage of the total population voting in the nation was 38. The percentages in the Solid South ranged from 5 in South Carolina to 26 in Florida. American Institute of Public Opinion, *The Gallup Political Almanac for 1946* (1946), pp. 226-27.

[8] The same, pp. 240-50; Louis Bean, "Who Will Win in November?" *New Republic* (Sept. 16, 1946), pp. 316-18; Arthur M. Schlesinger, Jr., "How We Will Vote," *The Atlantic Monthly*, Vol. 178 (October 1946), pp. 37-42.

[9] In Iowa, the people have shown a noticeable lack of interest in recent primaries.

[10] Compare M. R. Bendiner, "Party Platforms and the 1936 Campaign," *Editorial Research Reports*, Vol. 2 (Nov. 12, 1935), pp. 381-85.

[11] "Every contest, whether for a state office, a United States senatorship or a House seat, has issues of its own. And the remarkable thing is that these issues have so little connection with the prevailing national parties." The above refers to Wisconsin, Minnesota, Montana, Washington, Oregon, California, and Colorado. Raymond Moley in *Newsweek*, Sept. 2, 1940.

[12] Commenting on the 1942 "off-year" election, Clarence A. Berdahl says: "As a matter of fact, it becomes extremely difficult, if not impossible, to draw any conclusions from the election except that the people were somehow dissatisfied, probably with the lack up to that time of any important military victory. The results were evidently determined as much by local as by national considerations. In Minnesota, presumably an isolationist center, pro-Willkie and strongly internationalist Republicans were elected governor and senator, together with isolationist congressmen; in New York, an interventionist area, an anti-Willkie but moderately internationalist Republican was elected governor, while the most conspicuous anti-Willkie and isolationist Republican congressmen was also elected; in Illinois, generally conceded to be the strongest isolationist center, extreme isolationists were elected senator and congressman-at-large, although both had repudiated isolationism shortly before the election. New Deal and anti-New Deal Democrats were elected; conspicuous Democratic supporters of the war policies were defeated and more were elected. These results would seem to indicate that the war has actually done little or nothing to our party system—that our political parties continue to operate in about the same confused manner as in time of peace." Clarence A. Berdahl, "Political Parties and Elections," *American Political Science Review*, Vol. 37 (February 1943), p. 80.

[13] "The party organization had to be strong because, in order to afford any guarantee that the will of the people should actually be executed, all elected officers had to be pledged individually to follow a certain line of conduct, and the party had to assume responsibility for them, and had to formulate in advance what came to be called a platform. Upon this platform each candidate was supposed to stand, and its formal acceptance was demanded of each candidate for an important office. The individual candidate was thus necessarily

sunk in the party. It was largely for this reason that the individual professions of faith which under other governmental systems are often made by each candidate are practically unknown to American public life.

"It is mainly because of the absolute necessity for the coordination of the functions of politics and administration, a coordination which . . . could not be obtained in the governmental system, and must be found in the party organization, that party regularity, as it is called, has been so prized in the United States. . . .

"This strong party organization further was made necessary in the state and in the more complex local governments, viz. the cities, by the mere number of officers to be elected. . . .

"The party organization which took upon itself the burden of coordinating the functions of expressing and executing the will of the state in the American governmental system, had to be not merely strong but also permanent. . . ." Frank J. Goodnow, *Politics and Administration* (1900), pp. 105-07.

[14] Some states have a second or "run-off" primary to decide between the two leading candidates. This system puts an additional burden on the voter while intensifying conflict in the party.

[15] A survey in January 1940 indicated that 19 per cent of the voters called themselves independents and that neither party could claim even the nominal allegiance of anything like a majority of the electorate. It appeared that more than 11 million voters were unconcerned with party labels. "Institute of Public Opinion Analysis," *New York Times*, Jan. 14, 1940; Arthur C. Millspaugh, *Democracy, Efficiency, Stability* (1942), p. 337.

[16] Schlesinger, *Atlantic Monthly*, p. 42.

[17] The quotations are from Ernest Barker, *Reflections on Government* (1942), pp. 404-05.

[18] Examples of long political experience are found in the careers of McKinley, Theodore Roosevelt, Charles E. Hughes, Calvin Coolidge, and Franklin D. Roosevelt. Rising more rapidly, Grover Cleveland had been elected sheriff and governor; and Woodrow Wilson governor. Neither William H. Taft nor Herbert Hoover had held an elective office prior to his election as president, but both had been distinguished Cabinet members.

[19] Among presidential candidates since 1880, Wendell Willkie had not previously been a Republican, in politics, or in public office. William J. Bryan had been a member of Congress, Alton B. Parker a judge, and John W. Davis an ambassador. Harding had had long political experience but without distinction.

[20] An effort was made to extend the direct-primary principle to the nomination of presidential candidates; and in 1916 one half of the states had presidential primary laws. In a dozen or more states, the presidential primary is still used to test the strength of contenders, to indicate popular preference, and to instruct state delegations. The results, however, do not necessarily decide what the national convention will do. Buel W. Patch, "Decline of the Presidential Primary," *Editorial Research Reports*, Vol. 1 (Mar. 3, 1932), pp. 154-70.

[21] Of the 23 different men who have been major-party candidates since 1880, 19 have been residents of the Northeast, and 4 have come from west of the Mississippi. (Bryan, Hoover, Landon, and Truman.) The southern states have supplied not a single candidate. Of the 19 residents of the Northeast, 7 came from New York and 5 from Ohio. The other 7 were Hancock (Pennsylvania), Blaine (Maine), Harrison (Indiana), Wilson (New Jersey), Coolidge (Massachusetts), Davis (West Virginia), and Willkie (Indiana).

[22] Notable exceptions are Theodore Roosevelt, who was vice-presidential

candidate in 1900, Calvin Coolidge (1920), who certainly equaled Warren Harding in ability, and Earl Warren, Republican vice-presidential candidate in 1948.

[23] Carrol Reece, Chairman of the Republican National Committee, set forth the principle of party government as follows:

"Every Republican in Congress today represents both his party and his individual constituency. It was the party which elected him. He is a member of a team—one which he joined of his own free will and with full realization of the responsibilities he was assuming. . . .

"A successful team is one which executes the signals called by the duly chosen quarterback. Differences of opinion as to the choice of a particular play are ironed out in the huddles before the plays are called—not afterward. Team play is the first essential of success." *Washington Post*, Mar. 3, 1947; *New York Times*, Mar. 3, 1947.

But Senator Wayne Morse of Oregon replied as follows:

"It is Reece's fallacious contention that unless a Republican member of Congress follows the Republican leaders, he does not engage in Republican team play. As one Republican I deny that the group of Republicans for whom Carroll Reece serves as chore boy, represents the rank and file of registered Republican voters. . . .

"Middle-of-the-road liberal Republicans cannot team-work with the Reece type of Republicanism. We intend to carry this fight to the Republican voters of America and we are satisfied that they will demonstrate to Reece and his group that they want the Republican party to move forward with the Republican liberals and not backward with the Republican reactionaries." *New York Times*, Mar. 4, 1947.

In the spring of 1946, Secretary of Commerce Henry A. Wallace called for party responsibility on "fundamental issues."

"Unless a member of the majority party in Congress votes in favor of major issues upon which he and other members of his party were elected," Wallace declared, "the legislative branch of our Government ceases to function.

"New issues arise from time to time upon which parties have not taken stands in their platforms. When an important new issue arises, if the President, the President pro tem of the Senate, the Speaker of the House, the majority leaders in the Senate and House, and a party caucus agree upon it, the members of the majority party in Congress should, when the issue is up for a vote in Congress, be governed by such majority agreement." *New York Times*, Apr. 23, 1946. Six months later, Mr. Wallace himself, while retaining his Cabinet post, spoke publicly against the foreign policy announced by the leadership of his party. As modern American politics go, whether party responsibility is good or bad depends a good deal on whose ox is gored.

[24] George H. Sabine, "What Is the Matter with Representative Government," in *The People, Politics and the Politicians*, A. N. Christensen and E. M. Kirkpatrick, eds. (1941), p. 410. In 1937-38 Mr. William Green may have sent as many messages to members of Congress as did President Roosevelt. O. R. Altman, "Second and Third Sessions of the Seventy-fifth Congress, 1937-38," *American Political Science Review*, Vol. 32 (December 1938), p. 1120. "The agricultural bloc of the Senate within recent years has met more often than has the Democratic membership of the Senate." James F. Byrnes, in *The Organization of Congress*, Symposium on Congress by Members of Congress and Others. Joint Committee Print, 79 Cong., 1 sess., pp. 20-21. "House veterans of both world wars will be called together Monday to form a powerful perma-

nent caucus to work out a veterans' legislative program. Representative Prince H. Preston (D., Ga.), a member of a self-appointed bipartisan committee, said last night that the idea was for the caucus to unify 169 world war veterans in order to 'effectively sponsor legislation to aid our comrades.' " *Washington Post,* Jan. 9, 1947. To judge from its newspaper advertising, the American Federation of Labor considered the debate over labor legislation a struggle by organized labor against the National Association of Manufacturers. *New York Times,* May 24, 1947.

[25] Woodrow Wilson, *Constitutional Government in the United States* (1911), pp. 56-59.

[26] Quoted in *Washington Post,* July 20, 1946.

[27] On the basis of a study of vetoes during the 45 years from 1889 to 1934, Katherine A. Towle reached the following conclusions: "The period of politically divided or adverse Congresses covers 12 of the 45 years under consideration. In this period, there were 85 direct vetoes, and 37 (43.7 per cent) attempts to reverse the veto, of which number 13 (35.1 per cent) were successful, and 24 (64.8 per cent) unsuccessful. When the time element in the distribution of Congresses is considered, these figures assume importance, for they indicate that in the 12 years of politically divided or adverse Congresses the direct veto was exercised more than one and one-half times as often as in the 33 years of politically controlled Congresses; that, although within the respective groups themselves the percentages of both successful and unsuccessful attempts to override the veto were almost identical, four times as many attempts at reversal were resorted to in the years of politically divided or adverse Congresses as in those controlled by the President's party; and that in the former period, congressional reversal occurred approximately four times as frequently as in the latter." Katherine A. Towle, "The Presidential Veto Since 1889," *American Political Science Review,* Vol. 31 (February 1937), pp. 54-56.

[28] "This bi-partisan foreign policy has been confined within relatively narrow limits. It has applied to the United Nations. It has applied to peace treaties in Europe. It has applied to nothing else. I have had nothing to do, for example, with China policies or Pan American policies except within the United Nations, and at times I have been satisfied with neither. The first I ever heard of the Greek-Turkish policy was when the President disclosed his thoughts ten days ago at the White House. I do not complain. But I do not propose to be misunderstood. . . . I have said that we have no safe alternative but to uphold the President's hands at this dangerous hour." Senator Vandenberg, Statement to the Senate, *New York Times,* Mar. 19, 1947.

"Among the paramount factors to which we dare not deny due weight is this: To repudiate the President of the United States at such an hour could display a division and weakness which might involve far greater jeopardy than a sturdy display of united strength. We are not free to ignore the price of non-compliance." Senator Vandenberg, Speech in Senate, *New York Times,* Apr. 9, 1947.

"I intend to vote for the Greek and Turkish loans for the reason that the President's announcements have committed the United States to this policy in the eyes of the world, and to repudiate it now would destroy his prestige in the negotiations with the Russian Government, on the success of which ultimate peace depends." Senator Taft, Speech in Senate, *New York Times,* Apr. 11, 1947.

"In the field of foreign policy, this Congress has done its best to co-operate with the policies of the President. We realize that the Constitution and existing law confer upon the President almost complete power over the foreign policy of the United States. In general, I believe Congress should hesitate to interfere unless that policy involves us in the danger of an unnecessary war, or proposes to drain the resources of our taxpayers and our productive labor to an unreasonable degree."

"I believe it is a field where Congress should not, except with great provocation, give foreign countries a picture of a divided America. . . ." Senator Taft, Address at Columbus, Ohio, *New York Times,* Aug. 1, 1947.

[29] ". . . In fact the three—peace, freedom and world trade—are inseparable. . . .

". . . We are doing everything within our power to foster international co-operation. We have dedicated ourselves to its success.

"This is not, and it must never be, the policy of a single administration or a single party. It is the policy of all the people of the United States. We in America are unanimous in our determination to prevent another war.

"But some among us do not fully realize what we must do to carry out this policy. There still are those who seem to believe that we can confine our co-operation with other countries to political relationships; that we need not co-operate where economic questions are involved.

"This attitude has sometimes led to the assertion that there should be bipartisan support for the foreign policy of the United States, but that there need not be bi-partisan support for the foreign economic policy of the United States.

"Such a statement simply does not make sense.

"Our foreign relations, political and economic, are indivisible. . . ." President Truman, Address at Baylor University, *New York Times,* Mar. 7, 1947.

Universal military training "is no more an issue for partisan politics than is the whole subject of our national defense." *Washington Post,* Aug. 30, 1947. "We have determined on a bi-partisan foreign policy. Our ability to carry out our commitments under this policy is dependent upon our fiscal solvency. It would seem that a bi-partisan policy for retrenchment and economy should be the foundation stone on which to build our foreign policy." Senator Byrd, quoted by Arthur Krock, *New York Times,* May 25, 1947.

[30] Anne O'Hare McCormick in *New York Times,* July 17, 1948.

[31] Compare Hamilton Fish Armstrong, "Foreign Policy and Party Politics," in *Atlantic Monthly* (April 1947), pp. 56-63.

[32] Compare the following: "We might ask ourselves when it is that a bipartisan conduct of foreign affairs is necessary and workable. The answer, I think, is: when almost everyone agrees that the country needs a united foreign policy though it is not yet settled just what the policy ought to be. For whenever it is necessary to work out a bi-partisan arrangement, it is a sure sign that new decisions are in the making. Bi-partisanship is an arrangement by public-spirited men for dealing with those critical periods when a policy is forming but is not yet formed.

"If and when a policy is fully formed and proved, it ceases to be bi-partisan and becomes national." Walter Lippmann in the *Washington Post,* Nov. 9, 1946.

CHAPTER X

[1] "No aspect of the great elaboration of governmental functions during the past decade, of which further development is widely proposed, is more significant than the tendency to consider limited parts of the economic system without adequate consideration of their interrelationship with other parts, and the inclination to appraise limited phases of public policy without a proper under-

standing of their bearing on other phases. Efforts to deal with some parts of economic life are at times seriously hampered by the treatment given to other parts, and attempts to meet a particular problem by one plan are often nullified by other developments in public action. Moreover, larger social criteria are frequently neglected in the consideration of immediate problems, and once a program is adopted there is a strong tendency to focus attention on the problems of effective administration and to ignore questions concerning the wisdom of what it embodies." Leverett S. Lyon and Victor Abramson, *Government and Economic Life,* Vol. 2 (1940), p. 1287.

[2] "We are accustomed to thinking of Congress as the body which makes the laws, but to an extent greater than most people realize, Congress is now a revisionary body which influences but which does not itself make public policy. In considering legislation, Congress has what amounts to an item veto over presidential and bureaucratic proposals, and in some instances this revisionary power is used very extensively. But ordinarily neither Congress nor any agent of Congress thinks up the policy which should be followed and the laws which should be enacted. The initiative in originating legislation has passed almost entirely to the President and to the bureaucracy which he directs." Roland Young, *This Is Congress* (1943), pp. 7-8. Compare Lawrence H. Chamberlain, *The President, Congress and Legislation* (1946).

[3] In his excellent study of the legislative process (*The President, Congress and Legislation*), Chamberlain shows that, on various subjects of legislation, Congress is to be credited with the origination as well as with the accomplishment of legislation. He states: "The careful observer will not be taken in by the thesis that Congress has ceased to be an important factor in the process of law-making." (p. 307) While clarifying these points, however, Mr. Chamberlain shows, incidentally but convincingly, the deficiencies of Congress as a law-making organization and its inability on many occasions to take any action under its own power.

[4] "Since 1941 a series of independent surveys of the machinery and methods of our National Legislature have been made by public and private organizations. These surveys, including that by the Joint Committee on the Organization of Congress, have reached substantially the same conclusions as to the defects in our legislative structure and operation and as to appropriate correctives. They are agreed that Congress today is neither organized nor equipped to perform adequately its main functions of determining policy, authorizing administrative organization and appropriations to carry out policy, and supervising execution of the resultant programs.

"Devised to handle the simpler tasks of an earlier day, our legislative machinery and procedures are by common consent no longer competent to cope satisfactorily with the grave and complex problems of the postwar world. They must be modernized if we are to avoid an imminent break-down of the legislative branch of the National Government." *Legislative Reorganization Act of 1946,* Report of the Special Committee on the Organization of Congress, S. Rept. 1400, 79 Cong. 2 sess., pp. 1-2.

See also George Galloway, *Congress at the Crossroads,* Pt. 5 (1946); George Galloway, et al., American Political Science Association, Committee on Congress, "Second Progress Report," as of June 30, 1942, *American Political Science Review,* Vol. 36 (December 1942), pp. 1091-1102.

[5] Galloway, *Congress at the Crossroads,* p. 99. *Organization of Congress,* Hearings before the Joint Committee on the Organization of Congress, 79 Cong. 1 sess. (1945), pp. 105-06. Chamberlain, *The President, Congress and Legislation,* pp. 70-72.

[6] *Organization of Congress,* Hearings, pp. 9-10, 302.

[7] Galloway, *Congress at the Crossroads,* pp. 56-105, 195. The Legislative Reorganization Act of 1946 (60 Stat. 812) provides that the Ways and Means Committee and the Appropriations Committee of the House and the Finance Committee and the Committee on Appropriations of the Senate shall meet together at the beginning of a session to consider the revenues and expenditures of the government. The Employment Act of 1946 created a Joint Committee on the Economic Report. Other notable joint committees are Reduction of Nonessential Federal Expenditures and the Joint Committee on Atomic Energy.

[8] For a good summary of the arguments for and against bicameralism, see Alvin W. Johnson, *The Unicameral Legislature* (1938), pp. 45-75.

[9] Merlo J. Pusey, *Big Government—Can We Control It?* (1945), p. 124; Chamberlain, *The President, Congress and Legislation,* pp. 64-65.

[10] "But there are other reasons still more organic than these why the debates of Congress cannot, under our present system, have that serious purpose of search into the merits of policies and that definite and determinate party—or, if you will, partisan—aim without which they can never be effective for the instruction of public opinion, or the cleansing of political action. The chief of these reasons, because the parent of all the rest, is that there are in Congress no authoritative leaders who are the recognized spokesmen of their parties. Power is nowhere concentrated; it is rather deliberately and of set policy scattered amongst many small chiefs." Woodrow Wilson, *Congressional Government* (1913), pp. 91-92.

[11] The usual observation is that members of Congress are "representative" or "average." Estes Kefauver and Jack Levin say: "There are on the whole as good people in Congress as back home." (*Twentieth-century Congress,* 1947, p. 15.) This is true, if the average is meant; it is not true of many "back-home" districts, if reference is to the best.

[12] "Mr. Plumley: How many Members of the House do you suppose there are today that have read the bills which have been filed, or who know what they are all about?"

"Mr. Ramspeck: Mr. Plumley, I just do not want to say it for the record. I feel very few read the bills, or, for that matter know that they are coming up." *Organization of Congress,* Hearings, p. 298.

"Mr. Monroney: Today I venture to say, when an appropriation bill passes the House, not 10 per cent of the Members of Congress fully understand the fiscal matters involved in that bill." The same, pp. 678, 204.

"Mr. Michener: Yes. If you will pardon this one interjection—the public certainly does not know that a bill carrying, let us say, $23,000,000,000 for a department was determined in secret, that just a few Members of the Congress were permitted to participate in the preparation, and then that the House was called upon to act within 24 or 36 hours after the House got its first information as to what the bill contained." The same, p. 707.

For other examples of uninformed action, see Chamberlain, *The President, Congress and Legislation,* pp. 64-65, 70-72.

[13] Quoted in Vernon Louis Parrington, *Main Currents in American Thought* Vol. 2 (1939), p. 386.

[14] "Our representative legislative bodies have demonstrated their inadequacy for synthesizing group conflict into a unified conception of the public interest." E. Pendleton Herring, *Public Administration and the Public Interest* (1936), pp. 6-7.

[15] For example, the middle classes generally and the consumer interest.

[16] "In United States politics, the differences of attitude and interest are so

great among various regions, and the legislative representatives of those regions so free of direction by national leaders, that a majority may well support each of a dozen activities severally which, if combined in a single programme, would surely be defeated. (The majority for each of the several activities would be made up, of course, of a different combination of minorities.) In American government it does not pay to put all your functional eggs into one philosophical basket." Don K. Price, "American Government During 1946," *Public Administration,* Vol. 25 (1947), p. 81.

[17] "The long germinative period detectable in the genesis of most laws is of the utmost importance; it constitutes one of the most valuable contributions that a legislative body can make." Lawrence H. Chamberlain, "The President, Congress and Legislation," *Political Science Quarterly,* Vol. 61 (March 1946), pp. 57-59. This "long germinative period" too often represents pure dilatoriness or repeated obstruction. So far as the delaying function of Congress is concerned, one can agree with Chamberlain's view that "No other agency in a democracy is so well equipped by composition and organization to discharge this function." (The same.) "Congress did not enact regulatory legislation until seven chaotic years after radio-broadcasting had made its debut." Carl J. Friedrich and Evelyn Sternberg, "Congress and the Control of Radio-Broadcasting," *American Political Science Review,* Vol. 37 (October 1943), pp. 797-818.

[18] It was a filibuster in the Senate in March 1917 on a bill authorizing the President to arm merchant vessels that prompted 75 senators to sign a statement which read as follows:

"We desire this statement entered in the *Record* to establish the fact that the Senate favors the legislation and would pass it, if a vote could be had."

On the same day President Wilson issued the following public statement:

"In the immediate presence of a crisis fraught with more subtle and far-reaching possibilities of national danger than any the Government has known within the whole history of its international relations, the Congress has been unable to act either to safeguard the country or to vindicate the elementary rights of its citizens. More than 500 of the 531 members of the two Houses were ready and anxious to act; the House of Representatives had acted, by an overwhelming majority; but the Senate was unable to act because a little group of eleven Senators had determined that it should not. . . . The Senate of the United States is the only legislative body in the world which cannot act when its majority is ready for action. A little group of wilful men, representing no opinion but their own, have rendered the great government of the United States helpless and contemptible. . . ."

[19] For example, negotiations for the British loan were completed in December 1945, but the Senate did not begin committee hearings until March 5, 1946. On the bill to extend selective service (1946), the *New York Times* said editorially on May 15, 1946: "To begin with, there is not the slightest excuse for this delay in meeting the issue until the very eve of the expiration of the law. . . . It was away back on Sept. 6 of last year . . . that President Truman warned Congress of the necessity of action before May 15, 1946. . . .

"Yet Congress was so dilatory in this matter, so unwilling to face facts and apparently so afraid of its own political shadow that 216 days were permitted to pass before a committee of either branch of Congress even went so far as to report a bill to extend Selective Service."

The Greek-Turkish aid bill (1947) and unification of the armed services are further examples of what seem to be excessive delay. When Congress adjourned in 1947 and again in 1948, measures repeatedly urged by the Secretary of State were left in the log-jam of unfinished business.

[20] James Bryce, *American Commonwealth*, Vol. 1 (1910), p. 165.

[21] Charles A. Beard, *The Republic* (1943), p. 257.

[22] Kefauver and Levin cite two instances in which two men had the same seniority and the committee chairmanship was determined by alphabetical precedence. *Twentieth-century Congress*, pp. 134-35.

[23] Of 32 House leaders in the Republican Seventy-first Congress (1929-30), 21 were from the industrial Northeast; but in the Democratic Seventy-third Congress (1933-34), 22 were from the South. Both groups of leaders tended to be small-town or rural. More than two thirds of the Democratic leaders were from places of less than 50,000, and more than half from towns of less than 10,000. (Arthur C. Millspaugh, *Democracy, Efficiency, Stability*, 1942, p. 308.) Of 39 House leaders in the Democratic Seventy-ninth Congress (1945-46), 26 or 69.2 per cent were from the South and of 27 leaders in the Republican Eightieth Congress (1947-48), 21 or 77.8 per cent were from the Northeast. (The difference in the number of leaders is explained by the congressional reorganization which reduced the number of committees after 1946.) While the leaders in the Republican Eightieth Congress were predominantly from the industrial Northeast—a favorable indication—about two thirds appear to have had rural or small-town residences. The Republican, like the Democratic leaders came predominantly from the rock-ribbed or "safe" districts. Sixteen of the 27 received majorities in 1944 exceeding 60 per cent; and 24 received more than 55 per cent of the major party vote. *Gallup Political Almanac for 1946*, pp. 245-49.

[24] "The House of Representatives has some 40 standing committees. Ten of these committees have chairmen elected in 1932 or later—36 have chairmen elected earlier. Five of the 36 were elected in 1930. Three quarters of the committee chairmen were elected to Congress in the days when national issues were of the John Davis versus Calvin Coolidge, Cox versus Harding, or Smith versus Hoover type. Eleven of them were elected in 1918 or earlier." E. L. Oliver, "The Responsibility of Political Parties for Social Action," address delivered before the National Conference of Social Work, Seattle, Wash., June 28, 1938, cited in *The Organization of Congress*, Symposium on Congress by Members of Congress and Others, Joint Committee Print, 79 Cong. 1 sess. (August 1945), pp. 155-56. In 1947 of the 17 chairmen of committees concerned with public policy, 9 were first elected to Congress in 1928 or earlier.

[25] Bryce, *American Commonwealth*, Vol. 1, pp. 161-65. On committees with special reference to the Senate, see George H. Haynes, *The Senate of the United States: Its History and Practice*, Vol 1 (1938), pp. 271-316.

[26] 60 Stat. 812, 79 Cong. 2 sess.

[27] "Mr. Cox: Were you in the Senate in 1921?"

"Mr. Wadsworth: Yes."

"Mr. Cox: Do you recall the action of the Senate in working over the committee system, in reducing the number from 74 to 34?"

"Mr. Wadsworth: Vaguely."

"Mr. Cox: They got rid of 40 committees."

"Mr. Wadsworth: I remember it vaguely. I know a good many of us did not regard it as a great achievement in the way of reform."

"Mr. Cox: Mr. Chairman, you have been here a long time. Do you recall getting rid of the dead weight; do you recall that fight?"

"The Chairman: [Senator Robert M. LaFollette, Jr.] My recollection is the same as the recollection of Representative Wadsworth, that what we achieved was mostly pruning off the obviously dead branches of the committee tree." *Organization of Congress,* Hearings, pp. 95-96.

"These 81 "little legislatures' [in 1945] were by no means of equal magnitude and importance. More than half of them on both sides of the Capitol were classified as minor and relatively inactive so far as meetings, hearings, publications, and reports were concerned. Not more than 12 or 15 in each House were major committees dealing with public problems of national significance." Galloway, *Congress at the Crossroads,* pp. 89-90; the same, p. 54.

[28] "With fewer committees the crust of age at the top of the committees is now more than twice as thick as it was before." Philip S. Broughton, "Congress Is Far From Reorganized," *The New York Times Magazine* (May 18, 1947), p. 64.

[29] Estes Kefauver gives examples of duplication in his "Let's Cut Out These Congressional High Jinks," *American Magazine* (April 1948).

[30] The number of subcommittees had reached 146 on Apr. 13, 1947.

[31] Broughton, *New York Times Magazine,* p. 7; Arthur Krock, "Reorganization Gives Scant Aid to Congress," *New York Times,* July 6, 1947.

[32] Senator Vandenberg's prepared statement to the Senate Appropriations Committee, *New York Times,* June 10, 1948.

[33] The Republican party does considerably better than the Democrats. Republican co-ordination in the Eightieth Congress was exceptionally good.

[34] "This [Republican] conference body of 40 needed some sort of an executive directorship, just as a corporation has a board of directors. So, the conference elected a steering committee of nine members. On that steering committee, which is under the chairmanship of Senator Taft, we have all the principal leaders of the minority in the Senate. We have Senator White as a member of it, and he is floor leader of the minority. We have Senator Wherry, who is the whip of the minority on the floor. We have Senator Vandenberg who heads the conference itself, and therefore correlates the conference with the steering committee. In addition there are 6 other elected members. I am the secretary of that committee.

"The steering committee undertakes to do this over-all thing: to discuss problems of policy, to formulate a legislative program, and to consider problems of minority floor operations with the idea in mind of giving at least some guidance to the party members. The members of the conference are not bound by the decisions made in the steering committee or in the conference itself." Testimony of George H. E. Smith, in *Organization of Congress,* Hearings, p. 361.

[35] "In short, the Committee on Rules is to a large degree the governing committee of the House. To it the House has largely delegated the power vested in itself by the constitution to regulate its procedure." Galloway, *Congress at the Crossroads,* p. 112.

[36] In January 1935 President Roosevelt suggested that Congress take into consideration "the necessity for the development of interrelated planning of our national transportation." *Public Papers and Addresses,* Vol. 4, pp. 68-69. Along with his vetoes of labor bills, President Truman asked for the naming of a commission to review the whole field of labor legislation; and when he vetoed the tax reduction bill in 1947, he called for a general tax program "geared to the financial and economic needs of this country." Unfortunately, both recommendations resembled locking the stable after the horse had been stolen. A general tax program is at least fifty years overdue and the comprehensive study of labor relations should have preceded the enactment of the National Labor Relations Act of July 5, 1935. Still more unfortunately, because of the

time required for comprehensive studies, a proposal for one may be merely a scheme for political obstruction. The Taft-Hartley Labor Act, passed over the President's veto, provides for a joint congressional labor-management committee to study the whole problem of industrial relations. Following the President's veto of the income tax reduction bill on June 20, 1947, Representative Knutson, chairman of the House Committee on Ways and Means and of the Joint Committee on Internal Revenue Taxation stated that a comprehensive tax-revision bill would be ready in 1948.

[37] 60 Stat. 28, 79 Cong. 2 sess.

[38] The Joint Committee, according to Kefauver and Levin, "after considering the advice of many of its members and leading political scientists, recommended the establishment of majority and minority policy committees, four in all. These would consist of seven members from the majority and minority parties of each house, and function separately in each body. The recommendation was approved by the Senate. But part of the price of passage of the Reorganization Bill in the House was the striking out of this basic provision." *Twentieth-century Congress,* p. 129.

"To students of government the role of the speaker of the House in the dilution of the legislative reorganization bill was illuminating. As presiding officer of the House and high priest of its rules, he was naturally deeply interested in the proposed changes. As the central figure in policy making in the lower chamber, he faced a probable diminution of his power through the functions to be assigned to the proposed seven-man majority policy committee. As one of the Big Four who meet every Monday with the President while Congress is in session to consider the legislative program, perhaps he saw no need for superseding these smoothly working informal conferences by a formal joint legislative-executive council. And so these important sections of the bill had to be deleted before it could leave the speaker's table and receive the blessing of the Rules Committee." (Galloway, *Congress at the Cross Roads,* pp. 345-46.) After the House struck out this provision for policy committees, the Senate provided for its own policy committees in an appropriations-bill rider. The Republican policy committee of the Senate now serves as the steering committee. In the House, outstanding Republicans were put on the Rules Committee, and the majority members of that committee were made members of the Republican steering committee. "Here is at least a suggestion that the rule-makers will be held in check by and subject to the direction of a nucleus of policy-makers. . . . The Rules Committee could then be used to support and implement party policy, instead of exerting its power narrowly to advance or retard petty legislation or to give effect to the prejudices of some of its members." *Washington Post,* Jan. 16, 1947.

[39] In 1928 the Senate passed a bill for the registration of lobbyists; but in the House it remained pigeon-holed in the Judiciary Committee. (Haynes, *The Senate of the United States: Its History and Practice,* Vol. 1, pp. 499-500.) Registration was finally provided for in the Reorganization Act of 1946; but registration, while it may be desirable, is not likely to alter appreciably the pressure process.

[40] Henry Jones Ford, *Rise and Growth of American Politics* (1898), pp. 279-93; Wilson, *Congressional Government,* p. 13.

"The contemporary decline in the effectiveness and prestige of Congress in relation to the Executive branch reflects a trend true of representative assemblies generally. It is a concomitant of the rising power of the Executive and finds its inner explanation, *inter alia,* in the great expansion and centralization of governmental functions, the technical nature of modern public problems, the growth of the federal bureaucracy, the power of Executive patronage, the decline of leadership in Congress, and in the impact of the war emergency. The chances are that this trend may continue for some time. Dominance in our federal system has shifted to the Executive branch. Perhaps this is not a passing phase in the cycle of politics, but an underlying world-wide trend in institutional relations. State intervention in economic life and foreign wars calls for swifter decisions and quicker action than the present deliberative processes of parliamentary democracy usually bring forth." American Political Science Association, Committee on Congress, "Second Progress Report," June 30, 1942. *American Political Science Review*, Vol. 36 (December 1942), pp. 1091-1102. See also Karl Loewenstein, "The Balance Between Legislative and Executive Power: A Study in Comparative Constitutional Law," *University of Chicago Law Review* Vol. 5 (December 1937), pp. 583-84.

[41] In the field of domestic affairs, the basic and now accepted theory of presidential power or prerogative was set forth by Theodore Roosevelt as follows: "The most important factor in getting the right spirit in my administration . . . was my insistence upon the theory that the executive power was limited only by specific restrictions and prohibitions appearing in the Constitution or imposed by Congress under its constitutional powers. My view was that every executive officer, and above all every executive officer in high position was a steward of the people bound actively and affirmatively to do all he could for the people. . . . I decline to adopt the view that what was imperatively necessary for the nation could not be done by the President unless he could find some specific authorization to do it. . . . Under this interpretation of executive power I did and caused to be done many things not previously done by the President and the heads of the departments. I did not usurp power but I did greatly broaden the use of executive power." Quoted in Wilfred E. Binkley, *President and Congress* (1947), pp. 191-92.

The most extreme suggestion for delegation in a time of peace was made by Franklin D. Roosevelt in his first inaugural address on Mar. 4, 1933:

"It may be hoped that the normal balance of executive and legislative authority may be wholly adequate to meet the unprecedented task before us. But it may be that an unprecedented demand and need for undelayed action may call for temporary departure from that normal balance of public procedure.

"I am prepared under my constitutional duty to recommend the measures that a striken nation in the midst of a stricken world may require. These measures, or such other measures as the Congress may build out of its experience and wisdom, I shall seek, within my constitutional authority, to bring to speedy adoption.

"But in the event that the Congress shall fail to take one of these two courses, and in the event that the national emergency is still critical, I shall not evade the clear course of duty that will then confront me. I shall ask the Congress for the one remaining instrument to meet the crisis—broad executive power to wage a war against the emergency, as great as the power that would be given to me if we were in fact invaded by a foreign foe." *Public Papers and Addresses*, Vol. 2, pp. 12-16.

[42] The last-named reversal of the legislative process found embodiment in the Reorganization Act of 1939, which provided that the president's reorganization orders should be laid before the two houses and be subject to their veto by concurrent resolution at any time within 60 days. The Reorganization Act of 1945 (59 Stat. 613) had a similar provision.

[43] To save a measure of its power, Congress has in several instances retained for itself a power of veto by concurrent resolution. For example, in a number of wartime acts. Edward S. Corwin, *Total War and the Constitution* (1947), p. 45. Occasionally, a statute prescribes that an executive department shall obtain the consent of a congressional committee before taking action.

[44] "The President is at liberty, both in law and conscience, to be as big a man as he can. His capacity will set the limit; and if Congress be overborne by him, it will be no fault of the makers of the Constitution—it will be from no lack of constitutional powers on its part, but only because the President has the nation behind him, and Congress has not. He has no means of compelling Congress except through public opinion." Woodrow Wilson, *Constitutional Government in the United States* (1911), pp. 68-71.

[45] See Corwin, *Total War and the Constitution.*

[46] "Thus the atomic bomb is likely, if we take its menace with proper seriousness, to have considerable effect upon both our industrial and our constitutional structure. But now note that *the effect will not be confined to wartime . . . but will be spread through peacetime. The effects of the impact of total war on the Constitution will thus become imbedded in the peacetime Constitution.*" The same, p. 8.

[47] When he took office in 1933, Franklin D. Roosevelt asserted that "this nation asks for action, and action now." He assumed "unhesitatingly the leadership of this great army of our people dedicated to a disciplined attack upon our common problems." The people, he declared, had "registered a mandate that they want direct, vigorous action. They have asked for discipline and direction under leadership. They have made me the present instrument of their wishes." *Public Papers and Addresses,* Vol. 2, pp. 12-10.

[48] As President Wilson was at the end of his second term and as President Roosevelt seems to have been at the Yalta Conference.

[49] "No man entered the White House with less briefing of what was happening than Mr. Truman. Before he had had time to adjust himself, he had to go to Potsdam, and, in deference to Roosevelt-Morgenthau ideas, underwrote a scheme for a peace settlement which times have shown to have been plain lunacy." *Washington Post,* Sept. 27, 1947.

[50] Grant came from the Army.

[51] No test occurred of his qualifications as Commander-in-Chief of the Army and Navy.

[52] For an example, see President Truman's Address to Congress, Jan. 7, 1948.

[53] "If it were possible today for any President to give his full attention to military affairs, this step [unification of the armed forces] would not be necessary. But we all know that the President even now is much overworked and that he cannot permit himself to become entirely preoccupied by his duties as Commander-in-Chief. In wartime, of course, he will necessarily shift the balance of this attention toward military affairs, but it was our experience even in wartime that with all his great energy and deep understanding of military matters, President Roosevelt was not always able to give his personal guidance to the armed forces. And in peace, quite as much as in war, such guidance is urgently needed. . . ." Henry L. Stimson, Letter to Chairman of the Senate Armed Services Committee, *New York Times,* May 5, 1947.

[54] The conclusion that President Truman's Palestine policy sprang from considerations of party strategy is based on press reports and editorial and other interpretations in *New York Times,* Aug. 1, 1946, Oct. 7, 8, 1946, and Feb. 26, 1947; *Washington Post,* Aug. 16, 1946, Oct. 5, 7, 9, 1946; and Washington *Star,*

Oct. 8, 1946. Mr. Dewey, then candidate for Governor of New York, made a similar bid for the Jewish vote.

[55] For an admirable study of presidential commissions, see Carl Marcy, *Presidential Commissions* (1945).

[56] Herman Finer, *The Theory and Practice of Modern Government*, Vol 1 (1932), p. 164.

[57] As it did when Taft succeeded Theodore Roosevelt and Truman succeeded Franklin D. Roosevelt.

[58] "Taken by and large, the history of the Presidency is a history of aggrandizement, but the story is a highly discontinuous one. Of the thirty-one individuals who have filled the office only about one in three has contributed to the development of its powers; under other incumbents things have either stood still or gone backward." Edward S. Corwin, *The President: Office and Powers* (1940), pp. 17-30.

[59] Theodore Roosevelt, 7 years; Woodrow Wilson, 4 years; and Franklin D. Roosevelt, 7 years (1933 to 1939 inclusive).

[60] "A realistic appraisal of the President's endeavors and accomplishments between March 4, 1933 and the outbreak of the new World War six-and-a-half years later shows that almost every important domestic change began in the first three years—most of them in the first hundred days." George Fort Milton, *The Use of Presidential Power, 1789-1943* (1944), p. 274.

[61] Pendleton Herring describes Franklin D. Roosevelt's relations with the Seventy-third Congress as follows: "The presidential system was a game of touch and go between the chief executive and Congressional blocs played by procedural dodges and with bread and circuses for forfeits." *Presidential Leadership* (1940), p. 66. For examples of rejection by Congress of Franklin D. Roosevelt's leadership, see Walter H. C. Laves and Francis O. Wilcox, "American Government and Politics," *American Political Science Review* (April 1944), pp. 314-16.

[62] "In actual practice our system can respond quickly to emergency conditions once the public is convinced of the need. Presidential leadership sustained by a united people has power for any crisis.

"In a time of divided purposes Congress can so obstruct action that no president can have his will; but when the goal is clear the branches of government can move as one.

"Our governmental structure does not condemn us to inaction and delay; we are able to transcend the institutional devices that provide for checks and balances and deliberation." Herring, *Presidential Leadership*, pp. 140-41.

It has not been explained, however, just how a continuous, strong, and all-wise presidential leadership is to be obtained, or how, when we do happen to enjoy adequate leadership, the people can be "convinced of the need" for a quick response. Nor is it explained how long it will take for the goal to become clear or what the aggressor nation may accomplish while we are engaged in the painful process of making the goal clear. Nor are we told what we shall do when crisis becomes chronic; for it is evident that what we call the "strong executive" is a temporary and accidental phenomenon, even if it were thought to be a desirable one.

[63] Wilson, *Congressional Government*, pp. 12-13.

[64] Harold J. Laski argues that, when a crises comes, our political system "can discover the man to handle it," because "of the national recognition that energy and direction are required, and the man chosen is the party response to that recognition." *The American Presidency* (1940), pp. 52-53. Aside from the fact

that energy and direction are always required, this view seems to proceed from two untenable assumptions: (1) that the people foresee crises, and (2) that the parties, when they make their nomination, search around for the man best qualified to meet the crisis. Laski says: "The war of 1914 found Woodrow Wilson in office." Woodrow Wilson may or may not have been the best man for that crisis; but, in any case, he was nominated in 1912, when practically no one foresaw the First World War and our entrance into it. "The pattern of government in this country is an alternation of power both between administrations and within administrations which is dictated not by the needs of the country but by a time-cycle of the executive-legislative relationship." Thomas K. Finletter, *Can Representative Government Do The Job?* (1945), p. 16-17.

[65] "I have been confronted with a problem similar to the one which the Congress placed before me in the price control bill which it sent me on June 28, 1946. That bill was so damaging to price control that I vetoed it and addressed the country on the subject. Then, on July 25, the Congress sent me a second price control bill, in some respects worse than the first. The time was so late that I had to sign that bill in order to prevent the complete destruction of price control. But effective price control was impossible under the new law.

"If I had vetoed H. R. 3203, rent controls would end, and the prospects of another bill being sent to me would be negligible. I had no choice but to sign." President Truman's message to Congress on approval of the measure continuing modified rent controls, *New York Times,* July 1, 1947.

[66] In many cases, this mental attitude or habit takes the form of devotion to duty and high purpose, an aim to achieve effective administrative results through an extension of activities. In other cases, the motivation may be less praiseworthy—desire to hold and justify a remunerative job, jealousy of other bureaucrats, or will to power. Paul H. Appleby, *Big Democracy* (1945), p. 104.

[67] "Each group found its legislative spokesmen; its insistences found their ultimate governmental expression in the creation of a department, an agency, or a commission designed to exercise regulatory continuous intervention in its behalf; or occasionally, if two groups were clashing, in an arbitrating or regulatory agency." Ernest S. Griffith, "The Changing Pattern of Public Policy Formation," *American Political Science Review* (June 1944), p. 448.

"In simplest terms, the most characteristic task of government is the pulling together of diverse and often conflicting interests. Conversely, the most characteristic failing of government is its propensity for division within itself. From this angle, each major unit of governmental organization, under ideal conditions, should always be based upon more than a single predominant interest. But the pressures that emanate from the economic order and the political convenience of dealing with particular problems separately have combined to produce structural arrangements in the executive branch that make it harder rather than easier for government to fulfill its synthesizing role.

"We need only think of the denial of synthesis that results from the formation of clientele agencies.... The existence of clientele agencies is a continuing incentive to substitute for broadly defined public policy narrow policies linked with particular interests." Wayne Coy, "Basic Problems," in "Federal Executive Reorganization Re-examined," *American Political Science Review,* Vol. 40 (December 1946), p. 1128.

[68] ". . . Congress has an attitude toward executive machinery which is quite unique. It insists upon elaborate legislative restriction on the executive through the mechanism of statutory controls, and thus gives the President an alibi at all times for poor administration." Clarence A. Dykstra, "The Quest for Re-

sponsibility," *American Political Science Review,* Vol. 33 (February 1939), p. 18.

[69] "The groups, together with their legislative spokesmen and administrative agents, became so many separate centers of policy formation—and 'government by whirlpools' prevailed. Any compatibility between the programs of groups or their governmental expression was purely accidental. Behind the rituals and façades of the 'Quasi' and 'administrative law' lay the political realities of governmental intervention in group warfare." Griffith, *American Political Science Review,* p. 448.

[70] Because of "selfish urges" and "the natural tendency to resist 'interference' and to seek autonomy," it is of "fundamental national importance that bureaus be actually controllable and controlled by departments, and that departments be controllable and controlled by the President and the Congress." Appleby, *Big Democracy,* p. 104.

[71] The National Security Act of 1947 recognized this fact when it established a National Security Council, to "assess and appraise the objectives, commitments, and risks of the United States in relation to our actual and potential military power, in the interests of national security . . . and . . . consider policies on matters of common interest to the departments and agencies of the government concerned with the national security. . . ." (Public Law 253, 80 Cong. 1 sess.) The Secretary of State is only one of several members of this Council. The position of the State Department as co-ordinate rather than superior in the making of foreign policy was again emphasized when the president appointed his commissions to consider the bearing of our domestic economic situation and the Marshall proposal for aid to Europe. A similar indication appears in the Foreign Service Act of 1946 which gives the departments of Labor, Commerce, and Agriculture representation in the administration of the Foreign Service.

[72] Mr. Wallace's conflicts with President Truman and Secretary Byrnes and Mr. Baruch provide the most notorious and perhaps the most illuminating examples; but there have been other publicized instances, such as the relations between Secretary Hull on the one hand and Assistant Secretary Moley and Under Secretary Welles on the other, the difference betwen the State Department and the armed services over the Pacific trusteeships (*New York Times,* Oct. 29, 1946; *Washington Post,* Nov. 3, 1946) and over the arming of Latin-American countries (*Washington Post,* Apr. 16, 1947), the dispute between Army and Navy over the unification proposal (*New York Times,* Apr. 14, 1946), disagreements over Palestine (*New York Times,* May 23, 1946), the Braden-Messersmith feud over Argentina, divergences between occupation commanders and home officials, and disputes among American officials in Iran, China, and Greece.

[73] Don K. Price, "Staffing the Presidency," *American Political Science Review* (December 1946), p. 1168.

[74] "To certain highly influential Congressmen, our central control agencies such as the Civil Service Commission, the Bureau of the Budget, or the General Accounting Office must be looked upon as arms of Congress. Others would insist that these agencies must be more clearly recognized as arms of the Chief Exectuive. Such theoretical differences can give rise to very practical difficulties. Our central staff agencies are faced with a dilemma. They are expected to serve two masters. In 1943 Congress put the Budget Bureau to work in applying manpower ceilings. Congressmen have indicated clearly to the Civil Service Commission that they regard it as performing certain legislative functions delegated by Congress." Pendleton Herring, "Executive-Legislative

Responsibilities," *American Political Science Review,* Vol. 38 (December 1944), *The Organization of Congress,* Joint Committee Print, p. 103.

[75] "While administration is an outgrowth of legislation, so is legislation to a great extent nowadays an outgrowth of administration; and when it is, it should be initiated subject to a general control which is capable of evaluating the demands of the parts from the point of view of the whole." Corwin, *The President: Office and Powers,* pp. 300-01.

[76] "The President tries to control his department heads, and may even dismiss one now and then for differences over policy. But within the legislative branch it is a different matter. A congressman is his own subordinate. . . .

"This makes it hard for the President to consult with his department heads and direct their policies in the way—or rather, to the same degree—that a department head may count on the cooperation of his bureau chiefs in developing a common program. If the Secretary of Agriculture, for instance, has a new policy to consider, he must decide whether to discuss it confidentially first with the President or with the chairmen of the committees on agriculture in Congress. The President will probably want to coordinate the proposed policy with those of other departments. The committee chairmen, on the other hand, are likely to sympathize with the Secretary in thinking foremost of agriculture, and to ally themselves with the private groups that are the customers and constituents of his department.

"The explosion of the first atomic bomb raised issues that affected every department of government. Yet the first bill introduced with the support of the War Department had been drafted secretly for it by a group of private citizens, and was presented to the Congress without going through the usual channels of clearance by the President's Executive Office. The War Department showed the bill to the President personally and to several departments, but not others. Representative Andrew J. May and Senator Edwin C. Johnson, of the military affairs committee, introduced the bill with the intimation that it had top support. But it was soon clear that something was wrong. Other departments and other outside groups began to be heard. The Senate, with the support of the President, set up a special committee under Senator Brien McMahon to deal with atomic energy. Senator McMahon, with some help from the executive side, drafted his bill. The President backed it, and so, finally, did the Secretary of War. The McMahon bill was enacted.

"In our political practice, the main points in this little story are repeated again and again. An executive department gets the jump on the President by dealing with an interest group and a congressional committee. It presents its proposal to the public before the President—whether or not he hears of it personally—can tie it in with the programs of other departments. Sometimes the President can iron out the matter belatedly; sometimes he cannot do so at all; sometimes he never even hears of the issue." Price, *American Political Science Review,* pp. 1154-56.

[77] "The rank and file in the departments are exceedingly timid before Senators and Representatives, and the higher-ups range from exceedingly careful to cautious. . . . It is basic doctrine, invoked daily and never questioned, that everything done must be so done as to be ready for Congressional review." Appleby, *Big Democracy,* p. 157.

[78] Advice and consent to treaties by two thirds of the Senate.

[79] "[The] House Foreign Affairs Committee voted today to make a detailed study of the State Department's organization, personnel, and policies.

"Simultaneously, the committee moved to head off general investigations of the department by other House Committees. . . .

"At the same time, the committee recognized that various phases of foreign affairs, such as tariffs, foreign commerce and personnel, come under the primary jurisdiction of other committees.

"Likewise, it was recalled, the organization of the State Department would be under the jurisdiction of the House Committee on Expenditures in the Executive Departments as part of an inquiry into general government activities. Further, the Appropriations Committee's work requires detailed study of State Department's organization and activity.

"Consequently, the Foreign Affairs Committee suggested that in such cases it be permitted to have subcommittees sit in on hearings of other committees where the organization, personnel, and policies of the State Department were involved." *New York Times,* Jan. 29, 1947.

[80] Congress may resort to impeachment proceedings; but such proceedings, if not obsolete, cannot be considered an effective means for the supervision of administration.

[81] The indictment against the existing system of congressional control is impressive. It is basically control over details, not over essentials. It is negative and repressive rather than positive and constructive. It reflects fear rather than confidence. It is sometimes irresponsible. It is based on no rational plan, but is an accumulation of particulars whose consequences are seldom seen in perspective. Congress has done both too much and too little in trying to discharge this phase of its responsibilities. . . . A solution is complicated by the fact that Congress (the controlling body) is 'a numerous assembly' unaccustomed to close internal discipline, with a changing personnel periodically absent from the seat of government, whereas the public service (the agency to be controlled) constitutes a vast permanent hierarchy of trained, professional, and relatively disciplined officials." Leonard D. White, "Congressional Control of the Public Service," *American Political Science Review,* Vol. 34 (February 1945), p. 1.

[82] The Legislative Reorganization Act of 1946 (60 Stat. 812, 79 Cong. 2 sess.) aimed, through a reorganization of the committee system, provision of larger staffs, and of systematizing fiscal procedure, to improve congressional oversight of administration. Section 136 reads as follows: "To assist the Congress in appraising the administration of the laws and in developing such amendments or related legislation as it may deem necessary, each standing committee of the Senate and the House of Representatives shall exercise continuous watchfulness of the execution by the administrative agencies concerned of any laws, the subject matter of which is within the jurisdiction of such committee; and, for that purpose, shall study all pertinent reports and data submitted to the Congress by the agencies in the executive branch of the Government." To the extent, however, that the committee system established by the act compartmentalizes policy-making, it also compartmentalizes the control of administration and prevents congressional supervision of the bureaucracy as a whole. That the act made insufficient provision for the reorganization of administration is shown by the 1947 bills (H.R. 775 and S. 164) which provide for a special commission to study the organization of the executive branch.

[83] "The staff necessary for continuous inquiry could be maintained only at the risk of a harmful division of responsibility, while such a staff would still lack a first-hand sense of operations." Arthur W. Macmahon, "Congressional Oversight of Administration: The Power of the Purse—II," *Political Science Quarterly,* Vol. 58 (September 1943), pp. 413-14.

[84] In the Seventy-fifth Congress, Senator McKellar announced that "about three or four hundred nominations of postmasters have been submitted to the senators from the several states, and those senators have approved the nominations, which are now before the Senate. I ask unanimous consent that the nominations which have been approved by the senators be confirmed *en bloc* at this time, though they are not on the printed calendar." "Thus," says Altman, "the Senate confirmed an unknown number of anonymous postmasters." O. R. Altman, "Second and Third Sessions of the Seventy-fifth Congress, 1937-1938," *American Political Science Review,* Vol. 32 (December 1938), p. 1122.

[85] "Thus in their own interest as well as in the interest of their constituents, Congressmen themselves form a pressure group, or rather a number of small but intensive pressure groups, influencing, cajoling, threatening, or entreating the regulatory Commission which they have created." Friedrich and Sternberg, *American Political Science Review,* pp. 797, 807.

[86] For brief reviews of reorganization efforts, see Millspaugh, *Democracy, Efficiency, Stability,* pp. 188-204, 280-89; Lewis Meriam and Laurence F. Schmeckebier, *Reorganization of the National Government* (1939), pp. 182-228. On the general subject, see also "Federal Executive Reorganization Reexamined," *American Political Science Review,* Vol. 40 (December 1946), pp. 1124-68.

[87] "Resistance to more broadly conceived alterations in the administrative structure comes also from the legislative branch, and for several reasons. Lawmakers have read into executive reorganization the threat of presidential ascendancy. Besides, they are impressed with the low potential of popular enthusiasm for matters so technical and obscure. More important, no doubt, is their own stake in lack of organizational unity on the executive side. . . . [The] power of small groups in Congress over particular departments and bureaus would proportionately decrease if the legislative majority should assert general control over the executive branch as a whole. In the circumstances, one can understand why there is much legislative sentiment in favor of a state of executive organization allowing each prominent lawmaker to exert real influence in those areas of departmental business over which his committee holds sway. . . ." Coy, *American Political Science Review,* pp. 1129-30.

". . . The veto by Congress in 1946 of one of the plans submitted by the President, and the action of the House in disapproving all three plans, apparently because of the opposition of interest groups, illustrates both the real control retained by Congress and the difficulty in reorganizing agencies over the opposition of their clienteles." Joseph P. Harris, cited in "Wartime Currents and Peacetime Trends" the same, pp. 1149-50.

[88] "The assumption by the Senate that it is an executive council designed to check the Chief Executive in foreign policy helps to arouse suspicion and opposition on the part of Senators towards almost every move of the President. This tendency plays into the hands of those Senators who are guided by personal prejudice, animosity, and love of prerogative, as well as those who are active or latent candidates for the presidency." Kenneth Colegrove, *The American Senate and World Peace* (1944), p. 123.

[89] Localism, combined with the pressures of interest-groups, produces the kind of wasteful compromise known as log-rolling, which consists of giving every local and special interest what it demands and largely disregarding the general interest.

[90] Arguing against the Confederation, *The Federalist* pointed out that when

a minority is able to checkmate a majority, there will be "tedious delays; continual negotiation and intrigue; contemptible compromises of the public good. . . . [Upon] some occasions things will not admit of accommodation; and then the measures of government must be injuriously suspended, or fatally defeated." (Sesqui. Ed.), p. 136.

[91] For a good illustration, see Herring, *Presidential Leadership*, pp. 38-41.

[92] The great compromise on slavery beginning in the Constitutional Convention of 1789 and continued in the Missouri Compromise and the Kansas-Nebraska Bill did not prevent the Civil War, though it is possible to argue that these schemes postponed the inevitable conflict until the North could win it. On the other hand, few would deny the appropriateness of Andrew Jackson's uncompromising stand against nullification.

[93] "Congress shows novel zest for staffs of its own. In various ways it seeks to attach strings to action. How far can this double tendency be pushed under the presidential form of government without creating ambiguities of administrative responsibility? There is a related and deeper difficulty. Can a legislative body—the institutional virtue of which lies in the decentralized choice and diffused responsiveness of its individual members—act on details otherwise than through small groups within itself which, by their special biases, may distort the application of public policy and even destroy its integrity. . . . Mighty issues appear in the present assertiveness of Congress. Welcome as are the stirrings from the lethargy of its own institutional tradition, its restlessness holds at least as much portent as promise." Arthur W. Macmahon, "Congressional Oversight of Administration: The Power of the Purse—I," *Political Science Quarterly*, Vol. 58 (June 1943), pp. 161-90; and, the same, Pt. II, Vol. 58 (September 1943), pp. 380-81.

Acknowledgments are made to the following publishers for permission to quote from their publications: Appleton-Century-Crofts, Inc. (Edward McChesney Sait, *Political Institutions*, 1938); University of Chicago Press (Carl Brent Swisher, *Growth of Constitutional Power*, 1946); Cornell University Press (Charles Howard McIlwain, *Constitutionalism, Ancient and Modern*, 1947); Thomas Y. Crowell Company (George B. Galloway, *Congress at the Crossroads*, 1946, and Henry S. McKee, *Degenerate Democracy*, 1933); Harcourt, Brace and Company, Inc. (Thomas K. Finletter, *Can Representative Government Do the Job?* 1945); Harper and Brothers (Merlo J. Pusey, *Big Government—Can We Control It?* 1945); Houghton Mifflin Company (Carl Brent Swisher, *American Constitutional Development*, 1943); Alfred A. Knopf, Inc. (Paul H. Appleby, *Big Democracy*, 1945, and Roland Young, *This Is Congress*, 1943); McGraw-Hill Book Company, Inc. (William Yandell Elliott, *The Need for Constitutional Reform*, 1935, and Henry Hazlitt, *A New Constitution Now*, 1942); New York University Press (Edward S. Corwin, *The President: Office and Powers*, 1940); The University of North Carolina Press (C. Perry Patterson, *Presidential Government in the United States*, 1947); Rinehart and Company, Inc. (Alexander Hehmeyer, *Time for Change: A Proposal for a Second Constitutional Convention*, 1943, and Pendleton Herring, *Presidential Leadership*, 1940); Vanguard Press, Inc. (Kenneth Colegrove, *The American Senate and World Peace*, 1944); and the Viking Press, Inc. (Charles A. Beard, *The Republic*, 1945).

INDEX

INDEX